The Psychology of Prejudice and Discrimination

**Recent titles in
Race and Ethnicity in Psychology**

Sources of Stress and Relief for African American Women
Catherine Fisher Collins

Playing with Anger: Teaching Coping Skills to African American Boys through
Athletics and Culture
Howard C. Stevenson Jr., editor

The Psychology of Prejudice and Discrimination

VOLUME 4
DISABILITY, RELIGION, PHYSIQUE, AND OTHER TRAITS

Edited by
Jean Lau Chin

Foreword by
Joseph E. Trimble

PRAEGER PERSPECTIVES

Race and Ethnicity in Psychology
Jean Lau Chin, John D. Robinson, and Victor De La Cancela
Series Editors

PRAEGER

Westport, Connecticut
London

Library of Congress Cataloging-in-Publication Data

The psychology of prejudice and discrimination / edited by Jean Lau Chin ; foreword by Joseph E. Trimble.

    p. cm.—(Race and ethnicity in psychology, ISSN 1543-2203)

    Includes bibliographical references and index.

    ISBN 0-275-98234-3 (set : alk. paper)—ISBN 0-275-98235-1 (v. 1 : alk. paper)—ISBN 0-275-98236-X (v. 2 : alk. paper)—ISBN 0-275-98237-8 (v. 3 : alk. paper)—ISBN 0-275-98238-6 (v. 4 : alk. paper) 1. Prejudices—United States. I. Chin, Jean Lau. II. Series.

BF575.P9P79 2004

303.3'85'0973—dc22   2004042289

British Library Cataloguing in Publication Data is available.

Library of Congress Catalog Card Number: 2004042289

ISBN: 0-275-98234-3 (set)

        0-275-98235-1 (Vol. 1)

        0-275-98236-X (Vol. 2)

        0-275-98237-8 (Vol. 3)

        0-275-98238-6 (Vol. 4)

ISSN: 1543-2203

First published in 2004

Praeger Publishers, 88 Post Road West, Westport, CT 06881

An imprint of Greenwood Publishing Group, Inc.

www.praeger.com

Printed in the United States of America

∞™

The paper used in this book complies with the Permanent Paper Standard issued by the National Information Standards Organization (Z39.48-1984).

10 9 8 7 6 5 4 3 2 1

Contents

Foreword by Joseph E. Trimble   vii

Introduction by Jean Lau Chin   xiii

CHAPTER 1   Dress as a Manifest Aspect of Identity: 1
An Indian American Narrative
Leena Banerjee

CHAPTER 2   Spiritual Diversity and Clinical Practice   27
Ilene Serlin

CHAPTER 3   Prejudice toward People with Disabilities   51
*Asiah Mason, Helen D. Pratt, Dilip R. Patel,
Donald E. Greydanus, and Kareem Z. Yahya*

CHAPTER 4   Beyond the "Triple Whammy": Considering   95
Social Class as One Factor in Discrimination
against Persons with Disabilities
Martha E. Banks and Catherine A. Marshall

CHAPTER 5   Coping with Prejudice and Discrimination   111
Based on Weight
Anna M. Myers and Esther D. Rothblum

CHAPTER 6   Prejudice in an Era of Economic Globalization   135
and International Interdependence
Teru L. Morton

CHAPTER 7   The Sociocultural Abuse of Power: A Model   161
                for Shared Power
                BraVada Garrett-Akinsanya

CHAPTER 8   From Prejudice and Discrimination to   207
                Awareness and Acceptance
                Marie L. Miville, Jill M. Rohrbacker,
                and Angela B. Kim

CHAPTER 9   The Chicago Dinners: A Model for Community   233
                Engagement and Social Change
                Dietra Hawkins, Terri Johnson, and
                Josefina Alvarez

CHAPTER 10   When Diversity Becomes the Norm   253
                Donald Daughtry, Denise Twohey,
                David H. Whitcomb, Cindy Juntunen
                and Michael Loewy

Index   283

About the Series and the Series Editors   291

About the Advisers   293

About the Contributors   297

Foreword

Civilized men have gained notable mastery over energy, matter, and inanimate nature generally and are rapidly learning to control physical suffering and premature death. But, by contrast, we appear to be living in the Stone Age so far as our handling of human relations is concerned.

(Gordon W. Allport, 1954, p. ix)

Although written over fifty years ago, the haunting words of the eminent social psychologist Gordon W. Allport may ring true today. His intent then was to clarify the various elements of the enormously complex topic of prejudice. Since the writing of his now well-cited and highly regarded text on prejudice, social and behavioral scientists have made great strides in furthering our knowledge of the field. Since 1950, for example, thousands of books, journal articles, and book chapters have been devoted to studying prejudice and discrimination. Professor Allport would be somewhat pleased with the numbers because that was partly his expectation when he said, "So great is the ferment of investigation and theory in this area that in one sense our account will soon be dated. New experiments will supersede old, and formulations of various theories will be improved" (1954, p. xiii). But has there been that much improvement that we have moved away from a Stone Age understanding of human relations to a higher level of sophistication? The question begs for an answer, but that can wait until later.

Let me back up for a moment to explore another line of thought and inquiry that bears directly on the significance and importance of this wonderful set of books on the psychology of prejudice and discrimination. For as long as I can remember, I have been deeply interested in the origins of, motives in, and attitudes about genocide and ethnocide; as a young child I did not use those horrific terms, as I did not know them then. But I did know about their implied destructive implications from stories passed along by sensitive teachers, ancestors, and elders. The deep social psychological meaning of the constructs later became an intense interest of mine as a graduate student in the turbulent 1960s, an era filled with challenges and protestations of anything regarding civil rights, discrimination, racism, sexism, and prejudice. During that era I threw my mind and spirit into the study of Allport's writings on prejudice—not merely to study them, but to explore every nuance of his scholarly works to expand the depth of my understanding and expecting to come away with fewer questions and more answers. I was not disappointed in my exploration. I was baffled, though, because I recognized more so just how complicated it was to prevent and eradicate prejudice and discrimination.

As I write these thoughts, I am reminded of a sign that was once posted over the porch roof of an old restaurant and tavern in a rural South Dakota community adjacent to an American Indian reservation. The sign was hand-painted in white letters on a long slat of weathered wood; it was written in the Lakota language, and the English translation read, "No dogs or Indians allowed." The store was and is still owned by non-Indians. The offensive, derogatory sign is no longer there—likely torn down years ago by angry protestors from the nearby reservation. While the sign is gone, the attitude and intent of the message still linger in and around the rustic building, except that it is more insidious, pernicious, and guileful now. The prevailing prejudicial and loathsome attitude is a reflection of many of the residents of the small town. Many of the town's residents tolerate Native Americans because they dependent on them economically, but their bigoted and closed-minded convictions are unwilling to accept Native Americans as equals and provide them with freedom of movement and expression.

The wretched, mean-spirited, pernicious attitudes present in that rural South Dakota town symbolize the prevailing changes in attitudes and behavior across North America—the blatant signs are gone, but in many places and for many individuals the prejudicial attitudes persist, sometimes in sly and subtle forms. On other occasions they are overt and repulsive. Chapters in these volumes summarize and explore the social and psychological motives and reasoning behind the persistence of prejudicial attitudes and discriminatory practices. They go beyond the conclusions drawn by Professor Allport and other early writers on the topic and take us into domains represented by those who have experienced prejudice and discrimination firsthand, as did their ancestors. Indeed, a voice not included in early studies on prejudice and discrimination is intensified and deepened as more and more ethnic groups and women are represented in the social and behavioral sciences than in years gone by.

Stories and anecdotes, too, recounted by the rising groups of diverse scholars and researchers, lend a new authenticity to the literature. Some of the accounts provide a different perspective on historical events involving racial hatred that provide more thorough descriptions of the details and perspectives. Revisionist historical approaches have a place in the study of prejudice and discrimination because for so long the authentic voices of the victims were muffled and muted. For example, as a consequence of European contact, many Native American communities continue to experience individual and community trauma, a "wound to the soul of Native American people that is felt in agonizing proportions to this day" (Duran & Duran, 1995, p. 27). The cumulative trauma has been fueled by centuries of incurable diseases, massacres, forced relocation, unemployment, economic despair, poverty, forced removal of children to boarding schools, abuse, racism, loss of traditional lands, unscrupulous land mongering, betrayal, broken treaties—the list goes on. Brave Heart and DeBruyn (1998) and Duran and Duran (1995) maintain that postcolonial "historical and intergenerational trauma" has left a long trail of unresolved grief and a "soul wound" in Native American communities that contribute to high levels of social and individual problems such as alcoholism, suicide, homicide, domestic violence, child abuse, and negative career ideation. The presence of Native American scholars contributed a voice that was suppressed for decades because some feared the consequences if these scholars told their stories. The stories and accounts of past racial events and their corresponding trauma also were not told because there were few visible ethnic scholars available.

Decades ago the topics of prejudice and discrimination largely emphasized race and, more specifically, the racial experiences of black Americans. Over the years the topic has expanded to include the experiences of other ethnic groups, women, the elderly, those with disabilities, those with nonheterosexual orientations, and those with mixed ethnic heritages. The volumes edited by Jean Lau Chin expand the concepts of diversity and multiculturalism to add a broader, more inclusive dimension to the understanding of prejudice and discrimination. The addition of new voices to the field elevates public awareness to the sweeping effects of prejudice and discrimination and how they are deeply saturated throughout societies.

The amount of scholarly attention devoted to the study of prejudice and discrimination closely parallels the growth of ethnic diversity interests in psychology. Until about thirty years ago, psychology's mission appeared to be restricted to a limited population as references to blacks, Asian Americans, Native American and Alaska natives, Hispanics, Pacific Islanders, and Puerto Ricans were almost absent from the psychological literature; in fact, the words *culture* and *ethnic* were rarely used in psychological textbooks. The long absence of culture in the web of psychological inquiry did not go unnoticed. About three decades ago, ethnic minority and international psychologists began questioning what the American Psychological Association meant by its use of *human* and to whom the vast body of psychological knowledge applied. America's ethnic psychologists and those from other countries, as well as a small handful of North American psychologists, argued that American psychology did not include what constituted the world's population. They claimed that findings were biased, limited to studies involving college and university students and laboratory animals, and therefore not generalizable to all humans. Comprehensive literature reviews reinforced their accusations and observations.

Accusations of imperialism, cultural encapsulation, ethnocentrism, parochialism, and, in some circles of dissent, of "scientifically racist" studies, run the gamut of criticisms hurled at the field of psychology during that period. Robert Guthrie (1976), for example, writing in his strongly worded critique of psychology, *Even the Rat Was White*, argues that culture and context were not taken seriously in the history of psychological research. Given these conditions and the myopia of the profession, it is no small wonder that prejudice and discrimination were not given more widespread attention. The topic was not perceived as salient and important enough for extensive consideration. The four volumes in this set are a testament to the amount of change and emphasis that are focused on ethnicity, culture, and the topics of prejudice and discrimination.

The changing demographics in the United States call into question the relevance of a psychology that historically has not included ethnic and racial groups and that fostered a research agenda that was ethnocentric and bound by time and place. This can no longer be tolerated, as the rapid growth of ethnic minority groups in the United States amplifies the need for more attentiveness on the part of the social and behavioral sciences. Consider the population projections offered by the U.S. Bureau of the Census. By 2050, the U.S. population will reach over 400 million, about 47 percent larger than in 2000 (U.S. Bureau of the Census, 2001). The primary ethnic minority groups—specifically, Hispanics, blacks, Asian Americans, and Native American and Alaska Natives—will constitute almost 50 percent of the population in 2050. About 57 percent of the population under the age of eighteen, and 34 percent over the age of 65, will be ethnic minorities.

America never was and likely will not be a melting pot of different nationalities and ethnic groups for another century or two. As the mixture and size of ethnic groups increase, we are faced with the disturbing possibility that an increase in prejudice and discrimination will occur accordingly. Given this possibility, the topics covered in these volumes become even more worthy of serious consideration, especially the ones that emphasize prevention. Given the demographic changes and the topical changes that have occurred in the social and behavioral sciences, the extensive contents of these four volumes are a welcome addition to the field. Editor Jean Lau Chin and her long list of chapter authors are to be congratulated for their monumental effort. The volumes are packed with useful and wonderfully written material. Some is based on empirical findings, some on firsthand experiences. The blend of various writing styles and voice adds to the breadth of coverage of the topic. The many points of view provided by the contributors will help shape the direction of research and scholarly expression on a topic that has been around since the origins of humankind. We can hope that the contributions of these four volumes will move the field of human relations from a perceived Stone Age level of understanding to one where we believe we are moving closer to eliminating prejudice, discrimination, and the vile hatred they engender.

Joseph E. Trimble
Professor of Psychology
Western Washington University
Bellingham, WA
March 21, 2004

REFERENCES

Allport, G. W. (1954). *The nature of prejudice*. Garden City, NY: Doubleday.

Brave Heart, M. Y. H., & DeBruyn, L. (1998). The American Indian holocaust: Healing unresolved grief. *American Indian and Alaska Native Mental Health Research, 8*(2), 56–78.

Duran, E., & Duran, B. (1995). *Native American postcolonial psychology*. Albany, NY: State University of New York Press.

Guthrie, R. (1976). *Even the rat was white: A historical view of psychology*. New York: Harper & Row.

U.S. Bureau of the Census. (2001). *Census of the population: General population characteristics, 2000*. Washington, DC: Government Printing Office.

Introduction

Prejudice and discrimination are not new. The legacy of the Pilgrims and early pioneers suggested a homogenous, mainstream America. Our early emphasis on patriotism in the United States resulted in a false idealization of the melting pot myth. Prejudice and discrimination in American society were overt and permeated all levels of society, that is, legislation, government, education, and neighborhoods. In the 1960s, attempts to eradicate prejudice, discrimination, and racism were explicit—with an appeal to honor and value the diversity within different racial and ethnic groups. This soon extended to other dimensions of diversity, including gender, disability, and spirituality. However, long after the war to end slavery, the civil rights movement of the 1960s, desegregation in the schools, and the abolition of anti-Asian legislation—indeed, in the midst of growing public debate today regarding gay marriage—we still see the pernicious effects of prejudice and discrimination in U.S. society.

Prejudice and discrimination toward differences in race, ethnicity, gender, spirituality, and disability have had negative psychological consequences, and they continue in primarily covert forms. Bias and disparities still exist and result in inequity of services, opportunities, and practices in American society. Combating prejudice and discrimination in today's environment warrants some different strategies. We live in an environment of heightened anxiety due to war and terrorism. Thanks to technological advances in communication, travel, and the

Internet, news and information from all parts of the world are almost instantaneously brought to us. We live in a global economy with a narrowing of borders between countries and groups. Generations of immigrants have resulted in the U.S. population becoming so diverse that there may soon be no single majority group within most major cities. Technological advances have eliminated the biological advantage of males in strength and the biological "limitations" of women of childbearing age in the work environment. Yet, the more things change, the more they stay the same. Irrational and unjust perceptions of other people remain—more subtle, perhaps, but they remain.

This four-volume set, *The Psychology of Prejudice and Discrimination*, takes a fresh look at that issue that is embedded in today's global environment. Images, attitudes and perceptions that sustain prejudice and discrimination are more covert, but no less pernicious. What people say, believe, and do all reflect underlying bias. **We do not claim here to address every existing form of prejudice or discrimination, nor do we cite every possible group targeted today. What we offer are insights into a range from the most to least recognized, or openly discussed, forms of this injustice.** Each chapter offers new perspectives on standing issues, with practical information about how to cope with prejudice and discrimination. The "toolbox" at the end of each chapter suggests steps to be taken at different levels to combat prejudice and discrimination and to achieve change. At the individual level, self-reflection needs to occur by both the victims and perpetrators of discrimination. Practitioners, educators, and all who deliver services potentially impart a bias perpetuating prejudice and discrimination. At the systems level, communities and policymakers must join together and have the will to combat discrimination.

How does one remain "whole" or validate one's identity despite persistent assaults to self-esteem from prejudice and discrimination? How does one raise children or teach amid societal institutions that perpetuate bias? Culturally competent principles and practices are needed to provide a framework for managing diversity and valuing differences.

Volume 1, *Racism in America*, looks at stereotypes, racial bias, and race relations. How do we avoid internalizing racism or accepting negative messages about a group's ability and intrinsic worth? How do we address institutionalized racism that results in differential access to goods, service, and opportunities of society? Volume 2, *Ethnicity and Multiracial Identity*, looks at discrimination toward differences due to immigration, language, culture, and mixed race. Volume 3,

Bias Based on Gender and Sexual Orientation, looks at gender bias, women's issues, homophobia, and oppression of gay/lesbian life-styles. Volume 4, *Disability, Religion, Physique, and Other Traits*, strives to examine less-spotlighted bias against other forms of difference, and begins the difficult dialogue that must take place if we are to eradicate prejudice and discrimination.

Written for today's people and environment, these volumes are rich with anecdotes, stories, examples, and research. These stories illustrate the emotional impact of prejudice and discrimination throughout history and as it still strikes people's lives today. While the chapters spotlight psychology, they interweave history, politics, legislation, social change, education, and more. These interdisciplinary views reflect the broad contexts of prejudice and discrimination that ultimately affect identity, life adjustment, and well-being for every one of us.

Please take with you the strategies for change offered in the toolbox at the end of each chapter. Change needs to occur at all levels: individual, practitioner/educator, and community. The intent of the toolboxes is to move us from the emotional to the scholarly to action and empowerment. They are intended to encourage and compel readers to begin individual change that will spur community and social action. With each person who reads these volumes, gains understanding, and finds the motivation or method to help make his or her small part of the world a more just and open-minded place, we have moved closer to making our goal a reality.

Jean Lau Chin

CHAPTER 1

Dress as a Manifest Aspect of Identity: An Indian American Narrative

Leena Banerjee

This chapter discusses two salient but rarely-discussed aspects of cultural (ethnic-racial) identity and difference, those of dress and the way differences in dress are handled in public life in the United States. Dress stands alongside many other manifest (or socially visible) aspects of cultural identity, such as skin color, hair, appearance, language and accents, cuisines, ways of eating, ways of greeting, ways of sitting, ways of dancing, celebrations and ways of celebrating, and so on; and latent (or socially invisible) aspects of ethno-cultural identity such as values, knowledge, attitudes, expectations, belief systems, and so on. This chapter focuses on a personal narrative that chronicles the author's experiences as a first-generation immigrant with ethnic dress and identity in the public spheres of academia and the professional world in the United States. The narrative also familiarizes the reader with the author's pre-immigration cultural context, and moves on to discuss how she has grappled with the lessons learned from dealing with dress in the public sphere so that she could pass them down intergenerationally to her young daughter. Sociopolitical analysis of the history of the lack of diverse dress as a manifest aspect of identity in the U.S. public sphere is integrated into the chapter before the chapter makes concluding remarks and suggestions in the toolbox for change.

THE WAY YOU DRESS AND WHO YOU ARE: REFLECTIONS ON THE RELATIONSHIP BETWEEN THE TWO

Cultural identity contributes to a core and enduring sense of self. By being connected to a group, this sense of self anchors a sense of belonging and gives rise to feelings, attitudes, and meanings relative to that identity (Phinney, 1990). Cultural identity is used here as a broad term that includes both ethnic and racial identity. Culture as a broad category including color, region, class, language, customs, belief systems, gender, ability, and sexual orientation can include multiple dimensions.

> Therefore it can generate more flexible, fluid, encompassing mentalities in thinking about individual, communal, and national identity. It is a concept that is not always immediately apparent and can require getting to know people a little before labeling them. Culture is a changeable and adaptable concept unlike race which being based on unalterables such as color and appearance offers a rigid and closed set of categories, inviting stereotyping and a heightened sense of differences.
>
> As an alterable, multilayered concept it can be eminently suitable to the self definitional purposes of a diverse, democratic people because it can provide a framework for integration through the identification of commonalities and differences, and at the same time, absorb and reflect new realities and meanings that emerge from progressive exchanges in society. A multiculturalism coming of age among a free and diverse people can promote concepts of self definition that emphasize the dual needs for cohesion and distinctiveness which can engender trust, exchange and the experience of integration. (Banerjee, 2000, p. 17)

Cultural identity of the minority individual has received attention for several decades in the academic literature and has seen two very positive evolutions. One is that the development of ethnic identity that started out being conceptualized as a linear, invariant, stage-specific process (Cross, 1995; Ponteretto & Pederson, 1993; Phinney, 1990; Atkinson, Morten, & Sue, 1989) proceeding from a position of conscious or unconscious self-hatred through various stages of examination to eventual self-acceptance has been conceptualized first in a more interactive way (Helms, 1995; Carter, 1995; Parham, 1989) and currently in a nonlinear, variable, and fluid way (Yi & Shorter-Gooden, 1999). The second is that pathologization and negativity seen as inherent in the minority identity have given way to a much more balanced understanding of strengths, resiliencies, and oppressions inherent in it. An example of such a current approach to cultural identity is Yi and Shorter-Gooden's narrative identity model in which identity development is "fluid, dynamic and constructed in a relational (interpersonal) context" (1999, p. 18). Multiple developmental experiences and multiple sources and aspects of identity such as age, sex, color, SES, sexual orientation, ethnicity, and so on are acknowledged as important and influential in the process. The aim is to understand how individuals have chosen to create their own story by weaving together their strengths and challenges, pulling together the multiple strands into a coherent identity. The indication of a healthy cultural identity is that it feels authentic to the person, is coherent (that is, comprehensive and congruent with regard to the person's life information), gives the person a sense of order and unity, provides an overall sense of dignity and well-being, and promotes flexible adaptation to life circumstances.

One of the threads of such a cultural identity is dress, although this aspect has been fairly "neglected analytically" (Eicher, 1995, p. 1), in the social science literature and in public discourse. In other words, not much attention has been paid to it as yet as an aspect of a person's identity. Dress has been defined as including "modifications and supplements to the body, extending concern beyond apparel to allow appraisal of body and hair conformation, texture and color, scent and sound" (Eicher, 1995, p. ix). Culture defines proper and preferred dress, formal and informal dress, and expressions of "modesty and flamboyance, concealment and exposure" (Eicher, 1995, p. 3) as it relates to cultural parameters for mens', womens', and childrens' attire. Changes in culture through interaction with other groups or migration can lead to changes in dress that indicate it is indeed fluid and evolving.

As an aspect of cultural identity, dress offers the individual and group multiple potential psychological resources and meanings. These include being recognized and being found familiar as well as recognizing (that is, knowing and being known); feeling affinity and a sense of identification; feeling a sense of belonging; feeling distinctive; expressing individuality, mood, creativity, politics, and aesthetic style; feeling pride; feeling a link to a history and collective heritage; and finding a position in time and place in social relationships. For those of minority cultural identity, their ethnic dress offers them all of these avenues for meaning as well as the psychologically significant reality and struggle of the power differential between their ethnic dress and the dress of the dominant majority. Charisse Jones and Kumea Shorter-Gooden (2003) have in their recent book addressed this issue as it applies to the physical appearance of black women. They conclude as below on the basis of extensive surveys and in-depth interviews:

> The pressure to look like someone other than themselves, to look more European and less African, is enormous. And many Black women are pushed to obsession over their hair, their skin tone, and, increasingly their body size and shape. This is what we call the "lily complex," the belief that the only way to be beautiful is to look as close to "White" as possible. (Jones & Shorter-Gooden, 2003, p. 177)

The issue of ethnic dress poses similar challenges for the ethnic minority individual. Dress in the public sphere in the United States conforms and coalesces around certain recognizables with distinctly European roots. This goes along with the idea that in the United States, national cultural identity continues to be conceptualized with a white center and a cluster of minority identities in the periphery (Mukherjee, 1997). The notion of embracing in the public sphere the variety of ethnic dress inherent in a population as diverse and multicultural as the U.S. population seems conspicuous by its absence. Here again, diversity in dress has gone the way of diversity in other areas, such as language; an example of this is creating uniformity out of diversity in place of achieving unity, a far more complex process (Banerjee, 2002). The ethnic minority person is left needing to "look" as much like majority people as possible by dressing like them, so he or she can be seen as appropriate and acceptable at minimum in the public domain. The messages come through in the socialization and the media. The resulting sense of loss from having to discard customary ethnic dress in the public sphere may perhaps be most palpable for immigrant populations but is no less real as a part of the legacy of the price paid to survive and progress in the society for older generations of immigrants. On the other hand, not embracing the diversity available in spades domestically puts the population at a disadvantage in dealing with the world's inescapable diversity, as globalization becomes the order of the day in every sphere of human endeavor.

Some of this chapter is written in narrative form, as the author believes that personal voice has the potential to impact readers in a powerful way, to touch them somewhere that it matters, where apathy, naivete, and complacency no longer offer legitimate defenses. Weaving together personal narrative with scholarly analysis can also be compelling because it combines the authenticity of the narrative with the gravitas of the scholarly, placing the personal voice in the larger sociocultural context and providing an experiential glimpse into the issues of our times.

DRESS AND PROFESSIONAL IDENTITY: AN IMMIGRANT'S NARRATIVE

Aalap, or Allegro

When I arrived in the United States, I was twenty-two years old. I had a masters degree in clinical psychology from the University of Delhi in India and enrolled in the AAMFT (American Association for Marriage and Family Therapy)—an approved clinical PhD program at Virginia Tech Institute with a focused interest on the family systems paradigm and how to be helpful to families and children through its application. This was in the 1980s. In those early days in the United States, I used to dress in classic Indian style, in starched cotton saris usually hand-loomed, with traditional motifs in the summer and silks to keep warm in the winter. (The sari is an unstitched piece of fabric, usually six meters long, worn with a blouse and a long underskirt.) It expressed my taste and identity, my Indian-ness, my deep appreciation of indigenous, artistic creation of fabric and design, and the style and grace of the traditional apparel. My way of dressing—customary, ordinary, and comfortable to me—not only made me stand out in my predominantly white, western university environment in Virginia, but I felt like I was sticking out in a way that was incredibly awkward and uncomfortable. I would be greeted with the inevitable daily compliments about my dress from many, if not most, quarters. Sometimes these remarks would lead to other astonishing questions and remarks about India: "Do they have houses built of brick in India?" "Can you ride elephants over there in India?" I had professors hold open doors for me and stand up when I walked into the room, and in general around the campus I was aware of being stared at quite a bit. All of this conveyed to me a message about my exotic status that I did not want to have and gave me a great deal of unnecessary and what I felt to be the wrong kind of attention in place of a more matter-of-fact professional approach, which I desired.

Vilambit, or Slow Movement

Right before the first round of field placement interviews were to be held, the director of clinical training and a professor sat me down and asked me if I would consider wearing western dress in placement, suggesting that not doing so might create a barrier in the therapeutic process. My initial response was total shock. Nevertheless, I said to him that I would have to think this through before I could give him a response. I was not accustomed to wearing western dress. I was not accustomed to baring my legs, though I was very accustomed to baring my midriff! I cringed at the possibility of doing something that felt like changing my skin.

I had, however, made a long journey to the United States to learn about the practical applications of psychological knowledge that could benefit others, because access to such training was not readily available on my home turf. It was part of my initial breaking away from the ivory tower in which I had been formed, and I had a great deal of admiration for the practical use of knowledge made by my new professors and for their dedication to improving the quality of existence of those with whom they worked. I thought that if I had wanted an academic life solely, then I would refuse to shed my skin as it were, asking that my peers, students, superiors, and I deal with the differences in the process of interaction. In looking at the prospect of becoming a clinician and working with clients in a highly assimilative, conformist culture, I came to the conclusion that it was my professional responsibility to take the greater burden on myself. So, facilitating ease of engagement in the therapeutic process by adopting a western code of dress was something I chose to undertake as my professional responsibility. With great trepidation, I shared this with my clinical director and started investing in a new wardrobe. As I began to wear this new wardrobe, I felt a profound loss that is difficult to put into words. I also got something I had wanted when I first came through the door: just matter-of-fact treatment, and no second and third glances, stares, questions, excessive compliments, or misplaced chivalry.

Jugalbandi, or Minuette/Scherzo

Now, two decades later, I wear this western dress routinely with a definite stamp of Indian fabric and design. I have looked for and found organizations that sell such clothes in the United States and in India, and it is important to me that their enterprises be involved in resurrecting indigenous dyes, patterns, and fabrics and in empowering poor women and disabled people to earn livelihoods. I also travel frequently to India and buy fabrics there and have them tailored or buy the increasingly available "ready-made" clothes, both Indian and western. Developmentally, from late adolescence to early adulthood and beyond, I have gone through several milestones with respect to dress that have been significant to my identity. In late adolescence in India, I chose to wear traditional attire in college because at the time I felt it was congruent with my emerging taste and identity. I resonated with the style, artistry, grace, and femininity of classic Indian saris and the fact that they represented a legacy for me, a connection to how my mother, grandmothers, and aunts dressed. Externally I felt freedom to dress this way or a variety of other non-traditional ways, including dressing in western styles. This freedom was fairly typical in my upper-middle-class milieu. I was at home and felt a sense of congruence with myself as I dressed traditionally, and I felt comfortable in my world as well. As a result, I chose to wear traditional saris exclusively, unlike most of my peers at the time, who experimented with traditional and non-traditional attire, western and eastern, for reasons of their own.

Immigration to the United States initially left me still feeling at home in wearing the sari but challenged by external feedback and learning to cope with it. The request to change my style of dress came quickly enough and necessitated more radical steps than I may have taken myself without the external pressure. I chose to adapt to and incorporate western dress, which I liked (just not on me until then!) for reasons that made real sense to me and that I could accept. Nonetheless, the initial experience of wearing western dress felt incongruous and odd. This became moderated gradually by my essential openness to the new dress, my desire to adapt for good reasons, and by the practice of wearing it more. Incorporating Indian features into this dress added meaning and a deeper sense of good feeling and fit with who I was becoming through the process of immigration. My process, because of my early affiliations and circumstances of being a minority and immigrant, had much to do with expressing ethnic identity in a personally consonant and meaningful way. For a person in the majority, similar internal processes may not involve ethnically based majority–minority issues, but rather others, such as expression of personality, style, taste, and so on.

Over time, I have thought long and hard about what this experience of mine has had to offer in the dialogue on the evolution of multiculturalism within American culture, as this is indeed my new and chosen collective. The issue that sticks is not that one kind of dress is better than any other but that we have a culture, particularly in public or professional life, in which the freedom to wear different legitimate forms of cultural dress is restricted through an unexamined set of societal perceptions and expectations. As I have said before,

> Multiculturalism is the idea of a plural paradigm that allows retention and transformation of cultural identity through individual or collective choice rather than implicit or explicit coercion, thereby extending to each individual or collective an essential dignity. It fosters a climate of humanism and provides depth and resilience to a culture through access to its collective memories, better perspectives on oneself and others, collective wisdom and collective narrative stories that can be shared, exchanged, or blended freely in the exigencies of survival. Loss of cultural identity is a loss of cultural capital and a loss of opportunity to interact with multiple sources of meaning and expanded cultural resources. (Banerjee, 2002, p. 5)

It is toward this end of empowering ourselves to continually reach for multiculturalism that I write this as I have many other papers, in my own style of mixing the narrative with the scholarly.

DIFFERENCE IN DRESS REFLECTS A GAMUT OF CULTURAL DIFFERENCES: EXPERIENCES IN ACADEMIA

I was the only immigrant and the only full-time student of color in my entering doctoral cohort of ten students. The other student of color enrolled part-time and worked full-time, and so I saw her very little. Soon after I arrived in the program, my professors approached me and proposed that I take several multicultural courses as independent study units. Essentially they proposed that I read certain materials, digest and reflect on them, and discuss them with assigned professors. I warmed to the subject matter instantly. I felt excited about the proposal, but the fact that I was singled out in my cohort for this experience did not make sense to me. Indeed, even in those early days in the field and in this country, I felt something was amiss in this line of reasoning. I expressed my genuine interest in the course of study proposed and also suggested that my cohort as a whole could benefit from this exposure. My faculty politely thanked me for my thoughts and essentially said it was I and not they, in their view, who needed this instruction. They were offering me these opportunities so that I could acclimate and acculturate to my new environment, something my peers obviously did not have to do. I was quite unsettled with this answer, but decided that this was not a battle that I felt safe enough to take on at the time.

Many years later, I now see this as a product and reflection of the strong assimilationist, rather than multicultural, forces by which the American mainstream has been formed and which multiculturalism continues to face a very uphill struggle to change. This is indeed the assimilationist legacy of white conformity that is based on the belief that the peoples and cultures of northern and western Europe are more evolved and superior to all others, and therefore peoples of other groups must to adopt their mores (Banerjee, 2000). My professors were not trying to single me out, embarrass me, or offend me in any way. They were, out of respect for my potential and me, trying to groom me for success in the American mainstream by going out of their way. I genuinely believe that this was their intent in asking me to modify both my dress and my curriculum. However, in doing so by means that to me reflected unexamined assimilationist values and assumptions, they were unfairly singling me out and denying themselves and my peers a richer experience and dialogue that could have emerged from processes driven by diversity-owning multicultural values.

I dove into the courses and read multicultural literature in sociology, family sociology, psychology, and family therapy. I reveled in the extensive individual attention given to me by professors, and we had animated, soul-searching conversations in their individual offices when I met them for independent study appointments. In the end I made the most of what was offered, and the professors recognized me as something of an expert in multiculturalism in the department community, something I could hardly have expected and could hardly believe or accept. Nonetheless, when Celia Falicov's first book on multicultural issues, *Cultural Perspectives in Family Therapy*, was published, the editor of *Family Relations*, who was on our faculty, invited me to write a review of it. I was honored, and I did the job gladly (Banerjee, nee Roy, 1985).

PUTTING THE NARRATIVE INTO ETHNOCULTURAL CONTEXT

Roots

I identify as an Indian American psychologist and a first-generation immigrant. My professional activities run in three interrelated streams of teaching, practice (for me, synonymous with community-based service), and scholarship. I was born and raised in India in an upper-middle-class Bengali Brahmin family, the daughter of a lieutenant general of the Indian Artillery Corps of the Indian Army and a house-wife and stay-at-home mother whose engagement in community services of many kinds has been longstanding and tireless. I was the eldest of three sisters, who have gone on to be a professor of psychology, a distinguished professor of biochemistry, and an artist and animator who has exhibited independently. Besides this nuclear group, I grew up with a large extended family, along with many professional colleagues of my parents and neighbors and community members who were close enough to be called family. I grew up traveling the length and breadth of the Indian subcontinent and generally moved every two or three years during my childhood years due to my father's profession and my parents' consequent style of life. This pattern of life took me through quite a few wrenching goodbyes and also the thrill and anticipation of new people, places, homes, and schools. In time I realized that it contributed to the ease I have with transition and change, and indeed prepared me for the giant leap of faith involved in immigrating to the United States.

I grew up literate in Bengali, my mother tongue; Hindi, the Indian national language; English, the linguistic legacy of colonialism in India; and with a nodding acquaintance with a few other Indian and European languages besides. I also had lessons in the great classical language Sanskrit that Max Mueller defined as the mother or root of the Indo-European family of languages. I attended school in the northern Indian city of Allahabad in the Indo-Gangetic plain at the confluence of the great Indian rivers Ganga and Jamuna and the third mythic river Saraswati (which stands for knowledge). The school was proud of having educated two Indian prime ministers, Jawaharlal Nehru and Indira Gandhi, and I distinctly remember these and other illustrious alumni being held up for us as role models at the school. At fifteen I graduated high school, passing a board examination administered in India by the University of Cambridge in the United Kingdom, called Senior Cambridge.

During my high school years, besides being a bookworm and having a very tight band of friends, I remember the thrill of owning a bicycle by which I could make my independent way to and fro from school, a few miles each way, in the midst of fairly heavy and characteristically chaotic Indian traffic. I welcomed and relished this daily challenge, developing early competence and independence in making my way on the road. Metaphorically, it allowed me to break out a little from the sheltered environs of my upbringing and childhood.

After completing high school in the humanities and mathematics (there were no social science offerings at high school in those days), I spent a few months holidaying with my parents in Secunderabad in the Deccan plateau in southern India. My father was on the faculty of the Defence Management Institute in those days and was quite excited about the discipline of psychology as it related to management. He introduced me to a psychologist on the faculty and to their wonderful library. My innate human service interests were strongly ignited as I read the (largely western) literature in the discipline of psychology and conversed with the resident psychologist. Subsequently I applied to study psychology honors at the Universities of Delhi and Mumbai and received acceptances from both places, proceeding to accept the offer from the former.

EARLY PATHWAYS TO MULTICULTURAL COMMUNITY CLINICAL PSYCHOLOGY

Following a masters in clinical psychology from the University of Delhi, I was strongly inclined to step outside the ivory tower and become involved in real world service provision to the needy. Clarity on this goal came from projects such as an applied clinical class project in the masters program in which I did a mini-epidemiological survey of mental health needs of working poor families who served the university as janitors, gardeners, and so on. The need for intervention for mood and psychotic disorders was alarming, and the needed services were nowhere on the horizon. The same experience occurred when I did a research project on the state of services for the mentally handicapped in India for the All India Institute of Medical Sciences as a special project. The faculty around me at the time were involved in teaching and research, and practice opportunities for psychologists seemed to be confined to labor relations, industrial psychology, and organizational consultation. There were no role models or practice models for clinical or community psychology, the areas in which my interest had already begun to develop.

At this point I turned my sights to training and travel to the west to develop the expertise I wanted to have. In consulting with others about taking this course, the comments of Andre Beteille, an eminent and internationally renowned sociologist at the University of Delhi, remain in memory. He counseled that if I wanted to get on the conveyer belt of higher education and be served up to the market at the end of it all, I should go to the United States, and if I wanted to be handcrafted, then I should go to the United Kingdom: the two systems of higher education were very different. Coming from the society that I did, the handcrafted option felt more consonant and attractive. I competed for and won an Inlaks Scholarship, a merit scholarship that offered me the opportunity to pursue graduate studies at the University of Oxford in the United Kingdom. The admissions authorities, in consultation with the Department of Psychology at Oxford, assigned me to the supervision of eminent developmental psychologist Peter Bryant, Watts Professor of Psychology and Fellow of Wolfson College. Besides being a distinguished psychologist whose neo-Piagetian experimental work had substantially furthered our understanding of young children's development of perception and thinking, Peter was a human being of warmth, sincerity, and integrity; and a great mentor. We both quickly realized, however, that as well as we liked each other personally, we were mismatched professionally. He was a pure developmentalist and experimentalist, not a clinician or applied clinical researcher, and the closest that my interests could come to his were clinical-developmental, and he was not in a position to supervise this. Nor was anyone else in the largely experimental department of psychology at Oxford at the time. I could join Peter's experimental effort in understanding how young children's quantitative reasoning developed and how they processed numbers and graphs and so on, and become part of his dynamic and stimulating research group, but that did not seem in sync with me at the core. Looking back, it seems to me that the fact that this clarity came only after I was there in person in Oxford and had many conversations with Peter is testimony to the kind of international communications that were available and possible at the time more than twenty years ago, in contrast to the Internet age of the present day. Furthermore, speaking with practitioners in the United Kingdom at the time, it became clear that hands-on clinical training did not really occur in a very intensive or full-fledged way in their system until the postdoctoral level. This was helpful if frustrating information for me and resulted in my changing course and considering moving to the United States for further training.

By this time I was already aware of the family therapy literature. I remember having read Haley's statement that a revolution was occurring in the therapy room because more than one person (the whole family) was being seen in the clinician's office. I was immediately drawn to systemic ideas and practice and have long felt that my fit with it is attributable to my culture of origin and my way of being brought up. Being brought up in a collectivistic culture and owning many of its values makes me appreciate and understand the importance of the context over and in addition to the individual, when seeing emotional experience in the context of significant emotional relationships and valuing the engagement of the system in the intervention process.

I moved to Virginia Tech, to an AAMFT-accredited doctoral program. The Inlaks scholarship that came from a foundation belonging to an Indian woman, Indulakshmi Shivdesani, and which was administered by her Italian husband Count Nicola de Sella de Monteluce, carried over to Virginia Tech and set me up to receive the training I had been seeking.

My interest in serving the economically oppressed began in early childhood, growing up in India in a well-off family with considerable household help and witnessing great poverty all around me. I remember as a child of about five or six, living in our three-story ancestral home in Kolkata, observing particular homeless families lay claim to the footpath outside our home at dusk and set up their bedding, cook on their wood fires, and awake at the crack of dawn (which comes very early in the east) to bathe in the water from street hydrants. I still remember the laughter and play of the children bathing in the street at dawn, and the puzzled look on the face of the single woman who spoke to herself, and whom people called "mad." In the morning these folks would neatly wrap up all their belongings and disappear to return at dusk again. My internal responses as a young child observing all of this were those of abiding interest and an inexplicable sympathy, a mixture of awe in their hardiness and compassion for their hardships.

As an undergraduate at the University of Delhi's elite Lady Shri Ram College, I was a member of the National Honor Society and became involved in projects such as going into neighboring slums to bring literacy to housewives and mothers. I never failed to find a slum home that was spotlessly clean and tended with great care by the women I worked with, despite the overall squalor that lay all around outside. It is as if there was a great distinction between the private and public parts of space, with one owned with great respect and care and the other unclaimed, fetid, and overwhelming. The other aspects of those experiences were the warmth and generosity, the human kindness that was ever-present in the women I worked with, making my time spent with them very much an exchange in human terms, not a one-way street.

In time, in my life in the United States, I have focused my applied work on serving the economically oppressed and marginalized people of color. This allows me to reach out to some of the most challenged people through my clinical and professional skills and to the community and society through my social justice convictions. I have been a liberal all my life, growing up as a member of a privileged elite raised with a deep sense of responsibility to serve and give back and arriving eventually in the United States to experience being a minority immigrant. The latter experiences fueled my convictions to work in a more direct, visceral, and personal way than the former without the latter ever could have. Therein lies its value. I have expressed this before in a different way:

> In the process of immigration to the United States, I have personally lost the privilege of being among those who name everything. It is a privilege I have chosen to lose. In my pre-immigration life, I had the experience of a social context where privilege came for no good reason. In my post-immigration life, I have had the experience of a social context where discrimination comes for no good reason. The place in which I now stand in the fullness of the experiences of my life, with access to both kinds of contexts, I own as a unique place from which to give my voice to the cause of democratic social change. (Banerjee, 2002, pp. 14–15)

My experiences with the ever-present social impulse in the United States to take the different or unfamiliar—be it in dress, language, way of greeting, way of sitting, or anything else—and make it disappear or discount it has fueled my passion to advocate that core American culture evolve to its full multicultural potential. The advocacy comes through in the teaching and supervising I do with the next generation of clinicians I train, in the community-clinical service I do, and in the writing that I do to integrate personal narrative with scholarly analysis. Let me segue from the personal to the scholarly.

DRESS AS A MANIFEST ASPECT OF IDENTITY: A SCHOLARLY PERSPECTIVE

Anthropologists note that in environments in which intergroup differences are large, differentiation between groups tends to focus on

Figure 1. Original dress

Figure 2. The shift

Figure 3. Current dress

secondary or surface markers such as dress, language, and appearance. In environments where the differences between groups are small, differentiation tends to focus on primary markers such as kinship, commensurability, and religion (Sumberg, 1995; Nash, 1989). In America, where intergroup differences are large, appearance (or color and physiognomy) is frequently used to differentiate individuals and groups. Dress and language, the most changeable surface markers, disappear from the mainstream of life and thus reflect the power of assimilationist uniformity, the lack of value placed on lived diversity, and the social policy of white conformity that originated in the seventeenth century and left its definite mark on the society by the early twentieth century (Banerjee, 2002; Fairchild, 1926; Grant, 1916).

Dress is a manifest aspect of culture because it is socially visible and is therefore very important in social communication. It sets the stage for verbal interactions, the visual aspect of dress being primary in face-to-face interactions (Stone, 1962; Eicher & Sumberg, 1995). All forms of dress arise from cultural contexts and play a part in shaping those contexts as well. Dress can carry information on language, region, marriage customs, religious customs, and standards of beauty, and it can express emotional style and subjective experiences of identity (de Vos & Romanucci, 1982). Through the familiarity that it evokes, the information that it carries, and the subjective and affective responses that it engenders, the way of dressing a body can hinder or facilitate verbal or other communication (Sumberg, 1995).

Ethnic dress reflects collective self-image or identity and some of a culture's central values (Eicher & Sumberg, 1995). This is why ethnic dress can be an instrument of the preservation of group history and provide individuals with links to a meaningful heritage (Eicher, 1995). An example of this phenomenon is the headwrap as an item of dress among blacks, which in its style, underlying meanings, and functions is West African (Griebel, 1995). During slavery, the headwrap signified African origins and personal pride for blacks and a badge of servility for whites, a sign of devalued otherness. The headwrap survived brutal conditions of enslavement, a long history of privation, and many practical barriers to the continuance of material culture for blacks and is a small symbol of the depth, significance, and meaning of cultural markers in general. Those dual souls, described by W. E. B. Du Bois (1903) as souls forged in the crucible of racial slavery in America and a far older African one, are encoded in material form in the headwrap.

In the process of differentiation from one another, groups tend to use primary and secondary markers under different conditions, as has been mentioned before. Power differentials between the groups further complicate this interaction. In some cases, the larger group's recognition of the smaller group's culture (at points in history when it is politically feasible for the larger group) results in appropriating the smaller group's symbolism in such forms as dress, changing to some degree the symbol as well. For example, the Scottish highlanders' dress was recognized and popularized by the British in the mid-eighteenth century at a time when the British appeased the Scottish and secured their own power in political and demographic terms (Chapman, 1995). The kilt could be exploited for tourism and was thus transformed by the hand of the dominant outsider and the Scottish diaspora (Chapman, 1995). On the other hand, Bretons in France, whose growing population posed a threat to the French, lacked cultural support and recognition from the French until much later in time. This resulted in some Breton peasants giving up their traditional attire because of tension from the duality of their native attire appearing as elegant and in good taste in their own community and quaint and folklorish in the eyes of the French (Chapman, 1995).

A different outcome—mute assimilation—occurs when the power differential and access to resources between groups is perceived to be large. For example, young male Indians in the village of Shamanga in the Ecuador highlands, who traveled to the coast as migrant workers, adopted mestizo dress because foremen and co-workers mocked their Indian dress (Lentz, 1995). The women who remained in the village retained their dress, incorporating into it the colors and new fabrics from mestizo dress brought in by their men. These gendered strategies that the Indians of Shamanga adopted to survive economically and culturally came at the psychological price of internalized racism. Many elements of Indian culture, including dress, that were seen by the mestizos as primitive and negative were denied and internalized (Lentz, 1995, p. 290).

In the United States, mute assimilation of a wide cultural variation in minority cultures' dress is the norm in the mainstream of life. Ethnic dress is relegated to the realm of private social life or life in ethnic enclaves, indicating its lower status, recognition, and acceptance in the culture and society as a whole. The rich array of dress from the world's cultures is truncated by a culture yet to mature in its awareness and comfort with diversity.

World fashion or clothes such as business suits, t-shirts, jeans, athletic shoes, and so on can be considered to be the unofficial dress in the American mainstream. World fashion originates in the tailored garments of Europeans and is linked to urbanization (Eicher, 1995). Therefore, this unofficial national dress in America selects the symbols of European American culture among the many cultures represented by American peoples. The history of oppression as related to the Europeanization of dress has tenacious roots. Missionaries in the United States worked as hard to convert Dakota Indians to wearing European-style clothes as they did to converting them to Christianity (Eicher, 1995). Darwin and Dunlap (as cited in Eicher, 1995) argued that the myths inherited by the world in the last two centuries of economic and political ascendancy of European nations in the form of imperialism and colonialism includes the myth that wearing western dress implies moving up from primitivism to civilization.

Like culture itself, ethnic dress does not have to be a static reality. It is a domain of consumption that is particularly prone to change (Lentz, 1995) and is particularly adaptive. Can we imagine even for a moment, in this age of globalization, the U.S. mainstream transformed by the stamp of vibrancy of dress from all over the globe? Can we imagine how much richer our visual and cultural experiences could be, and how much more fluid, expansive, and multicultural our mentalities would need to be to navigate and interact with ease and knowledge in such an environment?

MY STORY AS IT LINKS TO MY DAUGHTER MIRA'S

My own struggles and transformation with dress in the public sphere stand as a model for my own daughter, Mira. Though she is still a young child, she is observant (as young children tend to be), and we often talk about dealing with differences in myriad forms, including dress. Earlier this year I was invited by her second-grade teacher to do a presentation on India. I happily agreed and arranged to be there on my daughter's seventh birthday along with my sons Rudy and Ives. On that day, I asked her and her eager-faced peers why they thought I was going to speak on India. Promptly came the reply "because you are from there." I elaborated that I was from here in America, but that I had come from India many years ago and so my roots were from there, and so were a part of Mira's. I went on to say that the other reason for talking about those roots of Mira's was that they were not spoken about or seen much in class. The children nodded in agreement and listened more intently. I unfurled a world map to place India in a geographical context relative to them. We talked about how long it takes Mira to fly over to see her grandparents (more than a day!). Children had questions about religion, terrain, climate, and language. Then I went on to focus the dialogue on dress, saying that there are so many things we could explore, but I wanted to offer them a chance to explore one of them that day, namely dress. I went up to the blackboard, drew two human figures, and dressed one in a female Indian costume, the sari, and the other in a male Indian counterpart, the churidar kurta. I wrote these words on the blackboard and we said them aloud together. I shared a Barbie doll in a sari that I had found in India recently and demonstrated draping myself in a sari as well. They seemed to be thrilled. My sons and I handed out activity sheets with human figures drawn on them, and they dove into dressing them in saris and churidar kurtas with the crayons and markers. Their colorful creations were wonderful. I went around to each child's desk and acknowledged each one individually, encouraging them to write the name of the outfit they had drawn and their own name on their sheet of paper, owning the lesson, so to speak. Afterward we celebrated with a mango fruit rollup snack that I had gotten from Little India.

Later the teacher reported to me that the children had really enjoyed the exposure to Indian dress and that they had continued to process the lesson in subsequent days. When I visited their spring open house a month later, their artwork from our time together was displayed all over their classroom as a multicultural activity. Most significant to me, which Mira said to me after we returned home from her class activity, was the statement "I thought they would make fun but they really loved what you did, Mom." I felt in that moment that she had gained an experience that gave her support, freedom, and permission to claim, in her own way in the public sphere of her classroom, dress that represented the distinctive minority part of her identity.

About six months later as I prepared to make a solo trip to India, Mira besieged me to be sure to bring her back a sari. In India I set about looking for a child-size sari and succeeded in acquiring a pale green silk sari for her. Upon mentioning her request to my family members in India, however, I was inundated with many more gifts of beautiful saris from them to her. She was thrilled and wanted to try out a bright red one with gold trim first. She was quite thrilled as she inspected herself in the mirror and twirled around, letting the gathers in her sari fan out. Then she said spontaneously that she wanted me to do the dress presentation at school for her eighth birthday as well, only this time she wanted me to drape her in one of her saris as well as part of the demonstration, where I had draped only myself in a sari the last time. It seemed to me that these dialogues, activities, and experiences had passed down to her a thread of her identity with regard to dress and as expressed through dress, and she had in her own way clearly claimed it.

DIVERSITY IN OUR CULTURE: DIVERSE NARRATIVES, NEW MIND-SETS, AND SOCIAL MIRRORING

This chapter is presented as a narrative that can serve as a psychologically powerful vehicle for weaving together in a coherent and comprehensive way the fabric of significant everyday experiences that shape our identities. Narratives can help us to make sense of and give meaning to a life of numerous experiences and daily challenges of coping with differences and "isms." This itself can be motivating and healing, deepening personal insights on self and context. Extensive and cogent narrative exposure to everyday struggles and issues faced by diverse ethnic minorities can serve readers by not only increasing knowledge but also empathy and readiness to work in diverse settings with diverse people.

Bringing diverse ethnic narratives into mainstream professional discourse opens up possibilities for rich and rewarding dialogue across groups. This type of activity is fundamentally important to diversification at the level of awareness and consciousness in the professional mainstream and in the societal mainstream. In other words, such activity can play a part in "carrying a robust and live multiculturalism into the heart and soul of the culture" (Banerjee, 2002, p. 7).

In my view, multiculturalism is an advantageous way for the mental health and human service professions to be oriented in the twenty-first century as the world continues to move toward a complex, communicationally, and technologically integrated and culturally diverse global village. Effective contributions in this context can come not from an avoidance of diversity or retreat to assimilationist processes but from interest, understanding, and ease with it.

We are not a society with a history or a culture that is at ease with differences, but one that is being actively challenged on this from many quarters, due to the democratic and open nature of our polity. We are also a young and dynamic society that has been transforming, and at the same time the phenomenon of racism has become subtler. It is thus less obviously present, but it is very often there in the demeanor, the slips, the seating patterns, the unconscious acts, and the hidden but conscious attitudes and behaviors. The personal desire to engage with these issues is important. It involves owning such painful realities that may directly contrast what we may want to believe about ourselves, and involves having the support of others who are similarly engaged and with whom triumphs and struggles on this journey can be meaningfully shared.

In the end, difference and diversity are lived issues and matters of personal choice and conviction. They cannot be mandated. So far as we live lives of voluntary segregation with limited real commitment to any diversity that challenges us in our personal lives and in our work, we remain impotent to impact the course of the profession and society with it. In this connection, I offer some thoughts in the context of how we name ourselves and others and the consequences of this, as it has clear relevance for the issue of dress as well (Banerjee, 2000). First, it is important to value heterogeneity itself (in place of uniformity), as in a heterogeneous society this would be a healthy act of self-owning. Thus in the context of dress, children, adolescents, and adults can be encouraged to explore and wear majority and minority forms of dress. They can create their own variations based on their creativity, taste, and the pragmatic considerations of weather, laundering, and so on. Societal mirroring of this heterogeneity of dress as both recognizable and valued, when replacing the exotic or outsider status currently given to it, would help in the multicultural evolution of social contexts of dress. Further, such fluidity in replacing more homogenous ways of thinking about dress would encourage mentalities that see subgroup boundaries as permeable and the border as a place of meaningful sharing (Saldivar, 1990). Once again, this would be a vital mind-set that could promote acceptance of diversity and multiculturalism not only with dress but with many other issues besides. The assumption here is not that multiculturalism is an absolute good for society. Rather "from a pragmatic and relative standpoint . . . in the context of a free and heterogenous society, it can be argued to be psychologically, socially and politically good because it can allow a healthy self-owning, a basis for egalitarianism and unification" (Banerjee, 2002, p. 4).

EXAMINED OR UNEXAMINED, DRESS IS SOCIALLY VISIBLE: HOW DIVERSE CAN WE BE?

Returning to the specific issue of ethnic dress, I have looked back many times with myriad feelings at my personal transformation and experiences. I choose to highlight it, as it is one of those silent but very socially salient issues, and therefore a subject of particular oppression in that context. No one raises it as an issue; no one really talks about it. I have felt that I was able to make a decision on professional dress that I found I could live with and have certainly come to terms with. I must add that I have worn a diamond nose stud for the last three decades, ever since I took lessons in bharatanatyam, a classical Indian dance form in Delhi. It was part of a dancer's traditional dress to have the right nostril pierced, and so I did. Though I gave up the dance form long ago and my traditional Indian clothes later on, I held on to the nose stud, which remains with me today. Somewhere, I said to myself, one draws a line!

The fact that the change in dress was asked of me is a barometer of how much we in the profession are able to tolerate diversity, respect people's manifest identities expressed in their dress, and indeed accept diversity as something inherent to our society—something that is at its heart and something that is our own. The historical practice has been to set the standard in terms of white American dress and subjugate all to it. This is the mute assimilation phenomenon referred to in the anthropological literature (Eicher & Sumberg, 1995). At the same time, the standards of dress in the profession reflect perceived expectations of the larger society. Catering to those expectations in the therapy room becomes necessary, since people come to see a therapist at times of stress and distress, and dealing with the unexpected and unrecognized can add to a person's stress. So we return to the larger question, one that bears reflection by each of us: how can we participate in the transformation of a core Eurocentric, assimilationist culture to a genuinely multicultural one that is congruent with the sociopolitical ideals of a plural, secular democracy?

Personally, I do not know that given the chance to do so tomorrow, I would or could return to the way I used to dress in India and when I first migrated to the United States. I do not know that we can walk down the same road twice. I see myself as an Indian American, and my western dress with an Indian stamp accurately reflects and proclaims my identity. My husband is white, and my children are growing up with Indian American, European American, and multicultural ethnic influences beyond the identities and choices of their parents. As immigration to the United States has been increasingly non-European and recent immigrants have been holding on and integrating culturally to some degree rather than giving up and integrating, more discussion about attitudes toward diversity of dress and other manifest aspects of ethnic identity, notably language (a vehicle to the heart of cultures), would be very worthwhile.

As Nash (1989) and Sumberg (1995) have pointed out, in vastly heterogeneous societies, surface markers or manifest aspects of difference are the first ones that people tend to and perhaps need to deal with, as they are socially visible and prominent. A traditional Arab American immigrant may be more effectively outreached in therapy by someone in traditional dress and familiar with cultural nuances and the Arabic language, as a bilingual Latino American may be by someone with bilingual facility. As ethnic minorities own their manifest and latent diversity and the Euro-American majority respects, accepts, and owns this diversity and replaces and reflects on the homogeneity of their own socialization and integration into the U.S. mainstream, progress on the path of creating multicultural professional cultures within a multicultural, democratic society can be made.

Toolbox for Change

For	Images/perceptions	Strategies for change
Individuals	Tailored garments of European origin are what one wears and expects to see at work. They denote American dress.	Reflect on homogenizing forces on dress in the public/professional sphere. Claim the choice to own and embrace distinct ways of dress and incorporate into own attire as desired, comfortable, and appropriate in the public sphere. Model and pass down this owning intergenerationally. Embrace heterogeneity of dress in the public sphere as representative of social diversity and freedom of expression.
Community	To fit in, to be recognized, to succeed, one must dress in this manner. Dress outside this genre is unfamiliar and less acceptable.	Raise awareness through programs offered to adults at community centers, churches, and other secular and religious organizations about the richness and meaning behind diversity in dress. Include corporate sponsors from textile, clothing, and affiliated industries. Advocate for informed, respectful representation of heterogeneity of dress in advertising by corporate businesses and by the media.

continued

Toolbox for Change (continued)

For	Images/perceptions	Strategies for change
Practitioners/ educators	Propriety/impropriety of dress is considered within mainstream notions and standards, not multicultural ones.	Include discussion of dress as a topic in multiculturalism in school and college curricula. Include workshops and hands-on experiential explorations of diversity in dress in children's art, summer school, after-school, and community programs. Introduce heterogeneity in the therapy room in parallel with the extent of visible heterogeneity in the larger community.

Homogeneity of dress based on Eurocentric standards is considered the appropriate dress for the public sphere in the United States. Successful and respected citizens dress in this way. The media, advertising, and garment industries are built on this assumption. Dress that is culturally appropriate in many non-European cultures for the public sphere is unincorporated in the U.S. public domain, and retains an exotic as well as a lower status insofar as it is mostly visible in ethnic enclaves in the private domain. This issue is little discussed and questioned and thus remains guided by the assumption that what is seen, known, and understood to be American dress is centrally connected with the cultural antecedents of its European immigrants, and peripherally with the cultures of all its other immigrants.

ACKNOWLEDGMENTS

Parts of this chapter appeared before in *Psychological Foundations*, the journal's winter 2002 special international issue. The author retained the copyrights for those materials.

The author acknowledges her debt to her father for his fine and aesthetic sartorial sense, to her mother for her commitment to keeping alive traditional weavers and weaves, and to the rich legacy left by anonymous weavers, artists, and craftswomen and men in India who have given their ideas, imaginations, sweat, and toil generation after generation to create beautiful fabrics that Indians and many others the world over have relished and enjoyed for centuries. Thanks are also gratefully extended to the author's son Rudy and friend Nicola Ragge for taking the two later photographs of her that appear in this chapter.

REFERENCES

Atkinson, D. R., Morten, G., & Sue, D. W. (Eds.). (1989). *Counseling American minorities: A cross-cultural perspective.* Dubuque, IA: William C. Brown.

Banerjee (nee Roy), L. (1985, April). Review of cultural perspectives in family therapy. In J. C. Falicov (Ed.), *Family relations.* National Council of Family Relations.

Banerjee, L. (2000). Through a child's eyes: What's in a name and other thoughts on social categorizations in America. *The Community Psychologist, 33*(2), 16–18.

Banerjee, L. (2002). Psychology and the reach of multiculturalism in American culture. In E. Davis-Russell (Ed.), *Multicultural education, research, intervention and training.* San Francisco: Jossey-Bass.

Carter, R. T. (1995). *The influence of race and racial identity in psychotherapy, towards a racially inclusive model.* New York: John Wiley.

Chapman, M. (1995). Freezing the frame: Dress and ethnicity in Brittany and Gaelic Scotland. In J. B. Eicher (Ed.), *Dress and ethnicity: Change across space and time.* Oxford: Berg Publishers.

Cross, W. (1995). The psychology of nigrescence: Revisiting the cross model. In J. G. Ponteretto, J. M. Casas, L. A. Suzuki, & D. M. Alexander (Eds.), *Handbook of multicultural counseling* (pp. 93–122). Thousand Oaks, CA: SAGE Publications, Inc.

de Vos, G., & Romanucci-Ross, L. (Eds.). (1982). *Ethnic identity: Cultural continuities and change.* Chicago: University of Chicago Press.

Du Bois, W. E. B. (1903). *The souls of black folks.* New York: Fawcett.

Eicher, J. B. (1995). Introduction: Dress as expression of ethnic identity. In J. B. Eicher (Ed.), *Dress and ethnicity: Change across space and time.* Oxford: Berg Publishers.

Eicher, J. B., & Sumberg, B. (1995). World fashion, ethnic and national dress. In J. B. Eicher (Ed.), *Dress and ethnicity: Change across space and time.* Oxford: Berg Publishers.

Fairchild, H. (1926). *The melting pot mistake.* Boston: Little Brown.

Grant, M. (1916). *The passing of the great race.* New York: Scribner.

Griebel, H. B. (1995). The West African origin of the African-American headwrap. In J. B. Eicher (Ed.), *Dress and ethnicity: Change across space and time.* Oxford: Berg Publishers.

Helms, J. E. (1995). An update of Helms's white and people of color racial identity models. In J. G. Ponteretto, J. M. Casas, L. A. Suzuki, & D. M. Alexander (Eds.), *Handbook of multicultural counseling* (pp. 181–198). Thousand Oaks, CA: SAGE Publications, Inc.

Jones, C., & Shorter-Gooden, K. (2003). *Shifting: The double lives of black women in America.* New York: Harper Collins.

Lentz, C. (1995). Ethnic conflict and changing dress codes: A case study of an Indian migrant village in highland Ecuador. In J. B. Eicher (Ed.), *Dress and ethnicity: Change across space and time.* Oxford: Berg Publishers.

Mukherjee, B. (1997). Beyond multiculturalism: Surviving in the nineties. In I. Reed (Ed.), *MultiAmerica: Essays on cultural war and cultural peace.* New York: Viking Press.

Nash, M. (1989). *The cauldron of ethnicity in the modern world.* Chicago: University Press.

Parham, T. (1989). Cycles of psychological nigresence. *The Counseling Psychologist, 17*(2), 187–226.

Phinney, J. (1990). Ethnic identity in adolescents and adults: Review of research. *Psychological Bulletin, 108,* 499–514.

Ponteretto, J., & Pederson, P. (1993). *Preventing prejudice.* Newbury Park, CA: SAGE Publications, Inc.

Saldivar, R. (1990). *Chicano narrative: Dialectics of difference.* Madison: University of Wisconsin Press.

Stone, G. (1962). Appearance and the self. In A. M. Rose (Ed.), *Human behavior and the social process: An interactionist approach.* New York: Routledge and Kegan Paul.

Sumberg, B. (1995). Dress and ethnic differentiation in the Niger Delta. In J. B. Eicher (Ed.), *Dress and ethnicity: Change across space and time.* Oxford: Berg Publishers.

Yi, K., & Shorter-Gooden, K. (1999). Ethnic identity formation: From stage theory to a constructivist narrative model. *Psychotherapy, 36*(1), 16–26.

CHAPTER 2

Spiritual Diversity and Clinical Practice

Ilene Serlin

What is the relevance of religious and spiritual diversity to the psychology of prejudice and discrimination? At the American Psychological Association's 1999 National Multicultural Conference and Summit, one of the three major themes was "spirituality as a basic dimension of the human condition" (Sue, Bingham, Porche-Burke, & Vasquez, 1999, p. 1065), which psychologists have an ethical mandate to address. While more crises of spirituality are being reported to therapists and more Americans are searching for meaning in their lives, however, psychologists are unable to help.

With the effects of globalization and the breakdown of traditional communities comes the freedom to intermarry and create one's own forms of religion and spirituality (Kristof, 2003; Serlin, 2001).While this may in some cases lead to increased openness and tolerance, it can also lead to backlashes of fear and discrimination. This form of discrimination is also found in response to other forms of cultural diversity. Stuart notes, "Despite innovative efforts to teach cultural competence, stereotypic thinking still clouds many evaluation and intervention efforts" (2004, p. 3). Research shows that most psychologists are not only unprepared to deal with these issues of religious and spiritual diversity, however, but actually have their own biases and prejudices against religion (Shafranske & Malony, 1990).

This chapter, therefore, builds on findings from APA's National Multicultural Conference and Summit in Newport Beach, California, which recommended that "psychology must break away from being a unidimensional science, that it must recognize the multifaceted layers of existence, that spirituality and meaning in the life context are important, and that psychology must balance its reductionistic tendencies with the knowledge that the whole is greater than the sum of its parts. Understanding that people are cultural and spiritual beings is a necessary condition for a psychology of human existence" (Sue et al., 1999, p. 1065).

Psychologists should be able to demonstrate religious and spiritual competency (Pope-David & Coleman, 1997), so this chapter proposes theoretical and clinical examples of how to teach psychologists this competence. It explores the relationship between religious and spiritual diversity and the psychology of prejudice and discrimination from the following three perspectives: the impact of globalization on religious and spiritual diversity; the relationships among religion, spirituality, and psychology; and the importance of religious and spiritual competency to clinical practice.

GLOBALIZATION AND RELIGIOUS AND SPIRITUAL DIVERSITY

Religious affiliations are changing rapidly across the globe as well as within our own country. Waves of immigration have made religious pluralism inevitable. Religion has always been a strong force in America (Kasmin & Lachman, 1993); since the American Revolution, when almost all Americans were Protestants (Hoge, 1996, p. 24), the religious makeup has changed. A Gallup poll from 1992 estimated that 56 percent of Americans were Protestant, 26 percent were Catholic, 2 percent Jewish, 7 percent other, and 9 percent marked no preference. Other figures show that the number of Muslims is increasing and is now between 1.5 percent and 2 percent of the population. Conservative Catholics have the highest birthrate, and the majority of immigrants today are Catholic, with 25 percent to 35 percent being Latino (Hoge, 1996, p. 25). Many people today are attracted to Zen and Tibetan Buddhism, Sufism, Hinduism, and contemplative or mystical branches of Christianity and Judaism. A national survey showed that 92 percent of all Americans said, "my religious faith is the most important influence in my life" (Bergin & Jensen, 1990, p. 5). Most Americans report that they believe in God, and 75 percent identify themselves as religious (Cadwallader, 1991), while more than 40 percent have admitted to a mystical experience or communication with transpersonal beings (Gallup & Castelli, 1989). Nine out of ten Americans say they pray, and 97 percent believe that their prayers are heard (Steere, 1997). Spiritually based rituals have been shown to be effective coping strategies for dealing with life stresses (Pargament, 1997), while the importance of religion is growing among married couples and identified as an "essential ingredient" in long-term satisfying marriages (Kaslow & Robison, 1996). Other individuals today choose new forms of religion or spirituality, or even more esoteric practices such as witchcraft and neo-paganism or earth-based goddess religions (Gimbutas, 1982; Neumann, 1955), while some develop a strictly personal form of spirituality. Recent figures show an increasing number of unaffiliated individuals, while many face unprecedented challenges about forming communities and relationships from new combinations of cultural backgrounds and traditions.

While research is beginning to track the impact of multicultural couples and families, however, there is relatively little on the effect of spiritual or religious diversity. These differences may include issues of child-rearing, family traditions, in-law and blended family issues, and personal versus traditional religious or spiritual practices. As globalization brings more interpersonal and interchangeable surroundings, people are losing their sense of place and local community. A community traditionally provided its members with a stable sense of identity, their place in the world, role models, support, and a set of values and beliefs to live by. Norms of moral behavior regulated relationships during courtship and marriage and provided a connection to the ancestors and continuity over time.

However, many individuals today are disconnected from that source of identity and stability. They are vulnerable and without traditional support structures (Sue, 1999). They may find the challenge of constructing a personal worldview of purpose and meaning overwhelming, become confused and depressed, and come to psychologists' offices with a *crisis of meaning*. According to the *San Francisco Chronicle*, the group of people who marked "no religion" (the so-called "nones") was "one of the fastest growing religious categories in the United States" (Lattin, 2003, p. A1). The path of creating a personal spirituality is lonely; on the other hand, a spiritual practice can buffer modern Americans in a stressful society.

Spirituality and mental health have a long history of connection in America, dating back to the Puritans' mission to reform society. Religion has been a voice against alcohol abuse, adultery, and forms of oppression. It has taken strong stands against issues like abortion, sex outside marriage, and sex between people of the same sex. From a societal perspective, issues of discrimination and prejudice are in effect inseparable from issues of religion and spirituality. Sensitivity to cultural differences helps us "recognize that traditional psychological concepts and theories were developed from a predominantly Euro-American context and may be limited in their applicability to the emerging racially and culturally diverse population in the United States" (Sue et al., 1999, p. 1063).

When their sense of meaning breaks down, instead of seeking counseling from priests or other religious figures, individuals may come to therapists with a crisis of meaning. There is a crucial role for psychologists to play in helping people sort out highly diverse cultural influences and make meaningful choices for themselves.

Clinical Vignette: Psychologists Need to Inquire about a Patient's Religious and Spiritual History at Intake

One client told me that she was having a difficult time putting together her own forms of spiritual practice. Her mother was a Southern Baptist and her father Catholic. She has memories of being in both churches, but doesn't have a church of her own. In fact, she describes her lack of roots in any one community as a source of psychological pain.

In our work together, she talked, drew, and danced out her cultural images. She used music from her own culture and explored feminine role models from those traditions. She needed new images to help her re-imagine herself as a woman, a lover, an artist, and a healer. By exploring a variety of images from other cultures and historical times, she could put together her own set of images. These gave her a sense of self that was more coherent, flexible, and resilient.

RELIGION, SPIRITUALITY, AND PSYCHOLOGY

Religion and psychology have only recently been separated; the Latin term *psychologia* was first used by Maruic about 1524 to refer to one of the three divisions of pneumatology, the science of spiritual beings and substances. *Pneuma* (spirit or religious aspect) was inseparable from *psyche*, or soul (Vande Kemp, 1996, p. 72). However, since that time, modern psychiatry and psychology have been trying to situate themselves as natural sciences, aiming to liberate man from religion (Needleman, 1983, p. 6). Positivist scientific psychology uses an exclusive method and view of truth, instead of the multiple epistemologies that are part of the history of knowledge. Psychology, once linked with philosophy, theology, and the arts, has followed medical psychiatry into science (Hillman, 1972). Returning religious and spiritual dimensions to psychology rebalances the positivist trend of modern psychology and is congruent with a broader feminist, narrative, and multicultural psychology whose epistemology is based on personal knowledge (Polanyi, 1958) and alternative ways of knowing (Polkinghorne, 1994).

Sue et al. challenge us to see the cultural component of these epistemological differences: "Moreover, a psychology based solely on the separation of science and spirituality and that uses primarily the segmented and reductionistic tenets of the natural sciences is one that may not be shared by three quarters of the world nor by the emerging culturally diverse groups in the United States" (Sue et al., 1999, p. 1065). Because of this, psychological theories are not necessarily generalizable across cultures. Included in this definition of culture is "subjective" culture, which "includes such elements as social norms, roles, beliefs, and values" and aspects of "spirituality and religion" (Betancourt & Lopez, 1993, p. 631). Cultural differences also affect research outcomes and threaten external validity.

Definition of Terms

Another problem with analyzing the impact of religious diversity and the psychology of discrimination is that definitions of religion and spirituality are confusing. The literature in psychology shows different definitions about to what extent experiences of religion or spirituality include a divine power, a set of beliefs or practices, and a cultural context. For example, the experience of spirituality in family therapy practice has been defined as "a relationship with a Transcendent Being that fosters a sense of meaning, purpose, and mission in life" (Hodge, 2000, pp. 218–219). Religion is usually associated with structured rituals or practices, while spirituality can be defined as a personal and direct experience of the sacred (R. Walsh, 1999, p. 3). Definitions of spirituality have also included an ecological and moral dimension, such as the sense of "connectedness" that spreads out to a compassionate concern for all beings (Elkins, Hedstrom, Jughes, Leaf, & Saunders, 1988) and "living in a manner consistent with their interior value framework" (Genia, 1990). In *Religion and the Clinical Practice of Psychology* (1996), Shafranske distinguishes five kinds of religious/spiritual practices: religious preference, church affiliation, church involvement, religious belief, and personal religious behavior. Wulff contrasts "cumulative tradition" as the "observable contents—temples, scriptures, myths, moral codes, social institutions, and so on—" with faith as the "essential and less variable personal quality . . . one's orientation toward oneself, other people, and the universe as they are experienced in the light of the transcendent dimension" (1996, p. 47). Whatever definitions are used to describe these dimensions of meaning and self-knowledge, however, they have been significantly left out of our value-free scientific psychology.

The split between religion and practice in society is mirrored in the split between religion and practice in the profession of psychology. Modern psychologists tried to position psychology as a science and thus separate it from its roots in religion and philosophy. Sigmund Freud (1927/1961), a product of the German Enlightenment, considered religion to be a defense against unacceptable impulses. Based on a belief in a father God and ritualistic practices, religion was "an illusion" (Freud, 1927/1961).

However, not all psychologists were against religion. There has always been an underground tradition of psychologists interested in consciousness and religion. For example, William James in *The Varieties of Religious Experience* considered religion to be more than the outer behaviors of religious practice and actually "an essential organ of our life, performing a function which no other portion of our nature can so successfully fulfill" (1902/1985, p. 49). Swiss psychiatrist Carl Jung (1932/1969) concluded, "Among all my patients in the second half of life—that is to say, over thirty-five—there has not been one whose problem in the last resort was not that of finding a religious outlook on life. It is safe to say that every one of them fell ill because he had lost what the living religions of every age have given to their followers, and none of them has been really healed who did not regain his religious outlook" (p. 334). Ferenczi described the therapeutic process as "redemption" and the "similarity of psychotherapeutic love to that love which permeates the Judeo-Christian tradition" (De Forest, 1954, p. 179). Erik Erikson valued the fact that religion connects us back to our deepest human longings, childhood needs, and basic ontological security. For humanistic psychologists, religion was less a regressive function than a progressive one, connecting human beings to the "farthest reaches of the human spirit" (Maslow, 1971). Gordon Allport (1950) was one of the first to describe and document a "mature religious sentiment" as well-differentiated, dynamic, directive, comprehensive, integral, and heuristic (Wulff, 1996, p. 60). The first to make the useful distinction between extrinsic and intrinsic spirituality, Allport discovered an important relationship between extrinsic religious attitudes, prejudice, and traits such as authoritarianism, ethnocentrism, dogmatism, and prejudice against blacks, gay men, and lesbians (Wulff, 1996, p. 61). Erich Fromm contrasted authoritarian religions that emphasized submission to a higher power, guilt, and sorrow with humanist religions that stressed optimal development of compassion, love, and a mature relationship with nature and other human beings. Abraham Maslow also saw religion as a path to human excellence, a life of integration and wholeness, and a mystical experience that was filled with wonder and awe. According to Victor Frankl (1959), religion helps us confront the void of disintegration and discover meaning, coherence, and integration. Psychiatrist Robert Assagioli extended the therapeutic goal of personality integration with spiritual dimensions in a process called "psychosynthesis."

Another link between religion and psychology concerns the relation of religion to mental health. Religion has been positively correlated with mental health: "Through its function of going beyond explanation to acceptance, faith instills a sense of meaning, coherence, and at times, courage in the face of confusion, disappointment, loss, suffering, and anomie" (Shafranske, 1996, p. 2). Crises of meaning can occur at any point in the life cycle, but are particularly apt to hit during times of transition like graduation from high school, marriage, birth of a child, loss of a loved one, and living with a life-threatening illness. Psychiatrist Roger Walsh notes that a spiritual approach to psychotherapy has been positively correlated with decreased anxiety and conflict, enhanced creativity, increased health and longevity, deeper empathy, greater marital satisfaction, and resiliency (1999). A negative relationship between religiosity and suicide, between religious commitment and drug use, and between church attendance and divorce; a positive relationship between religious participation and well-being for the elderly; lower levels of depression in college students; and a negative relationship between religiosity and suggestibility were reported by Gartner (1996). In addition, some religions experience prejudice more than others. Some non-western spiritual traditions like Buddhism are becoming more popular, but still face discrimination in mainstream Protestant America. How does a psychologist address these issues, and what kind of training should she or he have?

RELIGIOUS AND SPIRITUAL COMPETENCY

Religious and spiritual diversity are parts of a general understanding of the need for diversity-based psychology. Awareness of the need for multicultural competence in the training and practice of psychology was achieved with the Guidelines on Multicultural Education, Training, Research, Practice, and Organizational Change for Psychologists (American Psychological Association, 2003) and the APA's 2002 Ethical Principles and Code of Conduct (Knapp & VandeCreek, 2003). A new emphasis on training in diversity includes competence in religious and spiritual diversity (Manese, Saito, & Rodolfa, 2004). The multicultural guidelines for competency are applicable to spiritual and religious diversity. These include awareness of one's attitudes and beliefs, knowledge about cultural differences, and skills in working with diverse groups (Sue, Arredondo, & McDavis, 1992). In addition, the creation of a safe space for psychotherapy is an ethical practice. Pope, Sonne, and Holroyd (1993) listed several factors that contribute to what Manese et al. call a "safe diverse training and practice environment" (2004, p. 19), such as respect for the other and sensitivity and empathy for the other's experiences.

However, training in religious and spiritual competence is not available to most psychologists. In 1948, Allport examined fifty psychology textbooks published between 1928 and 1945 and concluded that "recent authors have virtually banished from their pages the essential problems of *the will, conscience, reasoning . . . self, subjective values*, and the *individual's world view*" (1948, p. 80). The profession has not changed much since that time (Shafranske, 1996, p. xv).

Yet some clients are reporting that they feel fragmented by having to consult both psychotherapists and pastors to address both relationship and spiritual issues (Griffith & Griffith, 1992); their needs are not being met. They need help navigating their spiritual and psychological confusion (Serlin, 1989b, 2000). Not only are most psychologists not trained to deal with these issues, but they may in fact have a bias against religion. They report feeling poorly prepared to deal with clients' religious and spiritual issues (Shafranske & Malony,

1990) or the psychological effects of globalization (Arnett, 2002, p. 774). They may over-medicate or over-pathologize their clients, missing an opportunity to help them discover the meaning of their symptoms and construct a new identity. Psychologists should not reduce all conflicts to inner psychological disorders, and they should acknowledge the very real impacts of religious and spiritual issues. They should have a clinical proficiency in religious and spiritual diversity issues. They have an "ethical responsibility" to teach it (Shafranske, 1996; Vaughan, 1987). Religious and spiritual competency includes a familiarity with differences between spirituality and religion, ability to differentiate between a healthy and pathological religious or spiritual experience, and an understanding of how spirituality can be both a problem and a helpful dimension in psychotherapy.

In response to the culture's increasing hunger for issues of meaning and purpose, psychiatry and psychology responded with the creation of a new diagnostic category called "religious or spiritual problems" in the 1994 *Diagnostic and Statistical Manual of Mental Disorders* (American Psychiatric Association, 1994). The role of spirituality is gaining notice in psychology (Tan, 2003; F. Walsh, 1999) and family therapy and couples counseling (Anderson & Worthen, 1997; Moules, 2000; Prest & Keller, 1993; Richards & Bergin, 1997; Rotz, Russell, & Wright, 1993). Some psychospiritual interventions have been empirically validated (Jacobs, 1992; Pargament, 1997; Worthington, Kurusu, McCullough, & Sandage, 1996) and correlated with religious attitudes of the therapist (DiBlasio, 1993; Moon, Willis, Bailey, & Kwansy, 1993). The first APA-accredited integrative doctoral degree was the Graduate School of Psychology at Fuller Theological Seminary, followed by Brigham Young University and others that offered courses like "Spiritual Issues in Family Therapy," which is offered in the masters in family therapy program at the University of San Diego (Patterson, Hayworth, Turner, & Raskin, 2000). A few organizations, like the Spiritual Emergency Network in Palo Alto, California, specially train counselors to recognize and help with "spiritual emergencies." Nontraditional programs exist in areas of creation spirituality, transpersonal psychology, and consciousness studies. Other programs have an East/West perspective on spirituality and psychology, like the Naropa Institute in Colorado, the California Institute of Integral Studies, and the Institute of Transpersonal Psychology.

Interest in the psychology of religion has grown also within the organized professional structures of psychology. In 1975, the American

Psychological Association formed a division called Psychology of Religion (Division 36). In 1961, the *Journal of Religion and Health* was founded, and in 1991 the *International Journal for the Psychology of Religion* was founded (Wulff, 1996, p. 45). Textbooks began appearing (Argyle & Beit-Hallahmi, 1975; Meadow & Kahoe, 1984; Spilke, Hood, & Gorsuch, 1985; Wulff, 1991).

Many crises of meaning, however, do not present floridly as spiritual or religious emergencies, but show up in our clients' everyday descriptions of inner emptiness and despair. Some clients describe the vague feeling of wanting to connect to something "beyond themselves," while others want to connect to a sense of meaning in their work. These spiritual crises are not psychiatric disorders that require treatment. They are existential and spiritual afflictions of the psyche.

Clinical Vignette: Psychologists Should Be Aware of the Role of Meaning in Their Patients' Lives

In my office, I see young people working for hi-tech or prestigious companies who find no meaning in their lives. They have "arrived" in their prime years of late twenties or early thirties, they are making large salaries, and they feel that they should be enjoying their lives. Instead, many are lonely, feel that what they are doing every day is pointless, and have trouble motivating themselves. Their lives have lost their meaning.

A crisis of meaning occurs also in their relationships. Why should they marry today? No longer a guarantee of security, relationships need a new reason for being. Some couples come to therapy to find more meaning in their lives together. Or they may discover that a relationship does not guarantee intimacy or stop their loneliness. New studies have shown that even intramarriage does not bring more intimacy than intermarriage (Heller & Wood, 2000, p. 245). What they miss is a sense of communion and connection that is often described as spiritual. The need for "reclaiming connection" to the basic web of relationships and life is a basic human right (Spretnak, 1991, p. 22).

Finally, relationships no longer provide a sense of home. Couples are transient, and few have family homes or families. Many young couples are desperate to make homes but cannot afford the high nationwide prices. Not only do they not have a literal home, but they also lack the neighborhood and web of family responsibilities to create a sense of place. Consequently, they are disoriented, flighty, and agitated. Spiritual practices teach them how to stay grounded in themselves.

THERAPEUTIC APPROACHES: A BRIEF HISTORY

A student training in religious and spiritual dimensions in psychotherapy needs to know the history of this field. Knowledge of these dimensions is ethically mandated, according to Guideline 2 of the Guidelines on Multicultural Education, which says, "Psychologists are encouraged to recognize the importance of multicultural sensitivity/responsiveness, knowledge and understanding about ethnically and racially different individuals (Manese et al., 2004, p. 18)." Understanding the historical resistances and splits between psychology and religion, as well as the history of psychological practices that embrace religious and spiritual diversity, is the foundation of such knowledge.

To provide some of that background knowledge, this chapter will provide a brief theoretical overview of historic and contemporary psychotherapeutic approaches that integrate spirituality into their theory and practices. The following section will summarize some of the major schools and briefly describe their traditions and approaches to the issue of spirituality and psychotherapy.

Integrative Movements

During Boston's Emmanuel Movement, psychotherapy used mental, moral, and spiritual methods to help sick people. After that movement, the clinical pastoral education (CPE) and pastoral counseling movements emerged as new specializations within psychology (Vande Kemp, 1996). The Christian Psychopathic Hospitals were founded in 1910, followed by private psychiatric hospitals with Christian therapy units. The field of hospital chaplaincy is a growing therapeutic application that is an attractive alternative to the traditional clinical psychology route, and its training programs can offer useful curricula to training programs in psychology and religion.

Existential Psychologies

Theologians and philosophers like Paul Tillich (1952) and Soren Kierkegaard (1844/1941) described existential states like anxiety, dread, fear, and trembling. Martin Buber (1922/1937) integrated Jewish mysticism with existentialism in the form of dialogue between man and God or man and man. Their astute psychological and phenomenological investigation into layers of the psyche contributed to a psychological understanding of the existential human condition. They had immediate influence on a new generation of American psychologists like Rollo May, James Bugental, and Irving Yalom, who developed existential and humanistic perspectives on psychotherapy (Bugental, 1976; May, 1940; Schneider & May, 1994; Yalom, 1980).

Transpersonal Psychology

Transpersonal psychologists critique western psychology for not going far enough. While western psychology can help us recognize dysfunctional patterns and free ourselves from our pasts, it lacks theory or practices to help us move beyond these patterns. Western psychology has a well-developed taxonomy of mental disorders, but almost nothing about mental "order" or, as the Buddhists say, "basic sanity," or extraordinary states of mind (Wilbur, 1981).

In 1969, Maslow and Sutich (Sutich, 1969) founded the *Journal of Transpersonal Psychology* and the Association for Transpersonal Psychology to explore "the farther reaches of human nature." Maslow defined transpersonal psychology as a "higher Fourth Psychology, transpersonal, transhuman, centered in the cosmos rather than in human needs and interest, going beyond humanness, identity, self-actualization and the like. . . . We need something 'bigger than we are' to be awed by and to commit ourselves to in a new, naturalistic, empirical, non-churchly sense, perhaps as Thorough and Whitman, William James and John Dewey did" (Maslow, 1968, pp. iii–iv). The early transpersonal theorists believed that consciousness existed as a phenomenon that could be systematically studied by science. It used clinical and experiential methods such as meditation to study inner states (Murphy & Donovan, 1997).

Abraham Maslow, president of the American Psychological Association from 1967–1968, helped establish transpersonal psychology in the United States. He theorized that human beings needed to first satisfy their basic needs for food and shelter, but then experienced a drive for higher states of consciousness (Maslow, 1971). Maslow identified such extraordinary states of mind as metavalues of "wholeness, perfection, completion, justice, aliveness, richness, simplicity, beauty, goodness, uniqueness, effortlessness, playfulness, truth, and self-sufficiency" (Hastings, 1999, p. 193). Today transpersonal psychology has its own national and international organization, journals, and wide popular interest (Frager, 1989; Fadiman & Frager, 1998).

Buddhist Psychology

Because the Buddhist method of inquiry into the phenomenology of mind is experiential, it includes the bodily experience of mind: namely, emotions. A Buddhist approach to psychotherapy, therefore, integrates body and mind through meditation and cultivation of the mind (Trungpa, 1969, 1983). In Sanskrit, for example, the words for "heart" and "mind" are part of the same reality or "citta" (Welwood, 1983, p. viii). The expanded mind brings expanded awareness that lets us see things in perspective, as they truly are, and it brings expanded compassion as well (Suzuki, 1949). The essence of Buddhist psychotherapy is the cultivation of compassion, or "maitri." In the encounter between client and therapist, both hearts awaken. The awakened heart is called "bodhicitta" (Welwood, 1983, p. 159), and the awakened state is called "Buddha nature." The goal of Buddhist psychology is to cultivate compassion to oneself first, seeing through the veil of illusions and self-deceptions to a clearer sense of reality.

Clinical Vignette: Psychologists Should Know How to Bring a Meditative State into Psychotherapy

Training exercises in spiritually and religiously diverse psychotherapy would include simple meditation exercises that are powerful non-invasive treatments for anxiety disorders and other psychological conditions. These practices, which include teaching a moment of mindful meditation, finding a calm center within and slowing down intentionally, also build preventive general resiliency and stability in most clients.

For example, a young female client was dating two people, and her head was literally spinning with choices. She couldn't think her way through them any more. I asked her if she would like to close her eyes and feel her breath, her weight, and her spine. As her breath became slow and steady, she felt her own rhythm. She was able to sense her interiority and feel at home in herself. She felt less panicked and could assess the situation more clearly, feeling a newly internalized locus of control.

Jungian Psychology

Jungian psychology contains a mythic soul and spiritual perspective on psychology. For the past several decades, our culture has had a new interest in Jungian psychology. People sense that something is missing in modern life, in everyday life and relationships. Some call it the quality of "soul," by which they mean the anima or animating principle of life. A number of imaginative and creative writers have written about soul, including poets Rumi and Emily Dickinson and psychologist James Hillman (1972). Individuals have had to look outside psychology to address life's essential issues; psychology should restore the cultural and mythic dimension of life to psychological practice (Serlin, 1988, 1989a).

Clinical Vignettes

Clients bring in images of the men and women in their families, for example, to see which archetypes run in their families and to search for more empowering images. They may be struggling with developmental or age-related crises, or may lack appropriate male role models. They don't know how to be. Young women experience jealousy and insecurity at their friends' weddings, and are anxious about what kind of women they want to become. Young men struggle with internalized self-criticism and can never live up to their fathers' expectations. Understanding their problem in the context of its developmental stage is an effective tool to help them deal with its stresses.

Jungian psychotherapy uses symbols and images to represent aspects of the Self. While some of them are explicitly religious, images themselves are processed in a non-rational part of the brain and have a natural affinity for religious and spiritual content. Therefore, another spiritual tool for a diverse psychotherapeutic practice is one of using images, dreams, artwork, etc. to convey psychological material. Seeing themselves in the context of parents, grandparents, geographical background, and family story helps give young people a needed sense of where they come from and to where they are going.

An increasingly common tool in family therapy is to tell the family stories and bring in pictures. Seeing similarities and differences between oneself and one's family of origin sharpens issues of what is genetic and what can be changed, and can help people make more appropriate choices about how to live their lives.

For example, one young man came from an extended Italian family. As he approached age thirty, he faced new pressures about being a man and establishing himself in the eyes of the community. Through imagery exercises, he began to visualize himself taking his place among the men of his tribe. He visualized the strengths that he inherited from the father he never saw to strengths from his uncles, grandfather, and other role models. He was able to deal with his impending marriage and discover his own unique way of becoming a man in his new partnership.

Men can also examine their relationship archetypes relative to the way they partner in relationships. They are encouraged to interchange images of "hero as conqueror" with images like "hero as healer" and Martin Luther King Jr.

A young Mexican American woman was struggling with multiple losses of both parents and her grandmother and her own issues of infertility. In a dream, she saw her grandmother, who reassured her that it was okay for her to die because she would be with her God. The client's grandmother was Catholic and believed that she would go to heaven and see the spirits of her ancestors. This reassurance gave my client enough strength to mourn her losses while still moving on to create her own life. She described, "I feel like I have a grip. I'm not losing it. I'm proud of myself."

BUILDING SPIRITUAL COMPETENCY IN CLINICAL TRAINING

Many psychologists are interested in incorporating a spiritual or religious dimension to their work, but don't know how. While spirituality includes alternative practices like meditation and imagery, it is primarily more of an attitude than a set of techniques.

The hallmarks of a *spiritual attitude* to psychotherapy and issues that underlie most sets of technique are the following:

The Here and Now

Buddhism teaches the truth of impermanence. Facing our mortality allows us to live more fully in the moment; a spiritual approach to psychotherapy emphasizes the present moment and the development of presence. We learn that we are always home in ourselves. Spiritual practices teach concentration and ways to calm the mind. Psychotherapeutic practices emphasize the importance of "fit" in clinical work rather than prestructured sessions (Maturana & Varela, 1992), continuing a trend started by the postmodern, feminist, and narrative therapists that focuses on strengths (Saleebey, 1997) and being in the body (Murphy & Donovan, 1997). The therapeutic reality is co-constructed, promoting a collaborative approach to therapy (Kok & Leskela, 1996).

Identity

We normally identify with our bundle of personality traits and neuroses, and think that is who we are; a spiritual approach knows that we are more. We normally identify with our jobs or roles; a spiritual approach teaches that even if these things crash, we have a deeper identity. We have moved from the "self" with a small *s*, as Jung described, to the "Self" with a large *S* (Jung, 1958). Beyond the narrow perspective of our insecure egos lies a larger egolessness and panoramic awareness, or "vipassana." Developing a larger awareness helps us get perspective on ourselves and our problems, and provides space for change to occur.

Transcendence

Buddhist psychoanalyst Ed Podvoll notes that a psychiatric history is usually the story of pain; instead, he teaches his students to take a "history of sanity," and he supports their "intrinsic instinct toward wakefulness." Behind the confusion of the neurosis is usually a deeper level of clarity.

Meaning

The search for meaning is an essentially human activity, but life may often feel meaningless. Victor Frankl (1959), coming out of a Nazi concentration camp, showed in his theory of logotherapy how the search for the meaning of these life events can itself overcome despair. Spiritual practices help us discover new meanings in the new spaces or emptiness (Buddhist "sunyata") that opens up. Discovering the meaning of an experience transforms knowledge into wisdom.

Compassion

Seeing and accepting ourselves as we truly are allows us to develop compassion toward ourselves and therefore to others. A spiritual practice trains the mind, which develops the discipline and courage to face life squarely. Through spiritual practices of "active love," we

The training toolbox consists of two levels: general guidelines of multicultural sensitivity and clinical methods to meet religious and spiritual psychotherapy needs. Clinical training, coursework, and research can develop new ways to help psychologists bring spiritual competence to working with issues of spiritual diversity in therapy today.

Level 1: Multicultural sensitivity

Be sensitive to one's own prejudices about religion and spirituality. Avoid efforts to avoid the subject. Instead, try to adopt a non-judgmental and exploratory approach that invites clients to share it with you.

Examine your countertransferential issues regarding confrontation with mortality, the void and meaninglessness, freedom and fate, and isolation and community.

Work collaboratively and respectfully, co-creating the understanding of the problem, central issues, and progress over time. Using approaches common to feminist, humanistic, and postmodern psychotherapies, therapists do not diagnose or pathologize spiritual issues in psychotherapy. Instead, they try to genuinely understand, with the client, the exact nature of the problem. They may be open about their own spiritual or religious perspectives, but not impose it on the therapy. Treatment goals are discussed together, and periodic check-ins give a sense of progress over time. While honoring the depths, they nevertheless focus on strengths.

Use of ethnographic interviewing and assessment techniques to help clients share the uniqueness of their worlds and religious and spiritual mixes.

Match therapists and method to client's background, which improves outcome (Morris, 2001).

Level 2: Clinical practices

Take a thorough **religious and spiritual history**. Ask about religion in the family of origin, belief in a transcendent being, cultural belief and rituals dealing with death, and history of spiritual practices and affiliations.

Assess for **spiritual strengths**. What coping mechanisms has the client demonstrated in the past to deal with loss, death, or change? What support system does the client have in terms of religious or spiritual friendships, mentorships, and community?

Introduce **spiritual practices into therapy**. Teach simple meditation and relaxation practices to help clients experience an expanded sense of self, connection, and internal locus of control.

honor our kinship and extend our compassion to others (Spretnak, 1991).

Home

Seeing a larger context than the self, we rediscover our larger connection to community and the universe. We find our sense of place: we belong. Some family therapists have developed practices such as spiritual genograms (Frame, 2002) and spiritual ecomaps (Hodge, 2000) to help couples perceive these connections in their own families and extended families.

CONCLUSION

Psychotherapists today face an exciting challenge. Their clients confront unheard-of changes in identity, mortality, and meaning. Many seek coherence and meaning by discovering their own forms of spirituality, but then need to bring this into larger contexts of relationship and community. By meeting the challenge of religious and spiritual diversity, psychologists fulfill their "ethical and social responsibility as a profession" and as a "scientific discipline" (Betancourt & Lopez, 1993, p. 636).

REFERENCES

Allport, G. W. (1948). *Psychology, in college reading and religion: A survey of college reading materials* (pp. 80–114). New Haven, CT: Yale University.

Allport, G. W. (1950). *The individual and his religion: A psychological interpretation.* New York: Macmillan.

American Psychiatric Association. (1994). *Diagnostic and statistical manual of mental disorders* (4th ed.). Washington, DC: Author.

American Psychological Association. (2003). Guidelines for multicultural education, training, research, practice, and organizational change for psychologists. *American Psychologist, 58*(5), 377–402.

Anderson, D. A., & Worthen, D. (1997). Exploring a fourth dimension: Spirituality as a resource for the couple therapist. *Journal of Marital and Family Therapy, 23,* 3–12.

Argyle, M., & Beit-Hallahmi, B. (1975). *The social psychology of religion.* London: Routledge & Kegan Paul.

Arnett, J. J. (2002). The psychology of globalization. *American Psychologist, 57*(10), 774–783.

Bergin, A. E., & Jensen, J. P. (1990). Religiosity of psychotherapists: A national survey. *Psychotherapy, 27*(1), 3–7.

Betancourt, H., & Lopez, S. R. (1993). The study of culture, ethnicity, and race in American psychology. *American Psychologist, 48*(6), 629–637.

Buber, M. (1937). *I and thou* (R. G. Smith, Trans.). Edinburgh, Scotland: T & T Clark. (Original work published 1922)

Bugental, J. (1976). *The search for existential identity.* San Francisco: Jossey-Bass.

Cadwallader, E. (1991). Depression and religion: Realities, perspectives, and directions. *Counseling and Values, 35*, 83–92.

De Forest, I. (1954). *The leaven of love: A development of the psychoanalytic theory and technique of Sandor Ferenczi.* New York: Harper.

DiBlasio, F. A. (1993). The role of social workers' religious beliefs in helping family members forgive. *Families in Society, 74*, 163–170.

Elkins, D. N., Hedstrom, L. J., Jughes, L. L., Leaf, J. A., & Saunders, C. (1988). Toward a humanistic-phenomenological spirituality: Definition, description and measurement. *Journal of Humanistic Psychology, 28*(4), 5–18.

Frager, R. (1989). Transpersonal psychology: Promise and prospects. In R. Valle and S. Halling (Eds.), *Beyond ego.* Los Angeles: Tarcher.

Frager, R., & Fadiman, J. (Eds.). (1998). *Personality and personal growth* (4th ed.). Palo Alto: Longman.

Frame, M. W. (2002). The spiritual genogram in family therapy. *Journal of Marital and Family Therapy, 26*(2), 211–216.

Frankl, V. (1959). *Man's search for meaning.* New York: Praeger.

Freud, S. (1961). The future of an illusion. In J. Strachey (Ed. and Trans.), *The standard edition of the complete psychological works of Sigmund Freud* (Vol. 21, pp. 1–56). London: Hogarth Press and the Institute of Psycho-Analysis. (Original work published 1927)

Gallup, G. J., & Castelli, J. (1989). *The people's religion: American faith in the 90's.* New York: Macmillan.

Gartner, J. (1996). Religious commitment, mental health, and prosocial behavior: A review of the empirical literature. In E. Shafranske (Ed.), *Religion and the clinical practice of psychology.* Washington, DC: American Psychological Association.

Genia, V. (1990). Religious development: A synthesis and reformulation. *Journal of Religion and Health, 29*(2), 85–99.

Gimbutas, M. (1982). *The goddesses and gods of Old Europe, 7000-3500 B.C.* Berkeley and Los Angeles: University of California Press.

Griffith, J. L., & Griffith, M. E. (1992). Therapeutic change in religious families: Working with the God construct. In L. Burton (Ed.), *Religion and the family* (pp. 63–86). Binghamton, NY: Haworth.

Hastings, A. (1999). Transpersonal psychology: The 4th force. In D. Moss (Ed.), *Humanistic and transpersonal psychology: A historical biographical sourcebook* (pp. 192–209). Westport, CT: Greenwood Press.

Heller, P. & Wood, B. (2000). The influence of religious and ethnic differences on marital intimacy: Intermarriage versus intramarriage. *Journal of Marital and Family Therapy, 26*(2), 241–252.

Hillman, J. (1972). *The myth of analysis: Three essays in archetypal psychology.* New York: Harper & Row.

Hodge, D. (2000). Spiritual ecomaps: A new diagrammatic tool for assessing marital and family spirituality. *Journal of Marital and Family Therapy, 26*(2), 217–228.

Hoge, D. R. (1996). Religion in America: The demographics of belief and affiliation. In E. Shafranske (Ed.), *Religion and the clinical practice of psychology.* Washington, DC: American Psychological Association.

Jacobs, J. L. (1992). Religious ritual and mental health. In J. Schumacher (Ed.), *Religion and mental health* (pp. 291–299). New York: Oxford University Press.

James, W. (1985). *The varieties of religious experience: A study in human nature.* Cambridge, MA: Harvard University Press. (Original work published 1902)

Jung, C. G. (1958). *Psychology and religion: West and East* (R. F. C. Hull, Trans.). In *Collected Works* (Vol. 2, Bollingen Series 30). New York: Pantheon Books.

Jung, C. G. (1969). Psychotherapists or the clergy. In H. Read, M. Fordham, & G. Adler (Eds.), *The collected works of C. G. Jung* (2nd ed., Vol. 11, pp. 327–347). Princeton, NJ: Princeton University Press. (Original work published 1932)

Kaslow, F., & Robinson, J. A. (1996). Long-term satisfying marriages: Perceptions and contributing factors. *American Journal of Family Therapy, 24*(2), 153–170.

Kasmin, B. A., & Lachman, S. P. (1993). *One nation under god: Religion in contemporary American society.* New York: Harmony Books.

Kierkegaard, S. (1941). *The sickness unto death: A Christian-psychological exposition for edification and awakening* (W. Lowrie, Trans.). Princeton, NJ: Princeton University Press. (Original work published 1844)

Knapp, S., & VandeCreek, L. (2003). An overview of the major changes in the 2002 APA ethics code. *Professional Psychology: Research and Practice, 34,* 219–224.

Kok, C. J., & Leskela, J. (1996). Solution-focused therapy in a psychiatric hospital. *Journal of Marital and Family Therapy, 22,* 397–406.

Kristof, N. (2003, December 6). Love and race. *The New York Times,* p. A33.

Lattin, D. (2003, December 4). Living the religious life of a none. *San Francisco Chronicle,* pp. A1, A19.

Manese, J., Saito, G., & Rodolfa, E. (2004, January). Diversity based psychology: What practitioners and trainers need to know. *Board of Psychology Update, 11,* 1–19.

Maslow, A. (1968). *Toward a psychology of being* (2nd ed.). New York: Van Nostrand.

Maslow, A. (1971). *The farther reaches of human nature.* New York: Viking.

Maturana, H. R., & Varela, F. J. (1992). *The tree of knowledge: The biological roots of human understanding* (Rev. ed., R. Paolucci, Trans.). Boston: Shambhala.

May, R. (1940). *The springs of creative living: A study of human nature and God.* New York: Abingdon-Cokesbury.

Meadow, M. J., & Kahoe, R. D. (1984). *Psychology of religion: Religion in individual lives.* New York: Harper & Row.

Moon, G., Willis, D., Bailey, J., & Kwansy, J. (1993). Self-reported use of Christian spiritual guidance techniques by Christian psychotherapists, pastoral counselors, and spiritual directors. *Journal of Psychology and Christianity, 12,* 24–37.

Morris, D. F. (2001). Clinical practices with African Americans: Juxtaposition of standard clinical practices and Afrocentrism. *Professional Psychology: Research and Practice, 32,* 563–572.

Moules, N. (2000). Postmodernism and the sacred: Reclaiming connection in our greater-than-human worlds. *Journal of Marital and Family Therapy, 26*(2), 229–240.

Murphy, M., & Donovan, S. (1997). *The physical and psychological effects of meditation* (2nd ed.). Sausalito, CA: Institute of Noetic Sciences.

Needleman, J. (1983). Psychiatry and the sacred. In J. Welwood (Ed.), *East/West approaches to psychotherapy and the healing relationship* (pp. 4–17). Boston: Shambhala.

Neumann, E. (1955). *The great mother.* Princeton, NJ: Princeton University Press.

Pargament, K. I. (1997). *The psychology of religion and coping.* New York: Guilford Press.

Patterson, J., Hayworth, M., Turner, C., & Raskin, M. (2000). Spiritual issues in family therapy: A graduate-level course. *Journal of Marital and Family Therapy, 26*(2), 199–210.

Polanyi, M. (1958). *Personal knowledge: Towards a post-critical philosophy.* Chicago: The University of Chicago Press.

Polkinghorne, D. (1994). A path of understanding for psychology. *Journal of Theoretical and Philosophical Psychology, 14,* 128–145.

Pope, K., Sonne, J., & Holroyd, J. (1993). *Sexual feelings in psychotherapy.* Washington, DC: American Psychological Association.

Pope-David, D. B., & Coleman, H. L. K. (Eds.) (1997). *Multicultural counseling competencies: Assessment education and training, and supervision.* Thousand Oaks, CA: SAGE Publications, Inc.

Prest, L. A., & Keller, J. F. (1993). Spirituality and family therapy: Spiritual beliefs, myths, and metaphors. *Journal of Marital and Family Therapy, 21,* 60–77.

Richards, P. S., & Bergin, A. E. (1997). *A spiritual strategy for counseling and psychotherapy.* Washington, DC: American Psychological Association.

Rotz, E., Russell, C. S., & Wright, D. W. (1993). The therapist who is perceived as "spiritually correct": Strategies for avoiding collusion with the "spiritually one-up" spouse. *Journal of Marital and Family Therapy, 19,* 369–375.

Saleebey, D. (Ed.). (1997). *The strengths perspective.* (2nd ed.). New York: Longman.

Schneider, K., & May, R. (1994). *The psychology of existence: An integrative, clinical perspective.* New York: McGraw Hill.

Serlin, I. (1988). *The last temptation of Christ.* Library journal. California: C. G. Jung Institute of San Francisco.

Serlin, I. (1989a). A psycho-spiritual body approach to a residential treatment of Catholic religious. *Journal of Transpersonal Psychology, 21*(2), 177–191.

Serlin, I. (1989b, Fall). From Buddhism and back. *Lilith Magazine, 21,* 23–24.

Serlin, I. A. (2000). Dance and religion. In W. C. Roof (Ed.), *Contemporary American Religion.* New York: Macmillan, Library Reference.

Serlin, I. A. (2001). Wandering God: A study in nomadic spirituality [Book review]. *The Journal of Transpersonal Psychology, 33*(1), 72–74.

Shafranske, E. P. (Ed.). (1996). *Religion and the clinical practice of psychology.* Washington, DC: American Psychological Association.

Shafranske, E. P., & Malony, H. N. (1990). Clinical psychologists' religious and spiritual orientations and their practice of psychotherapy. *Psychotherapy, 27,* 72–78.

Spilke, B., Hood, R. W., Jr., & Gorsuch, R. L. (1985). *The psychology of religion: An empirical approach.* Englewood Cliffs, NJ: Prentice Hall.

Spretnak, C. (1991). *States of grace: The recovery of meaning in the postmodern age.* New York: Harper Collins.

Steere, D. A. (1997). *Spiritual presence in psychotherapy: A guide for caregivers.* New York: Brunner/Mazel.

Stuart, R. (2004). Twelve practical suggestions for achieving multicultural competence. *Professional Psychology: Research and Practice, 35*(1), 3–9.

Sue, D. W., Arredondo, P., & McDavis, R. J. (1992). Multicultural counseling competencies and standards: A call to the profession. *Journal of Counseling and Development, 70,* 477–483.

Sue, D. W., Bingham, R. P., Porche-Burke, L., & Vasquez, M. (1999). The diversification of psychology: A multicultural revolution. *American Psychologist, 54*(12), 1061–1069.

Sue, S. (1999). Science, ethnicity, and bias: Where have we gone wrong? *American Psychologist, 54*(12), 1070–1077.

Sutich, A. (1969). Some considerations regarding transpersonal psychology. *Journal of Transpersonal Psychology, 1*, 11–20.

Suzuki, D. T. (1949). *Introduction to Zen Buddhism.* London: Rider.

Tan, S. Y. (2003). Integrating spiritual direction into psychotherapy: Ethical issues and guidelines. *Journal of Psychology and Theology, 31*, 14–23.

Tillich, P. (1952). *The courage to be.* New Haven, CT: Yale University Press.

Trungpa, C. (1969). *Meditation in action.* Boulder, CO: Shambhala Publications.

Trungpa, C. (1983). Becoming a full human being. In J. Welwood (Ed.), *Awakening the heart: East/West approaches to psychotherapy and the healing relationship* (pp. 126–131). Boston: Shambhala.

Vande Kemp, H. (1996). Historical perspective: Religion and clinical psychology in America. In E. Shafranske (Ed.), *Religion and the clinical practice of psychology.* Washington: APA Books.

Vaughan, F. (1987). A question of balance: Health and pathology in new religious movements. In D. Anthony, B. Ecker, & K. Wilbur (Eds.), *Spiritual choices: The problem of recognizing authentic pathos to inner transformation* (pp. 265–282). New York: Paragon House.

Walsh, F. (1998). Beliefs, spirituality, and transcendence. In M. McGoldrick (Ed.), *Re-visioning family therapy: Race, culture, and transcendence in clinical practice* (pp. 62–77). New York: Guilford Press.

Walsh, F. (Ed.). (1999). *Spiritual resources in family therapy.* New York: Guilford Press.

Walsh, R. (1999). *Essential spirituality.* New York: John Wiley.

Welwood, J. (1983). *Awakening the heart: East/West approaches to psychotherapy and the healing relationship.* Boston: Shambhala.

Wilbur, K. (1981). *No boundary.* Boston: Shambhala.

Worthington, E. L., Jr., Kurusu, T., McCullough, M. E., & Sandage, S. (1996). Empirical research on religion and psychotherapeutic processes and outcomes: A ten-year review and research prospectus. *Psychological Bulletin, 119*, 448–487.

Wulff, D. (1991). *Psychology of religion: Classic and contemporary views.* New York: Wiley.

Wulff, D. (1996). The psychology of religion: An overview. In E. Shafranske (Ed.), *Religion and the clinical practice of psychology.* Washington: APA Books.

Yalom, I. (1980). *Existential psychotherapy.* New York: Basic Books.

CHAPTER 3

Prejudice toward People with Disabilities

Asiah Mason
Helen D. Pratt
Dilip R. Patel
Donald E. Greydanus
Kareem Z. Yahya

Without knowledge of the roots of hostility we cannot hope to employ our intelligence effectively in controlling its destructiveness.

(Allport, 1954, p. xvii)

We are all affected by prejudice and discrimination (see Table 3.1); each of us is susceptible to it either as observers, perpetrators, or victims. We all have experienced it at some level. Some of the most extreme examples of the effects of prejudice include the Holocaust in Germany, the lynchings in the southern United States, and the ethnic cleansing in Africa and Bosnia. A more recent example is the bombing of the World Trade Center and the Pentagon on September 11, 2001. More subtle forms are common in our everyday lives (see Appendix, Case Example 1). For example, consider portrayals of people with disabilities, such as the limping villains in the movies, the stereotypical roles of East Indian families who can barely speak English and who own "all" of the Seven-Eleven stores, and media portrayals of successful and happy women as tall, skinny, and shapely.

Advances in medicine have changed the life expectancy of many individuals who survived their impairments. For example, the numbers of infants who are born premature and survive have increased dramatically; individuals diagnosed with cystic fibrosis, diabetes, and spina bifida now live into adulthood. The ability of medicine to save the lives of many individuals who suffer traumatic injuries also contributes to the increased numbers of individuals in our society who live and function with mental and physical impairments. Individuals who at one time did not survive past infancy or were hidden away in relatives' homes or placed in institutions are now active, contributing, and vital members of society. These individuals are vulnerable to the issues of prejudice and discrimination in every facet of their lives.

Examples of discrimination also surround us. More extreme forms of discrimination involve the denial of housing, medical care, or employment based on one's ethnicity, race, country of origin, or religion. A subtle

Table 3.1
Defining Prejudice, Discrimination, and Disability

Term	Definition
Prejudice	A negative attitude toward the members of some group, based solely on their membership in that group.
Discrimination	A negative action toward a group that is the target of prejudice (Baron & Byrne, 2003).
Disability	The condition of a person (1) having a physical or mental impairment that substantially limits him or her in some major life activity, and (2) having experienced discrimination resulting from this physical or mental impairment (*The Americans with Disabilities Act*, PL 504).
Prejudiced person	A person who adopts a negative belief or attitude about another person or group. That attitude refers to a general evaluation that a person holds of himself or herself, other people, objects, and issues (Petty, 1995). The prejudiced individual negatively evaluates and dislikes members of a group just because they belong to that particular group. The disliked individuals' personal characteristics, beliefs, or contributions to society are not considered by the prejudiced person; those factors have little or nothing to do with the prejudiced person's evaluation.

Table 3.1

Term	Definition
Physical or mental impairment	(1) Any physiological disorder or condition, cosmetic disfigurement, or anatomical loss affecting one or more of the following body systems: neurological, musculo-skeletal, special sense organs, respiratory (including speech organs), cardiovascular, reproductive, digestive, genitourinary, blood and lymphatic, skin, and endocrine; or (2) Any mental or psychological disorder, such as mental retardation, organic brain syndrome, emotional or mental illness, or specific learning disabilities. Major life activities means functions such as caring for oneself, performing manual tasks, walking, seeing, hearing, speaking, breathing, learning, and working.
Substantially limits	(1) Unable to perform a major life activity that the average person in the general population can perform; or (2) significantly restricted as to the condition, manner, or duration under which an individual can perform a particular major life activity as compared to the condition, manner, or duration under which the average person in the general population can perform that same major life activity.
Categories of disabilities	(1) By diagnosis (such as multiple sclerosis, asthma, or insulin-dependent diabetes), (2) by system affected (such as nervous, musculoskeletal, cardiovascular, pulmonary, visual, or auditory), (3) by onset (age at onset and speed of onset), or function loss (for example, quadriplegia or paraplegia).

example may involve asking a customer in a restaurant what his deaf friend wants to order, as if the deaf person cannot think for him/herself and does not even deserve the respect of receiving eye contact from the server. Another example involves assuming that a person with cerebral palsy is, prior to any interpersonal interactions, intellectually inferior and then, based on that assumption, talking down to the person as if he or she were a child with limited vocabulary.

Prejudice and discrimination may also result from any number of additional factors such as age, geographic origin, occupation, or even simply being overweight, rather than from race, gender, or ethnic background. Prejudice and discrimination are pervasive in our lives; regardless of their form or focus, they are real and damaging. Even the relatively subtle forms may have deleterious effects on the targeted individuals (Shelton, 2000).

This chapter is written from the professional and personal experiences of the authors. Each of us has trained to work with individuals who have disabilities, or has a personal disability, or has close family members who have one or more disabilities. We hope that these multiple perspectives will provide the reader with practical and useful information from a scholarly perspective. Our intent is to present "the psychology of prejudice and discrimination," *not* the "psychology of disability." It is crucial to clearly make this distinction for two reasons: first, the "disabled personality" does not exist, nor are there psychological problems that are "naturally associated" with having a disability. Second, in the past the idea of "psychology of disability" has led to an exaggerated perception that there are psychological differences between people *with* and those *without* disabilities. The recent findings in the human genome project have shown that human beings are more alike than they are different; the differences that do exist are minor.

This chapter also addresses the psychology of prejudice and discrimination toward persons with disabilities. First we provide definitions, historical information, legal information, medical information, and theoretical models from the science of social psychology to explain how prejudice and discrimination developed, were maintained, and were expressed toward persons with disabilities. Once this context is established, we will then present practical case studies with possible solutions.

A HISTORY OF PREJUDICE AND DISCRIMINATION

Throughout recorded human history, individuals or groups who were perceived as "different" from the main group have been vulnerable to appalling treatment and practices. Examples include abandonment, physical abuse, slavery, and infanticide. Cultural myths held that society needed to be protected from people with disabilities. These practices reflected a common societal fear that the so-called physically, mentally, and morally defective persons would degrade the human race (Szymanski & Trueba, 1999). It has been widely believed that most deviance is caused by hereditary factors that, if left unchecked, would result in widespread social problems.

Humanitarian reforms during the last half of the eighteenth century brought hopefulness to the treatment and eventual cure of people described as deviant. Unfortunately, when deviance wasn't cured and continued to be a major social problem, some professionals and societal leaders promoted measures to limit the perceived "harm" that social deviants might inflict on society. Supporters of this view became convinced that it was essential to sterilize and segregate large numbers of these social and mental "incompetents" (Hardman, Drew, & Egan, 2002). Laws were created to prohibit them from getting married. Since some concluded that that wasn't safe enough, laws were passed to require the targeted individuals to be sterilized to prevent them from bringing others like themselves into the world, thereby decreasing the numbers of so-called deviants. Additionally, these professionals strongly believed that the "disabled" were incapable of taking care of themselves, would be happier with people like themselves, and would be less of a burden on their families and their communities. Actions were taken to move large numbers of the "disabled" from their home communities to secluded special-care facilities. These facilities became commonly known as institutions. Institutions have had many different names, such as *special school*, *hospital*, *colony*, *prison*, and *asylum*.

By the early twentieth century, the number and size of institutions had increased, and the cost of maintaining these institutions was becoming astronomical. The focus shifted from containment to that of social control. Society was faced with the difficulties of managing large numbers of people without adequate financial resources. The solution was to strip away individuals' identities and force them into group regimentation. Individual rights were taken away and strict rules were enforced. Sadly, individuals were forced to wear institutional clothing, were given identification tags and numbers, and could not have personal possessions. More and more institution facilities were built (some with barred windows and high walls enclosing the grounds). This sad state continued until the early 1950s. In spite of the growth of the segregated institutions, most individuals with disabilities continued to live at home with their families.

The families of the persons with disabilities had to manage on their own because there wasn't much external support for them from state or community agencies. Many families who had children with disabilities did not get help for the children's basic needs, such as medical, social, or education services. Around this time, the civil rights movement was developing in the United States. Parents of children with disabilities modeled their organizational efforts after the civil rights movement. The United Cerebral Palsy Organization (UCP) was founded in 1949, and the National Association for Retarded children (NARC) began in 1950. The UCP and NARC joined other professional organizations already in existence (such as the National Association for the Deaf, the American Association on Mental Deficiency, the Council for Exceptional Children, and the American Federation for the Blind) to advocate for the rights of persons with disabilities (Hardman et al., 2002). These groups wanted to get accurate information to policymakers, professionals, and families. Each organization focused on the rights of people with disabilities to be included in family and community life and have access to medical treatment, social services, and education. Other parent groups followed, including those of the National Society for Autistic Children (1961) and the Association for Children with Learning Disabilities (1964) (Berry & Hardman, 1998).

These actions helped to cause philosophical changes in the United States that recognized and accepted that a range of differences existed among humans. Additionally, these efforts helped to lead to the inclusion of persons with disabilities into community settings, schools, places of employment, and neighborhood homes.

Access to education was considered a basic American value, reflecting the expectation that each individual should have an opportunity to learn and develop to be the best of his or her ability. However, many youth with disabilities did not have access, nor did they have equal access to an education. Youth with disabilities did not always receive their full measure of learning literacy, personal autonomy, economic self-sufficiency, personal fulfillment, and citizenship. Our schools often did not prepare all students to gain knowledge and apply what they learned in order to be productive workers and citizens (McLaughlin, Shepard, & O'Day, 1995). Full participation for everyone, regardless of race, cultural background, socioeconomic status, physical disability, or mental limitation, should be the goal for all students. Sadly, in the United States, it has taken more than two centuries to render this value into actual practice in educating students with disabilities.

THE INDIVIDUALS WITH DISABILITIES EDUCATION ACT

In 1975, the U.S. Congress saw the need to bring together the various pieces of state and federal legislation into one comprehensive national law. Public Law 94-142 (PL 94-142) made available a free and appropriate public education to nearly 4 million school-age students with disabilities in the United States between the ages of six and twenty-one. The law was renamed the Individuals with Disabilities Education Act (IDEA) in 1990 (see Table 3.2).

In 1986, Congress amended IDEA to include provisions for preschool-age students. Public Law 99-457 (PL 99-457) established a new mandate extending all the rights and protection of school-age children (ages six to twenty-one) to preschool (ages three to five) children with disabilities and mandated that they receive a free and appropriate public education. Another provision of PL 99-457 was the establishment of a state grant program for infants and toddlers up through two years old. Infants and toddlers who were developmentally delayed (as defined by each state) are eligible for services that include a multidisciplinary assessment and an individualized family service plan (IFSP). Although this provision did not mandate that states provide services to all infants and toddlers who were developmentally delayed, it did establish financial incentives for state participation.

THE AMERICANS WITH DISABILITIES ACT (ADA)

The struggles for civil rights for people with disabilities started with less visibility and became very visible when it was clear that these basic rights were at risk of not becoming law. Demonstrations were held, lawsuits were filed, and new organizations sprang up. Some of the names associated with the disability rights movement were Judith E. Heumann, Patrisha Wright, Wade Blank, Michael Auberger, and Justin Dart, and attorneys like Sidney Wolinsky and Stephen Gold. These leaders brought a revolution to disability rights. In 1973, the U.S. Congress passed an amendment to the Vocational Rehabilitation Act that included a provision prohibiting discrimination against persons with disabilities in federally assisted programs and activities. Section 504 of the Vocational Rehabilitation Act set the stage for passage of the most sweeping civil rights legislation in the United States since the Civil Rights Act of 1964: the Americans with Disabilities Act (ADA), signed

Table 3.2
Models of Disability

Model	Description
Moral	Disability brings shame to the person with disability because disability is a defect. This defect is caused by sins or moral lapse (Hahn, 1985). This disability represents the reification of sin, failure of faith, or evil.
	In cultures that emphasize family and group over individuals, the shame spreads to the group. The person and/or the family carries the blame for causing the disability (Florian, 1982).
	This model is prominent in many developing countries. To illustrate, the first author has a brother who was born deaf in Southeast Asia forty years ago. To this day, this author's mother believes that an act she committed caused her son to be born deaf, and that this deafness was given as a punishment from the gods. The mother has given many offerings to the gods asking to be forgiven for her past sin, so that her son can be given his ability to hear.
	Although the moral model is the oldest view of disability, it still very much exists and weaves through our language, culture, and ideology. In some cultures, the moral model is the most prevalent view (Chan, Lam, Wong, Leung, & Fang, 1988).
Medical	Main model accepted in the United States. This model takes the moral or sin out of disability.
	Disability is seen as a medical problem inside the person. The problem is that the body system has failed; disability is considered to be a pathology. Persons with disabilities are expected to be in the role of patient, being helped by the professionals. Cure is the ultimate goal of treatment.
Minority	Persons with disabilities, political scientists, and lawyers prefer to look at disability as the minority model (also called the "social model"). It views disability as social construction. The problems are not within the persons with disabilities but in the environment that fails to adapt to the persons with disabilities. The problems also lie in the negative attitudes of people without disabilities.
	Persons with disabilities are seen as a minority group in the same way that blacks are a minority group—they have been denied their civil rights, equal access, and protection. Key obstacles for any minority group are prejudice and discrimination, inferior housing, economic dependence, social isolation, disparate treatment, economic dependence, high unemployment, and a higher rate of institutionalization (Fleischer & Zames, 2001).

into law in 1990 (see Table 3.3). The purpose of the ADA is to prevent discrimination on the basis of disability in employment, programs, and services provided by state and local governments, goods and services provided by private companies, and commercial facilities.

The ADA charged the federal government with the responsibility of ensuring that these provisions be enforced on behalf of all people with disabilities (National Council on Disability, 1999). The intent of the ADA is to create a "fair and level playing field" for eligible persons with disabilities. To do so, the law specifies that reasonable accommodations need to be made to take into account each person's

Table 3.3
Individuals with Disabilities Education Act in 1990 (IDEA)

Item	Description
Criteria for receiving specialized services under IDEA	The individual must be identified as having one of the twelve disability conditions identified in federal law or their counterparts in the state's special education law: these conditions are mental retardation, specific learning disabilities, serious emotional disturbances (behavior disorders), speech or language impairments, vision loss (including blindness), hearing loss (including deafness), orthopedic impairments, other health impairments, deafness–blindness, multiple disabilities, autism, and traumatic brain injury. The individual must have a demonstrated need for specialized instruction and related service in order to receive an appropriate education.
Tenets that drive determination of eligibility for services, design of instructional programs, and education placement	Nondiscriminatory and multidisciplinary assessment of educational needs. Parental safeguards and involvement in developing each child's educational program. A free and appropriate public education. An individualized education program. Education in the least restrictive environment.

needs resulting from his or her disabilities. As defined in law, the principal test for a reasonable accommodation is its effectiveness: does the accommodation provide an opportunity for a person with a disability to achieve the same level of performance and to enjoy benefits equal to those of an average, similarly situated person without a disability?

The ADA in Education

The ADA has been important to parents and students with disabilities in helping them exercise their rights so they can have all of the resources they need to get a good and fair start in their lives, such as quality education. Today's schools must provide supports and services to two groups of students with disabilities. One group qualifies for special education services under the IDEA, based upon educational need. Another group, while not eligible for special education, meets the definition of disability under Section 504 of the Vocational Rehabilitation Act that was incorporated into the 1990 ADA (see Table 3.4).

Students eligible under ADA are entitled to reasonable accommodations or modifications as a means to "create a fair and level playing field" in their educational programs. A plan for individually designed instruction must be developed for each student qualified under the ADA. Numerous accommodations or modifications can be made for students, depending on identified need. Some examples include untimed tests, extra time to complete assignments, a change in seating arrangement to accommodate vision or hearing loss or distractibility, the opportunity to respond orally on assignments and tests, taped textbooks, access to peer tutoring, access to study carrels for independent work, and use of supplementary materials such as visual or auditory aids. The ADA definition of disability encompasses a broader group of students than those eligible under IDEA.

There are several perspectives or models and issues that are important to address in order to understand the experience of prejudice and discrimination for persons with disabilities (see Table 3.5). In addition to the historical (moral) perspective already covered, there are the medical perspectives and the minority perspectives.

MEDICAL ISSUES AND PERSPECTIVES FOR PERSONS WITH DISABILITIES

The most common model of looking at disabilities in United States is the medical model (also known as the disease model) and is worth

Table 3.4
Major Provisions of the Americans with Disabilities Act (ADA)

Term	Definition
Employment	ADA mandates that employers may not discriminate in any employment practices, including job application procedures, hiring, firing, advancement, compensation, training, and other terms, conditions, and privileges of employment. It applies to recruitment, advertising, tenure, layoff, leave, fringe benefits, and all other employment-related activities. The law applies to any business with fifteen or more employees.
Transportation	ADA requires that all new public transit buses, bus and train stations, and rail systems must be accessible to people with disabilities. Transit authorities must provide transportation services to individuals with disabilities who cannot use fixed-route bus services. All Amtrak stations must be accessible to people with disabilities by the year 2010. Discrimination by air carriers in areas other than employment is not covered by the ADA but rather by the Air Carrier Access Act (49 U.S.C. 1374 [c]).
Public accommodations	Restaurants, hotels, and retail stores may not discriminate against individuals with disabilities. Physical barriers in existing facilities must be removed, if removal is readily achievable. If not, alternative methods of providing the services must be offered. All new construction and alterations of facilities must be accessible.
Government	State and local agencies may not discriminate against qualified individuals with disabilities. All government facilities, services, and communications must be accessible to people with disabilities.

continued

Table 3.4 (continued)

Term	Definition
Telecommunications	The ADA requires that all companies offering telephone service to the general public must offer telephone relay services to individuals with hearing loss who use telecommunication devices or similar equipment.

discussing due to its prevalence. The medical model states that organisms have two dimensions: normalcy and pathology. The distinction between the two is that normalcy is defined as the absence of a biological problem, and pathology is defined as change in an organism caused by disease, which results in illness that destroys or disrupts the integrity of the organism. The premise accepted in many cultures is that being healthy is better than being sick. The person who has a biological problem is labeled the patient, and the deficits are then described as the patient's disease (Hardman et al., 2002).

The medical model came to being in the mid-1800s and took the morality and sin causalities out of disabilities. Since then, medical services for people with disabilities have evolved a great deal. Treatment used to be in a hospital or institutional setting. Today the medical professions work directly with the individual in the family and community settings. Physicians are often the first professionals with whom parents have contact concerning their child's disability. Parents are seeking to communicate with and receive advice from the physician about treatment, prognosis, and help learning how to deal with life after the discovery of the disabilities. Unfortunately, many physicians are not aware and do not know how to connect families with the resources they need. Therefore it is essential that physicians and families themselves learn about relevant community resources. These resources include support groups, other parents, social workers, and possibly other mental health professionals (Hardman et al., 2002).

Historically, the disability community has had a sensitive relationship with medical professionals. Frequently, individuals with disabilities view medical professionals as mainly concerned with reducing the numbers of people with disabilities by working on prevention or cure. The message received by persons with disabilities is "let's prevent people like us" from existing. There is a fear among the disability community that the medical model may resemble the earlier moral model of looking at disability (Silvers, 1998).

The authors brought up this model in this chapter not to "stereo-type" medical professionals as unresponsive to the needs of persons

Table 3.5
Utilizing Both the ADA and IDEA

	IDEA	ADA
Eligibility	IDEA identifies twelve categories of qualifying conditions.	ADA identifies students as disabled if they meet the definition of qualified handicapped [disabled] person (that is, student has or has had a physical or mental impairment that substantially limits a major life activity, or student is regarded as disabled by others).
Responsibility to provide a free and appropriate public education (FAPE)	Both require the provision of a free and appropriate education, including individually designed instruction, to students covered under specific eligibility criteria.	
Special education or general education	A student is eligible to receive IDEA services only if the child-study team determines that the student is disabled under one of the twelve qualifying conditions and requires special education. Eligible students receive special education and related services.	An eligible student meets the definition of qualified person with a disability: one who currently has or has had a physical or mental impairment that substantially limits a major life activity or who is regarded as disabled by others. The student is not required to need special education in order to be protected.

continued

Table 3.5 (continued)

	IDEA	**ADA**
Accessibility	IDEA requires that modifications be made, if necessary, to provide access to a free and appropriate education.	ADA includes regulations regarding building and program accessibility.
Enforcement	IDEA is enforced by the Office of Special Education Programs in the Department of Education.	ADA is enforced by the Office for Civil Rights in the Department of Justice.

with disabilities, but to bring awareness of the experience from the disabled persons' point of view when interacting with medical professionals. This awareness must be addressed and must be included in curricula addressing cultural awareness and sensitivity.

In an effort to describe functioning and disability, the World Health Organization approved the International Classification of Functioning, Disability and Health (ICF) in May 2001. In their briefing, the ICF defines disability as "an impairment of body structure or function, a limitation in activities, or a restriction in participation." The scope of disabilities is wide, ranging from congenital birth defects to disabilities acquired after a debilitating trauma.

Prejudice and discrimination differ among and between different types of disabilities. Individuals with obvious birth defects may face a greater challenge than individuals whose disability is less noticeable. In this section, we will look at the medical aspects of children with disabilities and the effects on the children and their families.

Though no two children are the same, most children grow and develop at an expected rate and sequence (see Table 3.6). For children born with physical defects, there often is no predictable pattern or sequence. Growth is often disrupted and milestones are often delayed (Molnar, 1992, p. 120). Physical defects influence and change the way a child interacts with the outside world. Objects will not feel the same, voices will sound different, exploration and learning will be limited, and the child's growth and development will be altered (Molnar, 1992). As a result, the child may face discrimination. There is also the risk that there will be a secondary lack of social skills. There is an expectation in society that a child with disabilities will be less socially adept. Interestingly, studies show that children with less-pronounced physical deficits are often more socially withdrawn than children with more pronounced impairments. It has been suggested that this is due to the higher expectations that are placed on them to perform and function as equals to their non-handicapped peers (Jellinek & Murphy, 1988).

Table 3.6
Examples of Medical Conditions with Potential for Prejudice/Discrimination

Medical condition	Description
Cerebral palsy	Prevalence estimated to be 1.5–2.5 per 1,000 among school-age children in the United States. Cerebral palsy results from a known or unknown insult to the brain during its early development, mainly before or sometime during birth. The condition is characterized by increased muscle tone, difficulties with movements, communication problems, and various orthopedic problems. Some individuals with cerebral palsy may have other medical problems including recurrent respiratory infections, hearing and vision problems, seizures, and developmental delay.
Meningomyelocele and other neural tube defects (NTD)	The prevalence of NTDs in the United States is estimated to be 1–2 per 1,000 births. Neural tube defects result from failure of the closure of the spine and/or the neural tube during development. Depending on what level of the spine is affected, such defects can result in paralysis of leg muscles. NTDs are also associated with other medical problems including various orthopedic deformities, hydrocephalus, seizures, growth failure, difficulties with bowel movements and bladder function, vision problems, learning difficulties and other cognitive difficulties, and sexual dysfunction.

continued

Table 3.6 (continued)

Medical condition	Description
Anomalies of the head and face	Congenital defects of the face and head can occur because of failure of normal development. Such defects may occur as isolated defects, a major example being cleft lip and palate; or they can be associated with other defects as part of a clinical genetic syndrome. Children with clefts of the lip and palate can have difficulties with feeding and swallowing, recurrent respiratory and ear infections, and problems with proper tooth development. These defects require multiple surgical procedures over time through the teenage years.
Severe skin disease	Many medical conditions are associated with skin rash or other lesions. Severe acne and various degrees of eczema are very common conditions. Although these may not result in specific disability, they are quite visible and are a cause of significant distress for the individual.
Cystic fibrosis	Chronic disease affecting many systems in the body. It is a genetically inherited condition characterized by thickened respiratory and other secretions that block normal clearance and result in multiple infections. Lung disease and intestinal disease cause many problems for individuals with cystic fibrosis. They may have foul-smelling breath, abdominal or intestinal bloating, recurrent diarrhea, decreased capacity for certain physical tasks, and males can have sexual problems.

Table 3.6

Medical condition	Description
Asthma	Asthma is a common medical condition affecting 15 percent of children, adolescents, and young adults. Depending on the severity of the condition, these individuals may face physical limitations and may at times have difficulties keeping up with peers. Some of them may become socially isolated. Stress can also trigger asthma attacks and make the condition worse. Individuals with asthma have to carry their medications with them and use them in the form of inhalers, often posing difficulties in social situations.

Children with mental disabilities face a different challenge. Children with intellectual impairment often suffer from more emotional and behavioral problems. A recent study by Dekker, Koot, van der Ende, and Verhulst (2002) evaluated children with and without intellectual disabilities. In a population of almost 3,000 children, it was shown that 50 percent of children with mental disabilities had a total score in the deviant range, compared to 18 percent of children without any mental impairment. The children with intellectual impairment suffered from higher incidence of attention problems, social problems, and aggressive behavior.

The manifestation of some disabilities may be subtle but can still have a significant impact on the quality of life for an individual with such a disability. A recent study by Witt, Riley, and Coiro (2003) showed that children with disabilities were more likely to be in poor health and have activity limitations. Divorce and separation were seen at higher rates in mothers of children with disabilities. Stress and poor health were also prevalent in mothers of children with disabilities. Families of children with disabilities experienced higher incidences of work, sleep, and financial difficulties.

Besides discrimination and prejudice, children with disabilities often have limited access to services, including education, health care, and entertainment. In addition to federally mandated laws like the

IDEA, resources such as the Internet have allowed individuals with disabilities to access to the world in unprecedented ways. Individuals can now participate in and navigate through the world without regard to physical, social, or emotional barriers. They can see other parts of the world and meet other people without moving farther than their computer screens. Furthermore, they can often bypass any social stigma associated with their disability. In virtual chatrooms and programs for instant messaging, the only identifying characteristic of a person is the login identity.

Minority Issues and Perspectives

Among persons with disabilities, the minority model is the perspective that most matches their daily living experiences. The central part of experiences faced by racial or gender minority groups is also the foundation of the societal experiences of persons with disabilities, such as the inferior status assigned to them based on negative stigmas held by the "able-bodied majority." The persons with disabilities are also expected to take in and accept the majority culture. They often become the targets of hate crimes and violence (it is sad that persons with disabilities are the only group not included in the Hate Crimes Act of 1999). Other issues include a lack of services appropriate for the persons with disabilities, such as mental health services with professionals trained to work with this population; higher rates of unemployment, dropping out of school, and substance abuse; a lack of representation in the political arena (to raise issues such as funding that are specific to the group); and insufficient assessment tools that have been appropriately standardized for persons with disabilities. There are also more negative than positive role models in media portrayals of persons with disabilities. Finally, there is an expectation that certain emotions, especially anger, are not acceptable. These emotions are used to further support the stigma assigned by the majority world.

The minority model (see Table 3.2) contends that disability is an experience created by the society and the environment. The minority view believes that humans can manipulate and alter their environment to make it welcoming for all people, regardless of impairments. The common issue of isolation for persons with disabilities is seen as something that can be avoided. Most outcomes (having impairments) can be corrected and are produced by stigmas and social environments (Silvers, 1998).

SOCIOPSYCHOLOGICAL PERSPECTIVES

Theories

To date, there are several theories about the origins of prejudicial attitudes that have been supported by considerable research. Most theorists agree that prejudice is determined by many factors. Prejudice needs to be looked at on multiple levels: physiological, emotional, social, and cultural.

Theories from social psychology contend that prejudice and discrimination serve several functions for the individual: they provide a context within which to organize information, and they allow for adaptation, classification, and the prevention of information overload in social contexts. The prominent theories of why prejudice exists and why prejudice persists are presented in Tables 3.7 and 3.8. Each society has different values, expectations, and evaluations of what is acceptable and unacceptable in their groups. We need to look at the individual because society varies greatly in terms of its overall levels of acceptance of violence, yet the ability to refrain from aggressive actions begins at the individual level (Baron & Byrne, 2003).

People who are prejudiced toward specific groups tend to process information about these groups differently from the way they process information about groups to which they are not prejudiced. In their minds (cognition), there are mental pictures or categories for different groups, some negative and some positive. They form negative pictures (categories) of the groups to whom they are prejudiced. Additionally, information relating to or supporting the prejudice is often given more attention, or processed more carefully than information that may contradict the negative view.

Human beings more accurately remember things that capture their attention. For example, imagine that the prejudiced person notices that a person who is leaving an auditorium in a wheelchair has difficulty opening a door. However, that person will not notice that the person in the wheelchair has just finished giving a lecture on his new invention. He or she will lend no importance to the fact that the person in the wheelchair has invented cars that do not use gasoline. The person misses that this invention will stop our dependence on oil and decrease our air pollution significantly! The prejudiced person is more likely to think, "Oh . . . that poor person in the wheelchair is not even capable of opening the door without help." As a result of such effects, prejudice becomes a kind of closed cognitive loop within a person and tends to become stronger over time.

Table 3.7
Prominent Social Theories of Why Prejudice Exists

Theory	Description
Social categorization	Gordon Allport (1954) suggested that the categorization of people into groups was necessary for adaptive functioning. Orderly living depends on it. It is necessary for us to categorize and file objects according to how they function and how they look so that we can reduce the complexity and difficulty of the physical world. It is also necessary for us to use social categorization (social filing system) to reduce the complexity of the social world. If we have to process and think about every single detail and aspect of all persons as individuals, we would quickly become overwhelmed and overload our cognitive processing and storage capacities.
Social learning: early experience	Prejudice is learned and developed in much the same way and through the same basic process as other attitudes. Children acquire negative attitudes toward various social groups the same way they acquire taste for different foods or traditions. They hear and experience such views expressed by parents, friends, teachers, and others, and because they are directly rewarded (with love, praise, and approval) for adopting these views. In addition to learning these attitudes by direct observation of others in their environment, children also learn the social norms/rules within their own group. These norms tell them what actions or attitudes are appropriate and important. Most persons choose to conform to most social norms of groups to which they belong.

Table 3.7

Theory	Description
Direct intergroup conflict: competition as a source of prejudice	Prejudice comes from competition among social groups over cherished and valued commodities or opportunities. Prejudice develops because of the struggle over jobs, adequate housing, good schools, and other desirable outcomes. Because of these struggles, competition continues, and the members of the groups involved come to see each other in increasingly negative terms. They label each other "enemies," view their own group as morally superior, and draw the boundaries between themselves and their opponents more and more tightly in negative ways.
Social identity theory	Prejudice develops when individuals enhance their self-esteem through identifying with positive attributes of specific social groups by devaluing other social groups. The individual views himself or herself as different from—and better than—his or her rivals, and prejudice arises out of this clash of social perceptions. People are motivated to create and uphold their self-esteem, and their different group memberships are connected to their self-esteem. To enhance our self-esteem, we can affiliate with social groups that already are considered attractive and successful, and/or try to view our social group memberships as positively as possible.

Even more potent is the fact that an attitude (prejudice) also involves negative feelings or emotions on the part of the prejudiced persons when they are in the presence of, or even think about, members of the groups they dislike (Vanman, Paul, Ito, & Miller, 1997). Prejudice can be automatic and can influence our behavior even when we are not aware that we have such views, and we might even vigorously deny that we hold them (Fazio & Hilden, 2001). Like other attitudes, prejudice also includes beliefs and expectations about

Table 3.8
Prominent Social Theories of Why Prejudice Persists

Theory	Description
Enhancing self-concept	We hold prejudiced views because doing so allows us to bolster our own self-image. When we put down a group toward whom we hold negative views, we affirm our own self-worth and feel superior in various ways. In other words, for some of us, prejudice may play an important role in protecting or enhancing our self-concept (Fein & Spencer, 1997).
Shortcuts	We hold prejudiced views to save us considerable cognitive effort. Stereotypes, in particular, seem to serve this function. Once stereotypes are formed, we don't have to bother engaging in careful, systematic processing; after all, because we "know" what members of this group are like, we can rely on quicker, shortcut processing and these preconceived beliefs. So our strong tendency to save mental effort seems to be another reason why prejudices are formed and persist.
Outgroup homogeneity	Members of the majority group view the groups that do not fit—or that are different and all exhibit the same (homogeneous) characteristics—in their characteristics, opinions, and behaviors as the "outgroup." The members of the majority or "ingroup" tend to recognize and appreciate their own ingroup diversity but do not recognize or appreciate differences within or among the outgroup members. They use phrases like "they are all alike" to discount diversity among outgroup members (Quattrone, 1986). Sadly, one implication of this process is that people tend to perceive a person with disabilities as just another anonymous group member rather than perceiving him or her as individual.

Table 3.8

Theory	Description
	As human beings, we tend to be prejudiced or discriminate against persons with disabilities because we have limited or no social exposure with them. As we interact with and have positive contacts with persons with disabilities, the level and nature of our prejudicial and discriminatory attitudes toward them change. This includes social categories such as men, women, blacks, the elderly, Latinos, gays, librarians, and waitresses.
Self-fulfilling prophecy	Our expectations about others may influence how we interact with them. Research on self-fulfilling prophecies suggests that the ways in which we interact with persons with disabilities may draw out our behaviors that confirm our preconceived negative expectations and stereotypes (Snyder, Tanke, & Berscheid, 1977). For example, if we expect someone with a severe physical disability to be hostile, we may interact with that person in a cold or distant fashion. This person may respond in kind—also behaving in a rather hostile fashion, thus confirming the original expectation. The person doesn't have to have a hostile personality or tendency for this prophecy to be fulfilled. It is only necessary that others expect the person to be hostile.

members of various groups—for instance, beliefs that all members of these groups show certain characteristics and traits.

When we think about a person with disabilities, it is important for us to link the personal experience of impairment with the social factors that create disability. It is argued that the community is the place where disability is constructed and experienced (Olkin & Howson, 1994). Disability is frequently called a social construct, meaning that the disability is best understood in terms of how society perceives disability. It is important for us to understand the perspective of persons with disabilities. Olkin (1999) notes that in the disabled community, there is an accepted understanding of what impairment and disability are:

- Impairment is the physical, sensory, cognitive, or systemic condition that directly imposes a reduction in certain functions; the locus of difficulty resides in the person.
- Disability is those barriers and reductions in function imposed by the physical and psychosocial environments; the locus of difficulty resides in the sociopolitical environment.

Working with persons with disabilities is the same as working with people who are from another culture. Persons with disabilities are bicultural, living in both a disability minority world and an "able-bodied majority" world.

There is commonality of experience among people with different types of disabilities. Being devalued for having a disability and learning to accept all aspects of the disability is shared by all. Having a disability does not mean that one will have psychological problems. However, for those persons with disabilities who experience psychological problems, devaluation and non-acceptance seem to be the primary causes of their difficulties. The natural solution to most of the specific psychological problems associated with disability will logically be personal validation and acceptance. Psychological problems experienced are not due to the mental disabilities per se, but to such abnormal stimuli as being devaluated in the eyes of others. Another psychologically damaging consequence of having a disability is the oppression that happens daily. That involves being regarded as a lesser being, inferior, not very capable, not very useful, possibly burdensome, unaesthetic, and (generally) one down. Devaluation and oppression by others (and themselves) are daily experiences for persons with disabilities.

Many authors on disability topics who themselves have disabilities have written that, given a level playing field, almost all persons with disabilities are capable of building a quality life (Vash, 1981; Olkin, 1999). The problems they encounter are the "able-bodied" people. Some examples of these are:

- The counselor who tells the parents that they have to grieve over the child they "did not have" before they can love their disabled child.
- The physicians who worked on the child's hands and legs as if the limbs were not attached to a whole person.

- The encouraging parents who assured their children that they could grow up to be anything they wanted to be, even when the children wanted to be ballerinas or football players (in spite of their wheelchairs).
- The colleges that told the person with a disability that he or she could not be accepted because he or she would not be able to "cut it" with the rest of the able-bodied on campus.
- The mother who did not want her son to marry a "disabled woman," or the father who didn't want the man with a disability to marry his daughter.
- The therapist who told the clients that they were in denial of their disabilities. (Olkin, 1999)

Each of these examples reflects efforts of professionals to "help" ease pain and suffering and to give hope; however, the impact on persons with disabilities or their families may not have been viewed so positively.

It is important to clarify some myths about persons with disabilities. First, research shows that the personalities of persons with disabilities are not different from personalities of persons without disabilities (Yuker, 1994). Second, the severity of the physical disability does not determine the severity of the individual's psychological problems (Olkin & Howson, 1994; Nosek, Fuhrer, & Potter, 1995). It is possible to have a severe physical disability in the absence of psychological problems.

Olkin (1999) contends that persons with disabilities are often told that the disabilities are in their heads: things they should deny or pretend do not exist. However, just imagine the effects of repeated devaluation of a person by those around that person and the impact of these experiences on the self-image and self-identity. Understanding the development of prejudicial attitudes and discrimination is important to helping the affected individuals survive such treatment. That understanding is also important for others who are not disabled to see how their behaviors affect the self-identity and behaviors of persons with disabilities.

Overcoming the commonly held notions of what it means to be disabled is not easily accomplished. According to theories in social psychology (see Table 8), one basis for making judgments about others is what is known as "central traits," such as a person's attractiveness and position in society (Asch, 1946). A person's perceived level of disability is a central trait. For example, most people have specific perceptions about persons in wheelchairs, and all of their future references about these persons will always revolve around the "wheelchairs" (that is, the disability). Research shows that most disabled people do not perceive their disability as the most important thing in their lives; however, others (non-disabled persons) perceive the disability as a *defining* aspect of the person with disabilities (Yuker, 1994).

People who are physically attractive (see Appendix, Case Example 2) are often assumed to be more competent, have more socially desirable personalities, and have happier and more successful lives than those of less-attractive peers (Collins & Zebrowitz, 1995). Individuals who are athletic, thin, and have physical features or characteristics valued by the majority culture are generally viewed as attractive. If such a person should suffer a physical disfigurement or become physically disabled, he or she will no longer be seen as attractive. Rarely are individuals in wheelchairs depicted as attractive or sexy in the mainstream media. Does disability in some way interfere with beauty? The answer, based on images of disabled people portrayed in the movies and other media, is yes! This is because disability is often used in the media as a metaphor for underlying character flaws or undesirable traits (Cahill & Norden, 2003).

It is the perspective of most persons with disabilities that able-bodied society has set up behavioral and affective norms that persons with disabilities must follow. For example, they are expected to be cheery, to not show any anger, and to be in mourning. They must be in full control of their emotions. If they show anger, they are said to be having adjustment problems. The message learned by persons with disabilities at a very early age is that the able-bodied group teaches that "you can live and work among us, as long as you are cheerful, and keep your disability away from our awareness; you must shield us from your difficulties" (Olkin, 1999, p. 96).

There is also the expectation that persons with disabilities should be grateful for what they have and all of the help they have received. If they present as cheerful, well adjusted, humble, and accepting, they are often embraced by members of the majority culture. This expectation is an added burden to the person with disability. Also, it would be nice if all of us could present with these behaviors and moods (grateful, cheerful, well adjusted) every day, but it is not realistic to expect such behaviors, and it is not fair to expect them from persons with disabilities.

It is common knowledge that many helping professionals view disability as a loss: a loss of the healthy or undamaged body, loss of function, or loss of the wished-for perfect child. Parents are often told to "mourn this loss" so that they can begin the processes of "adjust-ment" and acceptance of the child with disability. The authors are not saying that the mourning does not or should not occur. Wright (1983) makes a useful distinction between the "requirement of mourning" and the "period of mourning." In many instances, per-sons who sustain a disability may well experience a period of mourn-ing, with its components of sadness, loss, and grieving. But this is not inevitable or universal (Olkin, 1999). Another issue is that persons with disabilities are frequently told that they must be "brave," or "they must go on"; in the process, their challenges are often mini-mized. Individuals who do not conform to these very conflicting and contradictory "requirements" are seen as being in "denial" or having adjustment problems.

It is understandable that they experience continuous frustrations when interacting with professionals who are supposed to help them. The person with the disability is being made to perform several cog-nitively conflicting tasks: to learn to cognitively and physically accept and manage the disability while simultaneously pretending the dis-ability does not exist ("it's all in your head"), and to mourn the loss of a fully functioning body and at the same time show enthusiasm toward the rehabilitation process. Cognitive dissonance and emotional confusion then occur when a person is asked to perform competing cognitive processes (Baron & Byrne, 2003). Persons with disabilities are asked to deal with the debilitating powers of daily prejudice, stigma, and discrimination.

As we learned in the previous section, the cognitive self-identities of people with disabilities can be shaped by their experiences with preju-dice and discrimination, because they have the disabilities. This brings back the idea that the disability is much a social creation. We as a soci-ety can change the experience of persons with disabilities by providing equal playing fields, and the persons with disabilities can and will break the stigmas that the able-bodied use to negatively evaluate them.

The Disability Community

People born with deafness or hearing impairment have had to fight long and hard to prove to the hearing world that there is a deaf com-munity and deaf culture. Other persons with disabilities also consider themselves to belong to respective communities, for example, com-munities where the members have a sense of identity and are proud, and communities where members have their own language, history, priorities, humor, and norms. Persons with disabilities form a community with some features in common with other outgroups and many features specific to their community. The members of the disability community do not emphasize their diagnoses or medical conditions; instead they focus on their collective experiences. Social activism for disability rights and independent living are the focus of their attention, not rehabilitation. They also emphasize their rights to live and function in the majority communities.

Hardman et al. (2002) suggest that one way to measure the success of community services is to look at whether and how the services make a difference in one's life. Therefore, the quality of community services for person with disabilities can be evaluated by looking at the following four factors:

- Do service and supports promote personal autonomy?
- Do opportunities for social interaction and integration exist?
- Does the individual have a choice of lifestyle?
- Do opportunities for economic self-sufficiency exist?

SUGGESTED SOLUTIONS

If one takes a visit to the campus of Gallaudet University in Washington, DC, one will see a place where society has decided to respect a person's "impairment" (reduction in functions imposed by physical, sensory, cognitive, or systemic condition) and reduce or eliminate the experience of prejudice and discrimination due to a person's "disability" (reduction in functions imposed by the physical and psychosocial environment). One will see students in wheelchairs attending advanced biology classes where they can get to the buildings, enter the classrooms, and then find their choice of seats without any physical barriers or negative perceptions from others they pass. Persons born with deafness attend doctoral-level psychology classes with other hearing classmates. One may also see a professor giving a lecture on sociology or political science, where the professor has an interpreter using tactile sign language so he or she may understand students' questions, and the professor himself/herself has blindness and deafness. It is common to see students with cerebral palsy giving a presentation in the student government in which they are members, laboriously using American Sign Language to express themselves, while fellow students respectfully and patiently wait, while on the "white board" the PowerPoint slides of their presentations are displayed for all to follow. One will also see a student with a learning disability taking a test in a separate room with extra time permitted. A place where every classroom is equipped with technologies that provide equal access to persons of all walks of life, even if they cannot walk physically. There are interpreters for persons who cannot speak, persons who cannot hear, and for the able-bodied who cannot communicate using sign language.

The philosophy is equal access for all. Gallaudet is a place where the playing field is leveled so that higher education and jobs (on campus) are available to all individuals. Interestingly, large companies such as IBM and Apple Computer have recognized the potential consumers whom the students of Gallaudet will be in the future. They have wisely invested in technologies to support independence for the students in a variety of ways. Does prejudice exist at Gallaudet University? The authors are sure that some forms of prejudice exist. However, people are not defined by their disabilities; they are defined as college students seeking higher education. It is possible to change the social systems, attitudes, and behaviors to eliminate the experience of prejudice and discrimination toward persons with disabilities. Knowing this possibility allows us to take a look at how prejudice and discrimination can be eliminated.

As mentioned earlier in this chapter, disability is experienced physiologically, emotionally, socially, and culturally by the person with the disability (see Appendix). However, in this chapter we focused on the social construction of disability and the psychology of prejudice and discrimination toward persons with disabilities. In this concluding section, we would like to reflect on what we can do individually to change, using what we have learned, so as to reduce the experiences of prejudice and discrimination by persons with disabilities.

We are interested both in why prejudice exists and why it persists. We have looked at prejudice from a social-problem perspective. According to this perspective, prejudice is regarded as a problem with harmful consequences. The authors feel that prejudice needs to be eliminated in order that society may advance. Central to the strategies to reduce prejudice was the assumption that majority group members' negative attitudes toward minority group members were the main obstacle to well-balanced intergroup relations. Therefore, all the strategies to reduce prejudice must have, as their main goal, techniques to change the negative *attitudes* of majority group members. However, most recent studies are showing that it is more important to change the majority group *behaviors* than it is important to change the attitudes. It seems that attitudes sometimes influence behaviors, but behaviors always influence attitudes. The authors suggest that we address prejudice and discrimination toward persons with disabilities from both the attitude and behavior change strategies.

The best research finding so far about prejudice and discrimination is the significant role that the "ingroup versus outgroup" perception has in creating and maintaining prejudiced attitudes. The intergroup bias fuels the prejudiced attitude. It makes sense to address the problems of prejudice by using the information social psychologists have provided us. There are seven factors we have learned that can be acted on immediately:

1. Reducing intergroup bias using the "contact theory."
2. Showing the strengths and skills (not asking for pity or sympathy).
3. Getting the neighbors and community to behave more positively.
4. Getting professionals to reduce the "superior versus inferior" attitude.
5. Positively changing the effects of public education and the mass media on people with disabilities.
6. Political involvement.
7. Celebrating our sameness before pointing out our differences.

These factors are discussed below.

Reducing Intergroup Bias Using the "Contact Theory"

The most convincing strategy for reducing intergroup hostilities comes from the "contact theory." Social psychologists suggest that negative attitudes toward minority groups are at least partially due to ignorance of other groups in general. This ignorance is created and maintained by persistent segregation. One way to improve intergroup relations is to reduce ignorance between the groups about their members. Creating opportunities or contact between members of the different groups can do this. What is really important here is that the contact must be equal status contact between the majority and minority group members while working on common goals (Allport, 1954). For example, the common beliefs that able-bodied persons have about persons with disabilities are usually negative. The more contact that able-bodied persons have with the persons with disabilities, the more they will get to experience other aspects of them and not just the disabilities.

When the contact between the able-bodied person and the person with a disability involves them cooperating on a goal, and the cooperation is supported by the important people in their lives (boss, parents, etc.), the attitude toward disability improves. It makes sense that repeated contacts lead to the able-bodied person learning more information about the person with the disability (family, values, aspirations, joyful experiences, sense of humor, etc.) as a "whole" person. This leads to a reduction of negative feelings and thoughts about the disability.

Showing the Strengths and Skills (Not Asking for Pity or Sympathy)

When a person with a disability is seen as competent, others show a positive attitude toward him or her. This is especially true if the person is competent in areas that the able-bodied majority see as valuable (jobs, education, parenting, socializing). This is a catch-22 situation for the person with the disability. For example, the person cannot get an advanced education or a good job because he or she is seen as incompetent for not having an advanced education or a good job. We need to work at using our individual influence at the policymaking level to allow more access to education and jobs for persons with disabilities so all of us can benefit. Quality education and quality jobs should be basic rights for persons with disabilities. Think of the economic benefits possible if we reduce dependence on social welfare for persons with disabilities when we, the majority able-bodied, insist on equal access to all persons living in America.

Getting the Community and Neighbors to Behave More Positively

We tend to behave more positively toward people who are friendly and have strong social skills. This is true of the community's and the neighbor's behavior toward persons with disabilities; they tend to behave more positively toward a person with a disability when the person is friendly and has strong social skills. This is another catch-22 situation. It is difficult to behave in a friendly, sociable manner when you sense that others are awkward around you, and it is difficult to have a pleasant smile on your face when others are looking down on you or treating you as if you were inferior. Yet, many people think that a person with a disability is unfriendly, awkward, and inferior, and therefore they do not take the time to approach, invite, or relax around the person, and so the negative perception cycle goes on. It is true that we like to be with others who are pleasant to be around. However, the automatic prejudice attitude leads people with disabilities to feel an extra burden to deal with ("God forbid you should have a bad day") (Olkin, 1999).

Getting Professionals to Reduce the "Superior versus Inferior" Attitude

Researchers have found that professionals in all disciplines have more positive attitudes toward the client with a disability if the client is able to put the professional at ease. One of the factors that can help is perceiving the client as a person who can communicate effectively. Another factor is the client showing that he or she is comfortable or has accepted the disability; then professionals tend to have a more positive attitude. Also, if the client is more willing to discuss the disability, the professional will be more positive. All of these are factors that make professionals more comfortable and at ease—they are the ones who are supposed to be doing the comforting and the easing. So, professionals should be aware of who is getting paid to provide the support and services.

Positively Changing the Effects of Public Education and the Mass Media on Ordinary People

Public education is needed to help with the problems of prejudice toward persons with disabilities. The mass media have begun to report on the efforts of persons with disabilities to obtain their civil and human rights. They also have devised feature stories about the experiences of these persons. What is still missing is the ordinary portrayal of people who just happen to have disabilities going about the business of ordinary living in very nearly ordinary world. For example, they are rarely seen in bit parts or crowd scenes in fictional film and television presentations. When a person with a disability is shown in a main role, the disability is always a main theme, rather than the background concern it is in real life. These stereotypes lead to the harmful "us versus them" distinctions. Needed in the future are more images of disabled people as "plain folks," without over-dramatized attention to a single aspect of their disability.

Political Involvement

We need more persons with disabilities in public office. The majority group is afraid to vote for such people who are publicly active because they fear the people with disabilities will not be able to represent majority "able-bodied" views. The establishment of the League of Disabled Voters in Washington, DC may change the collective power of persons with disabilities and open the door for future candidates in public office.

This also ties into the fundraising campaign using sympathy to get donation. This old strategy needs to be replaced with a political force that demands equity and more public dollars to level the playing field for persons with disabilities when it comes to basic human rights (education, jobs, social activities, etc.).

Celebrate Our Sameness before Pointing Out Our Differences

It is politically correct at this time to say "celebrate our differences." We know that all the research is showing that prejudice stems from focusing on our differences. We try to find what is different about the outgroup even if the group is made up for pointless games or training purposes. If group boundaries maintain and perpetuate intergroup biases, a reasonable strategy for reducing such biases would be to decrease the importance of group boundaries. The main goal is to decrease reliance on category-based, or "we" versus "they," processing. For example, showing that the outgroup members have diverse opinions is helpful in reducing prejudice. Another example is encouraging ingroup members to respond to outgroup members as individuals rather than as a group. This encouragement leads to reductions in intergroup bias (Langer, Bashner, & Chanowitz, 1985).

When new subgroups are formed using both people who used to be in the ingroup and people who used to be in the outgroup, the new group members seem to pay less attention or have less need for categorization, and intergroup bias is reduced. When people from the outgroup and people from the ingroup are put together in situations where they have to cooperate and work on a common goal that is rewarding to both groups, this cooperation has the effect of reducing intergroup biases (Worchel, 1986). What happens in these two situations is that the members of the ingroup and the outgroup get to experience personal interactions with each other. The false negative perceptions give way to more real, personal experiences.

CONCLUSION

In the end, we seem to be faced with two conflicting goals. First, we know that we need to reduce the use of categories for intergroup perception because they lead to biased or prejudiced attitudes. Second, we want to encourage a multicultural society and celebrate diversity. We are struggling to find ways to make these two goals work. Even social scientists are puzzled about which path is best for us to take. Based on what we know about outgroup perception research, we feel it is important to be careful about deciding how to decrease prejudice. We need first to find and emphasize how we are more alike and what we have in common. If we were to encourage celebration of our differences in the absence of celebrating our similarities first, we could have the effect of heightening or sharpening the perception that our groups are really different from each other (that is, by making intergroup boundaries more important). Social psychologists have pointed out some of the potential dangers of encouraging the perception that we are different. It is not the authors' intention to say that we should not celebrate our differences. The authors are only saying that society needs to use the information we have learned and to use it objectively. In order to celebrate differences, society must first find and celebrate commonality (similarities) and encourage inclusion between groups and individuals (Devine, 1995).

Finally, there is hope, because people in the United States generally show more favorable attitudes toward disability than do people in other countries (Westbrook, Legge, & Pennay, 1993). Nationality is an important determinant of attitudes toward disability. It suggests that broad social movements and political factors can have a substantial effect on the lives of persons with disabilities by affecting the attitudes of the populace toward them. We still have a lot of work to do, and we can look forward to a lot more humanity. Daily technological advances are making the world much more accessible to persons with disabilities (for example, text and instant messaging, the Internet, universal designs, accessible taxis, and "smart classrooms"). Again, a visit to Gallaudet University campus will be sure to inspire artists, engineers, parents, and children with a barrier-free environment and its possibilities for the society at large. Most of all, all visitors will notice that *impairment does not mean disabilities*. The prejudice and discrimination experienced by persons with disabilities outside of the campus disappears on campus. Society can alter and build physical environments that are welcoming. People can learn and adjust their social values.

> The man who doesn't make up his mind to cultivate the habit of thinking misses the greatest pleasures in life.
> —Thomas A. Edison

Toolbox for Change

For	Images/perceptions	Strategies for change
Individuals	"Us versus them." "Those people are all alike." Persons with disabilities are depressed, grouchy, and not friendly. Persons with disabilities are too consumed with their disabilities to be interested in friendships and socializing.	Reduce intergroup bias using the contact theory. Invite your neighbor with a disability to come over for tea or go over for a visit and chat. Organize a block party and make it accessible for all your neighbors (including the person with a disability). Imagine what the children can learn.
Community/ society	Persons with disabilities must rely on charity and social welfare to survive in society. Persons with disabilities can't do important work or benefit from higher education. "They are not like us." "They are very different from us. They cannot possibly represent us in political office." "They don't vote, so their opinions don't matter." "They are all alike."	Showcase the strengths and skills (don't ask for pity and sympathy). Show persons with disabilities doing important jobs, contributing to society, being tax-paying citizens with a civil right to funding (decrease or eliminate the need to showcase disabilities as pity inducers to solicit donation money). Reduce intergroup bias using the contact theory – Churches, schools, and neighborhood organizations can arrange for social or volunteer interactions between the outgroups. Political involvement: League of Disabled Voters is gaining strength in political and voting force. Encourage and support political involvement of students with disabilities so they can become active in political roles in the future.

continued

For	Images/perceptions	Strategies for change
		Celebrate sameness before pointing out our differences. Create celebrations of humanities, commonalities, inclusions along with celebration of diversities.
Practitioners/ educators	Persons with disabilities are depressed, grouchy, and not friendly.	Set examples by behaving positively and nonjudgmental toward persons with disabilities.
	Persons with disabilities are too consumed with their disabilities to be interested in friendships and socializing.	Show persons with disabilities doing important jobs, contributing to society, being tax-paying citizens with a civil right to funding (decrease or eliminate the need to showcase disabilities as pity inducers to solicit donation money).
	You are the client; therefore, you are inferior. I am the professional; therefore, I am superior.	
	Persons with disabilities are scary, mentally unstable, and cognitively impaired.	Get professionals to reduce the "superior versus inferior" attitude. Do not insist on the response you think should be, or what you think it would be like if you had a disability.
	They will be overcome with magical cures.	Respect the person with a disability as a consumer of your services, not as an inferior being in need of your help.
		In public education and the mass media, show that persons with disabilities do, enjoy, and suffer from ordinary things in life.
		Be humane and be humble.

APPENDIX: CASE EXAMPLES FOR DISCUSSION OF PREJUDICE AND DISCRIMINATION ISSUES

Case Example 1

Roger is a seventeen-year-old male who attends a school for deaf students. He has cerebral palsy and a severe hearing impairment. Roger lives in two worlds. One world is where young men his age hang out at the mall, lift weights to impress the teenage girls, and drive using their newly obtained driving permits. His other world is where he and his school friends swerve back and forth without his awareness at times, comparing wheelchairs to others who pass by him and to peers who live in sweat pants, not for the sloppy look but for the convenience of not having zippers. The typical hairstyle is a very close buzz cut, not for the hair fashion but for the lack of mobility to style his own hair. He lives in a bicultural world. One is the majority able-bodied world and the other the minority world of the disabled community.

When Roger goes out to eat at restaurants with his family, he is often faced with the limitations of the eating environments. Sometimes his parents have jokingly remarked that they would just rather stay in and be sure that they got to eat before hunger made the whole family cranky and ruined the whole outing experience. For example, many restaurants do not have barrier-free access; seating is limited to a few tables, meaning that the family often has to endure long waits to get a table that accommodates a wheel chair.

Roger is very worried about his disabilities and how they will affect his health. But these don't seem to wear him down as much as his worries about his interpersonal relationships (or lack of them). Roger dreams about having a girlfriend, desires sexual experiences, and is afraid of growing old alone. He is worried about the financial costs of his independence when he cannot even get a part-time job to give him pocket money. He is exhausted and frustrated from his experience of not having access to buildings and events.

For a very long time, Roger was taught to look and behave like his non-disabled friends. He was trained to deny his disabilities. Roger did not have any friends in his neighborhood who also had disabilities. Roger had never met another person who had cerebral palsy and/or deafness and happened to live a successful, happy life. Roger has been told numerous times that his disabilities are problems only if he lets them become problems.

It is understandable that Roger wants to avoid people who are just like him; he often tries to point out how he is "not like them"—other people with physical disabilities. He is not like them except for his wheelchair, crutches, limp, fatigue, and negative reaction of others. In his neighborhood, Roger is usually the only person with a disability. What he sees reflected back to him is the picture of non-disabled people. Roger often catches himself having negative attitudes toward other people with disabilities. He sees how others view disability, and thus he has absorbed and learned how to view disability just like any non-disabled teenager in his "majority" world. Roger's self-identity has been shaped by his environment. His own attitude and prejudices hurt him and make him reject himself.

Case Example 2

Mark has a subtle disability that, nonetheless, has had profound effects on him. Mark is blind in one eye. Though at first this seems like a minor handicap, its sequellae are more far-reaching than one might expect. Each eye sees a slightly different image. As with most human beings, Mark's brain uses the two images seen by each eye and the distance between the eyes to measure depth. This is known as stereoscopic or binocular vision. Because Mark can see with only one eye, he cannot perceive depth. Simple tasks such as playing catch, shaking hands, or picking up objects are very difficult for a person with no depth perception. This disability prevented Mark from playing sports like softball, tennis, and football. He always felt he had to explain to those who questioned his lack of athletic endeavors why he did not play sports. Sometimes he found himself making up elaborate stories to explain his "lack" of participation rather than tell another person—especially a male peer—the truth. Even as an adult, Mark is cautious about making such a disclosure. He does not want to be different—he does not want to expose himself to rejection or ridicule. Mark was an excellent student in school and excelled academically, and he is a very successful adult. Yet he too still worries about the issues of prejudice and discrimination against persons with disabilities.

Case Example 3

Audrey was diagnosed with eczema when she was three months old. Her skin was often scaly, cracked, red, and oozed yellow drainage. Her mother was the only person who could tolerate cuddling

her and loving her. No matter how many medications were prescribed and interventions employed, Audrey's appearance was not
pleasant. Audrey had a beautiful smile and bright eyes, and was a
happy baby when she was not suffering discomfort from her dermato-
logical condition. As Audrey grew, her family learned ways to keep
her condition under better control. She seldom was a mass of ugly
scales, red patches, and sores. Most of the time her outbreaks were in
less-visible places (such as behind her knees, under her arms, inside
the bend of her elbows, on her neck, or on the backs of her hands).
Unfortunately, when her peers or strangers did see places where her
eczema was showing, they did not want to touch Audrey. They often
recoiled and stared at her darkened or scaly skin. As Audrey became
a teenager, she was often isolated and unable to establish a steady
group of friends. Audrey often cried about this but developed
healthy coping strategies because she had a loving set of parents, siblings, and relatives. She did have people who loved her and accepted
her as she was. Audrey grew up engrossed in books and learned to
write beautiful stories. She became a very successful researcher and
often talks to youth about the importance of self-acceptance and
learning to manage the negative reactions of others.

Case Example 4

Harry, a nine-year-old black male, stuttered severely. He often refused to talk in front of other people in order to avoid being laughed
or to avoid having others focus on him and his speech. Harry hated
being pulled out of class to go to speech therapy. He would often
cry before school and attempt to stay home on the days he had speech
therapy. With his parents' insistence, Harry did go to school. His
speech therapist was able to help him learn to control his stuttering
in therapy sessions. He also learned to control his speech at home and
with close friends; however, he was so nervous in class that he refused to read out loud. He often refused to talk in front of classmates.
He could not tolerate their reactions to his struggles. By the time
Harry entered the fourth grade, he was placed in a classroom with a
teacher who was patient, supportive, and empathetic. This teacher
had a son who also stuttered as a child and understood Harry's issues.
She talked to the class about helping Harry feel safe enough to practice his talking out loud. She would ask Harry to read in reading
group. She would allow him to struggle with a word until he could
pronounce it without interference from his stuttering. She had the

class listen and be patient, too. Within the first six months of Harry's fourth grade year, Harry no longer stuttered. This teacher, the therapist, and his classmates created a "safe" environment for Harry to gain confidence and practice and to overcome his disability.

Case Example 5

Alice is an individual who suffered a traumatic injury and became disabled. She now faces discrimination and prejudice on a daily basis. This young woman was in a tragic automobile accident. Prior to the accident, she was a healthy, attractive young woman with no medical problems. She was popular and enjoyed the benefits of being young, intelligent, and pretty. Though she was very fortunate to survive the initial insult of the accident, she sustained major injuries to her face that left her permanently disfigured. She also shattered her pelvis, leaving her wheelchair-bound for several years while she underwent numerous surgeries and physical therapy. Throughout her reconstructive surgery and physical rehabilitation, she was subject to prejudice and discrimination on several levels. The most painful for her was the change in the way people responded and reacted to alterations in her face, body, and person. Simple things that she once enjoyed, such as shopping, turned into heartbreaking experiences filled with finger-pointing and sideways glances. She often could not get anyone to help her with her purchases. She became invisible. The salespeople who once flocked to the young woman to show her beautiful dresses, various shades of lipstick, and other merchandise now frequently ignored her attempts to buy their goods.

REFERENCES

Allport, G. W. (1954). *The nature of prejudice.* Reading, MA: Addison-Wesley.
Asch, S. E. (1946). Forming impressions of personality. *Journal of Abnormal and Social Psychology, 41,* 258–290.
Baron, R. A., & Byrne, D. (2003). *Social psychology: Attitudes, evaluating the social world.* Boston: Allyn & Bacon.
Berry, J., & Hardman, M. L. (1998). *Lifespan perspectives on the family and disability.* Boston: Allyn & Bacon.
Cahill, M. A., & Norden, M. F. (2003). Hollywood's portrayals of disabled women. In A. Hans & A. Patri (Eds.), *Women, disability, and identity* (pp. 56–75). New Delhi, India: SAGE Publications, Pvt. Ltd.

Chan, F., Lam, C., Wong, K. D., Leung, P., & Fang, X. F. (1988). Counseling Chinese-Americans with disabilities. *Journal of Applied Rehabilitation Counseling, 19,* 21–25.

Collins, M. A., & Zebrowitz, L. A. (1995). The contributions of appearance to occupational outcomes in civilian and military settings. *Journal of Applied Social Psychology, 25,* 129–163.

Dekker, M. C., Koot, H. M., van der Ende, J., & Verhulst, F. C. (2002). Emotional and behavioral problems in children and adolescents with and without intellectual disability. *Journal of Child Psychology and Psychiatry, 43*(8), 1087–1098.

Devine, P. G. (1995). Prejudice and out-group perception. In A. Tesser (Ed.), *Advanced social psychology* (pp. 467–524). Boston: McGraw-Hill.

Fazio, R. H., & Hilden, L. E. (2001). Emotional reactions to a seemingly prejudiced response: The role of automatically activated racial attitudes and motivation to control prejudice reactions. *Personality and Social Psychology Bulletin, 27,* 538–549.

Fein, S., & Spencer, S. J. (1997). Prejudice as self-image maintenance: Affirming the self through derogating others. *Journal of Personality and Social Psychology, 73,* 31–44.

Fleischer, D. Z., & Zames, F. (2001). *The disability rights movement: From charity to confrontation.* Philadelphia, PA: Temple University Press.

Florian, V. (1982). Cross-cultural differences in attitudes towards disabled persons: A study of Jewish and Arab youth in Israel. *International Journal of Intercultural Relations, 6,* 291–299.

Hahn, H. (1985). Changing perception of disability and the future of rehabilitation. In L. G. Perlman & G. F. Austin (Eds.), *Social influences in rehabilitation planning: Blueprint for the 21st century* [A report of the ninth Mary E. Switzer Memorial Seminar] (pp. 53–64). Alexandria, VA: National Rehabilitation Association.

Hardman, M. L., Drew, C. J., & Egan, M. W. (2002). *Human exceptionality: Society, school, and family.* Boston: Allyn & Bacon.

Jellinek, M. S., & Murphy, J. M. (1988). Screening for psychosocial disorders in pediatric practice. *American Journal of Disabled Children, 142,* 1153.

Langer, E. J., Bashner, R. S., & Chanowitz, B. (1985). Decreasing prejudice by increasing discrimination. *Journal of Personality and Social Psychology, 49,* 113–120.

McLaughlin, M. W., Shepard, L. A., & O' Day, J. A. (1995). *Improving education through standards-based reform: A report by the National Academy of Education Panel on Standards-Based Education Reform.* Stanford, CA: The National Academy of Education.

Molnar, G. E. (1992). *Pediatric rehabilitation.* Baltimore: Williams and Wilkins.

National Council on Disability. (1999). *National disability policy: A progress report, November, 1997–October, 1998.* Washington, DC: National Council on Disability.

Nosek, M., Fuhrer, M., & Potter, C. (1995). Life satisfaction of people with physical disabilities: Relationship to personal assistance, disability status, and handicap. *Rehabilitation Psychology, 40,* 191–202.

Olkin, R. (1999). *What psychotherapists should know about disability.* New York: Guilford Press.

Olkin, R., & Howson, L. (1994). Attitudes toward and images of physical disability. *Journal of Social Behavior and Personality, 9,* 81–96.

Petty, R. E. (1995). Attitude change. In A. Tesser (Ed.), *Advanced Social Psychology* (pp. 195–255). New York. McGraw-Hill.

Quattrone, G. A. (1986). On the perception of a group's variability. In S. Worchel & W. G. Austin (Eds.), *Psychology of intergroup relations* (2nd ed.). Chicago: Nelson-Hall.

Shelton, J. N. (2000). A reconceptualization of how we study issues of racial prejudice. *Personality and Social Psychology Review, 4,* 374–390.

Silvers, A. (1998) Formal justice. In A. Silvers, D. Wasserman, & M. B. Mahowald (Eds.), *Disability, difference, discrimination: Perspectives on justice in bioethics and public policy.* Lanham, MD: Rowan & Littlefield.

Snyder, M., Tanke, E. D., & Berscheid, E. (1977). Social perception and interpersonal behavior: On the self-fulfilling nature of social stereotypes. *Journal of Personality and Social Psychology, 35,* 656–666.

Szymanski, E. M., & Trueba, H. T. (1999) Castification of people with disabilities: Potential disempowering aspects of classification in disability services. In R. P. Marinelli & A. E. Dell Orto (Eds.), *The psychological and social impact of disability* (4th ed., pp. 195–209). New York: Springer.

Vanman, E. J., Paul, B. Y., Ito, T. A., & Miller, N. (1997). The modern face of prejudice and structure features that moderate the effect of cooperation on affect. *Journal of Personality and Social Psychology, 73,* 941–959.

Vash, C. L. (1981). *The psychology of disability.* New York: Springer.

Westbrook, M. T., Legge, V., & Pennay, M. (1993). Attitudes towards disabilities in a multicultural society. *Social Science Medicine, 36,* 615–623.

Witt, W. P., Riley, A. W., & Coiro, M. J. (2003). Childhood functional status, family stressors, and psychosocial adjustment among school-aged children with disabilities in the United States. *Archives of Pediatric and Adolescent Medicine, 157*(7), 687–695.

Worchel, S. (1986). The role of cooperation in reducing intergroup conflict. In S. Worchel & W. G. Austin (Eds.), *Psychology of intergroup relations* (2nd ed., pp. 288–304). Chicago: Nelson-Hall.

Wright, B. A. (1983). *Physical disability: A psychosocial approach* (2nd ed.). New York: Harper & Row.

Yuker, H. E. (1994). Variables that influence attitudes toward persons with disabilities: Conclusions from the data [Special issue]. *Journal of Social Behavior and Personality, 9,* 3–22.

CHAPTER 4

Beyond the "Triple Whammy": Considering Social Class as One Factor in Discrimination against Persons with Disabilities

Martha E. Banks
Catherine A. Marshall

For more than twenty years, researchers have documented the double discrimination that women with disabilities face in society and in the workplace (Banks, 2003a, 2003b; Banks & Ackerman, 2003; Crawford & Ostrove, 2003; Feldman & Tegart, 2003; Lesh & Marshall, 1984; Williams & Upadhyay, 2003). Women continue to face unsupportive workplace environments and unrealistic workplace expectations (Neal-Barnett & Mendelson, 2003; Vande Kemp, Chen, Erickson, & Friesen, 2003). As only one example, the Arizona Job Service advises via a handout given to those registering for their services as a requirement of receiving unemployment insurance that "there are some responses that present a more positive image than others. . . . DO NOT use 'Child-care'" (n.d., p. 9) as a reason for having left a previous job. In the recent experience of one of the authors (CAM), a university administrator asserted in a staff meeting, "Child care is a woman's personal problem." Thus we are left to posit that not only might disability status, but also a woman's children, still be seen as personal "problems" that women (and certainly some men) must "overcome" in order to fully participate in education and the workplace, including professional positions (Wilson, 2003). Payment for quality childcare is generally understood to be a costly component of one's budget and also challenging for low-income families.

In addition to the "double whammy" of being female and disabled is a third level of discrimination that people of color with disabilities experience (Corbett, 2003; Feist-Price & Wright, 2003; Feldman & Tegart, 2003; Mukherjee, Reis, & Heller, 2003; Nabors & Pettee, 2003; Neal-Barnett & Mendelson, 2003; Vande Kemp, Chen, Erickson, & Friesen, 2003; Vernon, 1999; Yee, Nguyen, & Ha, 2003). Such discrimination, a "triple whammy" based on culture, can be expected to be particularly damaging for persons whose cultural values do not mesh with the individualistic, capitalistic values of mainstream America. An example is taken from the Arizona Job Service's one-page flyer entitled *Job Search Tips*, which includes "*Go alone (Job search is not teamwork)*" (n.d., italics added). Such advice might be deemed necessary for successful employment in Arizona, but it is not consistent with the values of some Native people. As one former state of Arizona vocational rehabilitation counselor reported (Marshall, Longie, Du Bois, & Flamand, 2003) in regard to his tribe:

> When we're talking about [our] tribally enrolled members, I think we have always been—I hate to use the word—isolated; we've always been our little community where a lot of our people never go out of the parameters of the community. So when they go to Phoenix Indian Hospital, they see other Native Americans. There's an adjustment even though it's Native Americans. They [the trainees] were so used to living in their community, with the exception of one who is very out-going, for the rest of them it was like a culture shock. Just the travel in itself—because a lot of them are afraid to leave the community. . . . I think about two of them, that it was very difficult for them to go to a new place away from their community. . . . I guess the best way I can answer that is when I was growing up, if I went on a job search I needed to take my friend with me, somebody. . . . What a lot of the people in the community do—say there's a landscaping job, "Hey, so and so, come with me. There is a job opening." They will never want to do it by themselves—they need that somebody to go apply with them. And sometimes it works against them because the other person might be hired and the guy that knew about the job would not be hired. But the idea is that for a lot of people, with these kind of things, they buddy up to somebody. It's another support system that they have. I did it. I went down there, went to school; I needed to go with somebody. I don't do it anymore, but a long time ago I used to. (p. 26)

WHICH COMES FIRST: LOW INCOME OR DISABILITY?

Former U.S. Senator Paul Simon recently noted that "today, there are more young African American males in prison than in college. If we provided greater assistance to those wanting to go to trade school or college, we could dramatically reduce our crime rate . . ." (Simon, 2003, p. B16). We understand that many of these young men may have learning disabilities or other developmental disabilities. Further, we understand that men from middle-class and upper-class backgrounds typically do not go to prison, even if they have committed crimes. Thus in terms of discrimination, one formula for incarceration in the United States would be: African American male plus a disability plus a low-income background.

Such incarceration is an example of the class distancing described by Lott (2002). Adelman (2003) and Wise (2003) each provide a brief overview of the history that has led to racial disparities in socioeconomic status (Moon & Rolison, 1998; St. Jean & Feagin, 1998). Past overt discrimination has provided financial foundations for European Americans; those foundations took forms that allowed intergenerational transfer of wealth not available to people of color, resulting in continued financial inequities. European Americans continue to utilize stereotypical thinking, albeit subconsciously, to evaluate people of color for training and employment (Dovidio, Gaertner, Kawakami, & Hodson, 2002; Lott & Saxon, 2002), thereby limiting current access to financial power.

Similar discrimination has occurred, with relative impunity, regarding ability status. Until the enactment of the Americans with Disabilities Act, it was difficult for people with disabilities to obtain gainful employment consistent with their abilities. In individual situations, people with disabilities, especially people of color, encounter barriers in their attempts to gain employment and relevant training. Group data, however, reveal continuing ethnic, gender, age, geographic (urban–rural), and ability disparities in employment and income (Dunham et al., 1998; Fujiura, 2000; McNeil, 2001; Szalda-Petree, Seekins, & Innes, 1999; Wray, 1996). This is particularly troubling as there are significant ethnic and gender disparities in the prevalence of disabilities (Bradsher, 1996; Jans & Stoddard, 1999; Johnson & Marshall, 2001; Stoddard, Jans, Ripple, & Kraus, 1998).

Significant differences have also been found in Canada in regard to disabling conditions, ethnicity, and socioeconomic status; for example, "chronic diseases such as arthritis, rheumatism, diabetes, heart problems, cancer, and hypertension are much more common, often twice as common, for Aboriginal persons, who also have generally much lower socioeconomic status (SES) than non-Aboriginals. For instance, Aboriginal men have a rate of diabetes three times the rate of non-Aboriginal men; for women, the ratio is 5 to 1" (Phipps, 2003, p. 11). Overall, researchers found the following:

> Disability or activity limitation is much more common among individuals with incomes in the bottom 30% of the income distribution (32% for men; 28% for women) compared to those at the top of the income distribution (12% for men; 16% for women). The direction of causality, however, is particularly unclear. That is, it is possible that low income leads to activity limitation, but it is also possible that activity limitation, by limiting paid work possibilities, leads to low income.

It might be expected that as people become increasingly aware of past discrimination that special efforts would be made to provide opportunities for those who have been historical victims of discrimination; such progress has been slow. For example, although psychologists are guided by ethical principles informed, in part, by the ADA and civil rights legislation, it is still difficult for psychology graduate students to receive accommodation needed for education in the field (Vande Kemp et al., 2003).

In advocating for increased federal grant (not loan) assistance for education, Simon (2003) referred to the historic success of the GI Bill and how the educational opportunities provided to returning veterans after Word War II produced professionals such as engineers, accountants, teachers, scientists, physicians, and others whose work "lifted the standard of living of the nation and raised the educational expectations of their children and future generations." He noted that "as the average educational level went up, income also rose" (p. B16). Issues of poverty and disability have historically been raised in terms of "which comes first?" Is it that low-income, low-wage occupations result in higher rates of disability; or is it that given a disability, the high cost of living results in poverty? From the field of public health we know that "there is considerable evidence that social position is an over-arching determinant of health status. . . . Social class affects lifestyle, environment, and the utilization of services; it remains an important predictor of good and poor health in our society" (Turnock, 1997, p. 39).

One solution at least in regard to increasing socioeconomic status is that public vocational rehabilitation programs should ensure the highest possible level of education and training in rehabilitation plans in order to optimize incomes and quality of life for persons with disabilities (Marshall, Sanderson, Johnson, & Kvedar, 2003). Clearly, we are not in agreement with Thomas and Weinrach (2002), who "encourage future VR counselors to help their clients make realistic appraisals of likely [educational and vocational] outcomes in view of their own social context" (pp. 88–89), thereby countenancing "lower expectations" as being both reasonable and desirable. These authors wrote, for example, that since "[b]lacks, as a group, are more likely to have incomes below the poverty level," it might be best to consider the "social context" and focus on "achieving realistic vocational re-habilitation goals" (pp. 82–83).

In terms of environmental barriers, money can make the difference of whether or not a barrier results in a handicapping condition for the person with a disability. Clearly, if defined only in terms of environ-mental barriers as some disability advocates suggest, a low-income individual may not be able to purchase those services or material goods that can make access possible and therefore might not be able to "buy out" his/her disability status. To the extent such a "buy out" of disability status is possible, identifying as having a disability or not may become a choice open only to those of economic means.

HEALTH, DISABILITY, AND SOCIAL CLASS

> You call it my ill health; I would call it a part of my strength. Not that I really want illnesses.
>
> —Lauraine Barlow (In press)

Understandably, disability advocates have worked to dissociate defi-nitions and concepts of disability from definitions and concepts of health. In a recent textbook serving to educate professionals in public health, the authors of *Dimensions of Community Health* (Miller & Price, 1998) provide a diagram of the consequences of the lack of adequate health care and/or appropriate intervention. At the bottom of the diagram, the student is confronted with two apparently equal calamities from the authors' perspective: death and disability. We know that disability does not equate with death; we know that disability can be a source of pride, of well-being, and of community. We know that for some individuals with a disability, life is not something to be avoided or prevented. Yet, we also know that from a human rights and social justice perspective, those individuals and cultural groups whose health has been compromised due to racist or classist denial of appropriate access to medical information and health care, may not choose to be affiliated with the disability community and may not "really want illnesses." The recent commentary of Aboriginal woman Lauraine Barlow, who has several chronic illnesses and depression, and who believes that she and her family were denied important medical information and intervention because of their race (and one might argue class as well), illustrates this point.

> **Interviewer**: Do you see yourself as having a disability?
> **Lauraine Barlow**: No, I don't. But there would be a lot of people who would argue against that because I can't work—that's a disability—they can't work so they don't contribute to society, that's a disability.
> **Lauraine's husband, Edward**: Society in general—others, automatically put you in that category. Like colour is a disability in society, straight up. . . . Being different also is making the person work extra harder. See, you can have a brilliant brain, but if you are a coloured person, they're going to keep putting you under the microscope. First little mistake and they'll be pointing the finger. It is like that anywhere.
> **Lauraine**: If you had asked me what's *normal*, I would say, having a lot of people around and everybody just accepting each other for what they are and learning from one another.
> **Interviewer**: We talked about whether or not you considered your health to be a disability.
> **Lauraine**: You call it my ill health, I would call it a part of my strength. Not that I really want illnesses. . . . Makes me more determined and he [Edward] can tell you about that. . . . My eldest son is always saying, mum, slow down, what am I going do with you old girl? And I say, but I'm not ready to slow down. My body may be deteriorating, but my mind is still very much alive. As long as I can talk—I may not be able to run fast, but I still can talk fast. (Barlow, In press)

Liu et al. (2004) reported an extensive review of the literature, motivated by their observation that "along with race and gender, social class is regarded as one of the three important cultural cornerstones in multicultural theory and research" (p. 3). These investigators reviewed 3,915 articles and found 710 that referred to social class, using an amazing "448 different words to describe social class" (p. 3). While it is important to note their conclusion that "the use of 448 key words to describe social class and social class-related constructs might be related to the confusion and infrequent use of social class in counseling research" (p. 16), it is equally important to note several outcomes of their review that were associated with measures of social class. For example, regarding physical health concerns that might lead to disability, they reported that "not only do lower social class individuals have less access to health resources, but lower class women are at a higher risk for depression, obesity, and diabetes than are higher social class women. Lower social class individuals also have a higher tendency for coronary heart disease and tend toward higher alcohol use when compared with higher social class individuals" (p. 7).

The review of Liu et al. (2004) also found social class differences based on race and gender. They reported that "[b]lacks were three times more likely to be living in poverty than [w]hites (24% vs. 8%, respectively), and for Hispanics, the poverty rate was 23%. . . . Additionally, women made about 72 cents for every dollar men made, down from 74 cents in 1996" (p. 3).

Further, these researchers found that, for women, because divorce so often affected their socio-economic status, "social class identity was fluid rather than static [and] regardless of their objective social class, as determined by income, education, and occupation, the women had to contend with their own internal sense of social class identity, which sometimes was congruent with the objective social class but sometimes was incongruent and in conflict" (p. 6).

Conley (1999) described the intergenerational effects of racial discrimination on differences in accumulated wealth, which are more reflective of social class than income. In 2001, the average wealth or net worth of African American families was about one-sixth that of European American families (Kennickell, 2003). "In 2001, the typical Black household had a net worth of just $19,000 (including home equity), compared with $121,000 for whites. Blacks had 16% of the median wealth of whites, up from 5% in 1989. At this rate it will take until 2099 to reach parity in median wealth" (Muhammad, Davis, Lui, & Leondar-Wright, 2004, p. 1).

In considering the relationships between health and poverty status, we know, for example, that "more than half (55%) of American Indians/Alaskan Natives have incomes below 200% of the federal poverty level" and this is correlated with "a higher burden of illness, injury and premature mortality than non-Hispanic [w]hites" (Katz, 2004, p. 13). What is less clear are intervening variables that may differentiate factors exclusively related to socioeconomic status and those also associated with social class. Again we note the extensive review by Liu et al. (2004), who concluded that "the definition and measurement of social class have been inconsistent and confusing" (p. 8), yet who also argued for the importance of considering this construct as "people regarded as not part of a particular social class group may be targets of prejudice and discrimination (i.e., classism) as a means for people in the social class group to maintain their position or group coherence and identity" (p. 8). They argue for a measure of social class that is subjective and that "allows people to determine their own social position rather than being placed into a category and position" (p. 7) rather than have class based, for instance, on the socioeconomic status of the moment; such a measure of social class then would allow researchers to use "social class in intentional and meaningful ways" (p. 16) to explore and understand the intersections of people's lives as they navigate health, education, work, and economic stability.

ACCESS TO EDUCATION, WORK, AND ECONOMIC STABILITY

As discussed earlier in this chapter, issues of social justice and people with disabilities are intertwined with issues of access to education, work, and the hope in most people's lives for economic stability. Blustein et al. (2002) explored the role of social class in the transition from school to work under the premise that "social class is a major factor in the work lives of people, reflecting a significant source of marginalization in our culture for those who are from poor and working-class backgrounds" (p. 311). They noted the need for further research into "the complex relationship between race and class" and called for a "serious study of the role of social class in the work lives of youth and adults across diverse cultural contexts" (p. 321). These researchers noted that "wealth is becoming increasingly concentrated in the upper strata of society, which is impacting the vocational trajectories of many poor and working class individuals" and, as only one example given here, cited the 1992 research of Timothy J. Owens, who "concluded that individuals from the upper social classes were more likely to attend college, whereas members of the lower social classes were more likely to transition directly to work or enter the military" (p. 311) after leaving high school. (This research finding brings to mind the experience of a Chicano graduate student in rehabilitation counseling who reported this during the U.S. conflict in Vietnam. He noted fellow high school students looking at college options, and he recalled his school counselor suggesting a school-to-work transition option between branches of the armed forces.) Blustein et al. (2002) concluded from their research that "the lack of access to financial resources, coupled with the difficulties posed by poor housing and inadequate health care, may leave individuals from LSES [lower socioeconomic status] backgrounds feeling more fragmented emotionally and, at times, overwhelmed by their life circumstances. . . . Our findings suggest that individuals from poor and working-class backgrounds may be attempting to resolve various vocational development tasks with a clear disadvantage" (pp. 320, 322).

Consider the possibility that an LSES individual approaching "vocational development tasks with a clear disadvantage" also has a cognitive disability, an emotional disability, or a physical disability. Consider the possibility that this individual with a cognitive disability is also a person of color or a woman whose vocational choice may well lead her to earn "about 72 cents for every dollar" a man would make. In considering concerns beyond the triple whammy, "the pervasive role of social class in creating a different starting gate for the development and implementation of a meaningful work life" is clear (Blustein et al., 2002, p. 320).

Yet, Lee and Dean (2004) have written of the "invisibility of immigrants and people of color from social class discourse" (p. 19) and that "generations of working-class people, who constitute the largest working population in the country, as well as those people living in poverty (approximately 10 percent of the U.S. population), remain relatively silent from the social class discourse (i.e., underemphasized and understudied)" (p. 20). In their critique of the work of Liu et al. (2004), Lee and Dean noted the "powerful effects of social class disparities on mental health" and concluded, "clearly, the stakes are high if researchers overlook the needs and concerns of people across the wide spectrum of social classes" (p. 23). Lee and Dean urged us to "[t]hink more thoroughly about the complexity of modern life in the United States for the growing majority of Americans—working-class immigrants and their families. . . . Many uneducated, unskilled immigrants with few resources remain encumbered by low paying, labor-intensive working-class jobs offering scant job security and limited opportunities for growth. . . . For many of these immigrant families of color, the American dream is simply unattainable—a myth" (pp. 21–22).

In the end, perhaps we know more about the intersections of low income, access to education, work, and *death* than we know about the same factors and disability. When low-income jobs result in disability, we are not always informed. For example, how many women indeed suffer from preventable carpal tunnel syndrome from long days at the keyboard or swiping item after item in groceries, drugstores, and superstores of all types over the United States? Yet, we can find almost daily accounts of the death of immigrants from Mexico, in attempts to walk across deserts to "low-wage manual jobs that most American workers won't do" (Diamond, 2004, 1D). Diamond also reported a finding by Washington-based research group The Urban Institute that "immigrants today hold 20 percent of the nation's low-wage jobs, even though they comprise 11 percent of the population" (p. 3D). To what extent do these low-wage jobs, most likely labor intensive, result in disability? Again, we can assume that these jobs, apart from the "disability equals death" formula so deplorable from a public health perspective, might well result in disability, if not death. The history of arduous labor leading to disability and lack of provision for health service or work relief for members of lower socioeconomic classes has been demonstrated in archeological studies of American slaves of African descent. Examination of the bodies of Africans buried in New York revealed that adolescents and many adults (male and female) showed exaggerated development of lifting muscles (deltoid and pectoral crests of the humeri) and early degeneration of the vertebral column and shoulder. Evidence of trauma to the skull as well as "parry" fractures of the lower arm suggest an unusually high incidence of accidents and violence (Blakey, 2001, p. 405).

Today, poor immigrants endure terrible work conditions and are vulnerable to poor nutrition and infection without adequate health care, similar to the situation of African slaves in the United States. Based on an Associated Press investigation, Pritchard (2004) reported that "the jobs that lure Mexican workers to the United States are killing them in a worsening epidemic that is now claiming a victim a day. . . . These accidental deaths are almost always preventable and often gruesome: Workers are impaled, shredded in machinery, buried alive" (p. A5).

Prichard gave examples of jobs where Mexicans have been killed and wrote that

> what's happening to Mexicans is exceptional in scope and scale. Mexicans are nearly twice as likely as the rest of the immigrant population to die at work.
>
> Mexicans died cutting North Carolina tobacco and Nebraska beef, felling trees in Colorado and welding a balcony in Florida, trimming grass at a Las Vegas golf course and falling from scaffolding in Georgia. . . . Two brothers . . . died building a suburban high school that at 15 and 16, they might have attended. They were buried in a trench when the walls of sandy soil collapsed. (p. A5)

A representative from the Centers for Disease Control was quoted as saying, "They're considered disposable" (Pritchard, 2004, A5).

SUMMARY

This chapter has only begun to look at issues beyond the "triple whammy"—issues of discrimination and prejudice when disability, gender, and culture are considered within the context of a fourth dimension, social class. The implications of disability status and the disability experience, given a low-income environment, need to be further explored and understood. We need to understand how individuals from low-income environments both identify as having a disability and make choices regarding education and career goals—most importantly, the extent to which these choices might be restricted by class, by gender, or by mainstream expectations associated with People of Color. Definitions of disability are understood to be culturally specific, and as we move to a definition of disability that might also be environmentally specific, we need to ensure that such definitions do not also become class-specific.

Much of the research that has been useful for understanding the complexity of class as a critical variable in the understanding of the lives of people with disabilities has been conducted outside of the United States. Albers et al. (1999) examined economic consequences of disability. Sociodemographic predictors of treatment success and failure for people with disabilities was addressed by Becker, Hojsted, Sjogren, and Eriksen (1998); Bhandari, Louw, and Reddy (1999); Frumkin, Walker, and Friedman-Jimenez (1999); Mayer et al. (1998); and Stronks, van de Mheen, van den Bos, and Mackenbach (1995). Those are excellent models for the study of class status as both a contributor and consequence of disability.

NOTE

The authors contributed equally to this chapter.

REFERENCES

Adelman, L. (2003). *A long history of racial preferences—for whites.* Retrieved August 25, 2003, from http://www.pbs.org/race/000_About/002_04-background-03–02.htm

Albers, J. M., Kuper, H. H., van Riel, P. L., Prevoo, M. L., van't Hof, M. A., van Gestel, A. M., et al. (1999). Socio-economic consequences of rheumatoid arthritis in the first years of the disease. *Rheumatology (Oxford), 38,* 423–430.

Arizona Job Service. (n.d.). *Tips to assist you in your job search* (Handout). Phoenix: Arizona Department of Economic Security.

Banks, M. E. (2003a). Disability in the family: A life span perspective. *Cultural Diversity and Ethnic Minority Psychology, 9*, 367–384.

Banks, M. E. (2003b). Preface. In M. E. Banks & E. Kaschak (Eds.), *Women with visible and invisible disabilities: Multiple intersections, multiple issues, multiple therapies* (pp. xxiii–xli). New York: Haworth Press.

Banks, M. E., & Ackerman, R. J. (2003). All things being unequal: Culturally relevant roads to employment. In F. E. Menz & D. F. Thomas (Eds.), *Bridging gaps: Refining the disability research agenda for rehabilitation and the social sciences—Conference proceedings* (pp. 35–63). Menomonie, WI: University of Wisconsin-Stout, Stout Vocational Rehabilitation Institute, Research and Training Centers.

Barlow, L. (In press). Lauraine's story: "If I'd only known" and resilience factors in Aboriginal culture. In C. A. Marshall & E. Kendall (Eds.), *When women paint a story: Participatory action research, indigenous ways of knowing, and stories of culture and community.* Manuscript submitted for publication.

Becker, N., Hojsted, J., Sjogren, P., & Eriksen, J. (1998). Sociodemographic predictors of treatment outcome in chronic non-malignant pain patients: Do patients receiving or applying for disability pension benefit from multidisciplinary pain treatment? *Pain, 77*, 279–287.

Bhandari, M., Louw, D., & Reddy, K. (1999). Predictors of return to work after anterior cervical discectomy. *Journal of Spinal Disorders, 12*, 94–98.

Blakey, M. L. (2001). Bioarchaeology of the African Diaspora in the Americas: Its origins and scope. *Annual Review of Anthropology, 30*, 387–422.

Blustein D. L., Chaves, A. P., Diemer, M. A., Gallagher, L. A., Marshall, K. G., Sirim, S., & Bahti, K. S. (2002). Voices of the forgotten half: The role of social class in the school-to-work transition. *Journal of Counseling Psychology, 49*(3), 311–323.

Bradsher, J. E. (1996, January). *Disability among racial and ethnic groups.* (Disability Statistics Abstract, No. 10). Washington, DC: U.S. Department of Education, National Institute on Disability and Rehabilitation Research.

Conley, D. (1999). *Being black, living in the red: Race, wealth, and social policy in America.* Berkeley, CA: University of California Press.

Corbett, C. A. (2003). Special issues in psychotherapy for minority deaf women. In M. E. Banks & E. Kaschak (Eds.), *Women with visible and invisible disabilities: Multiple intersections, multiple issues, multiple therapies* (pp. 311–329). New York: Haworth Press.

Crawford, D., & Ostrove, J. M. (2003). Representations of disability and the interpersonal relationships of women with disabilities. In M. E.

Banks & E. Kaschak (Eds.), *Women with visible and invisible disabilities: Multiple intersections, multiple issues, multiple therapies* (pp. 179–194). New York: Haworth Press.

Diamond, M. L. (2004, March 16). Low-wage jobs going unfilled. *Tucson Citizen*, 1D.

Dovidio, J. F., Gaertner, S. E., Kawakami, K., & Hodson, G. (2002). Why can't we just get along? Interpersonal biases and interracial distrust. *Cultural Diversity and Ethnic Minority Psychology, 8*, 88–102.

Dunham, M. D., Holliday, G. A., Douget, R. M., Koller, J. R., Presberry, R., & Wooderson, S. (1998). Vocational rehabilitation outcomes of African American adults with specific learning disabilities. *Journal of Rehabilitation, 64*(3), 36–41.

Feist-Price, S., & Wright, L. B. (2003). African American women living with HIV/AIDS: Mental health issues. In M. E. Banks & E. Kaschak (Eds.), *Women with visible and invisible disabilities: Multiple intersections, multiple issues, multiple therapies* (pp. 27–44). New York: Haworth Press.

Feldman, S. I., & Tegart, G. (2003). Keep moving: Conceptions of illness and disability of middle-aged African-American women with arthritis. In M. E. Banks & E. Kaschak (Eds.), *Women with visible and invisible disabilities: Multiple intersections, multiple issues, multiple therapies* (pp. 127–143). New York: Haworth Press.

Frumkin, H., Walker, E. D., & Friedman-Jimenez, G. (1999). Minority workers and communities. *Occupational Medicine, 14*, 495–517.

Fujiura, G. T. (2000). The implications of emerging demographics: A commentary on the meaning of race and income inequity to disability policy. *Journal of Disability Policy Studies, 11*, 66–75.

Jans, L., & Stoddard, S. (1999). *Chartbook on women and disability in the United States. An InfoUse report*. Washington, DC: U.S. Department of Education, National Institute on Disability and Rehabilitation Research. Retrieved August 25, 2004, from http://www.infouse.com/disabilitydata/

Johnson, S. R., & Marshall, C. A. (2001). Best practices for serving American Indians in vocational rehabilitation. In C. A. Marshall (Ed.), *Rehabilitation and American Indians with disabilities: A handbook for administrators, practitioners, and researchers* (pp. 99–112). Athens, GA: Elliott & Fitzpatrick.

Katz, R. J. (2004). Addressing the health care needs of American Indians and Alaska Natives. *American Journal of Public Health, 94*(1), 13–14.

Kennickell, A. B. (2003, September). *A rolling tide: Changes in the distribution of wealth in the U.S., 1989–2001*. Washington, DC: Federal Reserve Board.

Lee, R. M., & Dean, B. L. (2004). Middle-class mythology in an age of immigration and segmented assimilation: Implications for counseling psychology. *Journal of Counseling Psychology, 51*(1), 19–24.

Lesh, K., & Marshall, C. (1984). Rehabilitation: Focus on disabled women as a special population. *Journal of Applied Rehabilitation Counseling, 15*(1), 18–21.

Liu, W. M., Ali, S. R., Soleck, G., Hopps, J., Dunston, K., & Pickett, T., Jr. (2004). Using social class in counseling psychology research. *Journal of Counseling Psychology, 51*(1), 3–18.

Lott, B. (2002). Cognitive and behavioral distancing from the poor. *American Psychologist, 57*, 100–110.

Lott, B., & Saxon, S. (2002). The influence of ethnicity, social class and context on judgments about U.S. women. *Journal of Social Psychology, 142*, 481–499.

Marshall, C. A., Longie, B. J., Du Bois, B., & Flamand, H. (2003). Follow-up analysis of a model job training demonstration project: A 10-year return to the Phoenix Indian Medical Center. Unpublished manuscript, Northern Arizona University, Flagstaff.

Marshall, C. A., Sanderson, P. L., Johnson, S. R., & Kvedar, J. C. (2003). Considering class, culture, and access in rehabilitation intervention and research. In F. E. Menz & D. F. Thomas (Eds.), *Bridging gaps: Refining the disability research agenda for rehabilitation and the social sciences—Conference proceedings* [May 29–31, 2002, Washington, DC] (pp. 199–210). Menomonie: University of Wisconsin–Stout, Stout Vocational Rehabilitation Institute, Research and Training Centers.

Mayer, T., McMahon, M. J., Gatchel, R. J., Sparks, B., Wright, A., & Pegues, P. (1998, discussion 606). Socioeconomic outcomes of combined spine surgery and functional restoration in workers' compensation spinal disorders with matched controls. *Spine, 23*, 598–605.

McNeil, J. (2001, February). Americans with disabilities: Household economic studies, 1997. *Current Population Reports.* Washington, DC: U.S. Department of Commerce, Economics and Statistics Administration, U.S. Census Bureau.

Miller, D. F., & Price, J. H. (1998). *Dimensions of community health* (5th ed.). New York: McGraw-Hill.

Moon, D. G., & Rolison, G. L. (1998). Communication of classism. In M. L. Hecht (Ed.), *Communicating prejudice* (pp. 122–135). Thousand Oaks, CA: SAGE Publications, Inc.

Muhammad, D., Davis, A., Lui, M., & Leondar-Wright, B. (2004, January 15). *The state of the dream 2004: Enduring disparities in black and white.* Boston: United for a Fair Economy.

Mukherjee, D., Reis, J. P., & Heller, W. (2003). Women living with traumatic brain injury: Social isolation, emotional functioning and implications for psychotherapy. In M. E. Banks & E. Kaschak (Eds.), *Women with visible and invisible disabilities: Multiple intersections, multiple issues, multiple therapies* (pp. 1–26). New York: Haworth Press.

Nabors, N. A., & Pettee, M. F. (2003). Womanist therapy with African American women with disabilities. In M. E. Banks & E. Kaschak (Eds.),

Women with visible and invisible disabilities: Multiple intersections, multiple issues, multiple therapies (pp. 331–341). New York: Haworth Press.

Neal-Barnett, A. M., & Mendelson, L. L. (2003). Obsessive compulsive disorder in the workplace: An invisible disability. In M. E. Banks & E. Kaschak (Eds.), *Women with visible and invisible disabilities: Multiple intersections, multiple issues, multiple therapies* (pp. 169–178). New York: Haworth Press.

Phipps, S. (2003). The impact of poverty on health: A scan of research literature. In *Poverty and Health, CPHI Collected Papers.* Canadian Institute for Health Information. Available at www.cihi.ca.

Pritchard, J. (2004, March 14). Mexicans more likely to die on U.S. jobs. *Arizona Daily Star*, p. A5.

Simon, P. (2003). A GI Bill for today. *The Chronicle Review*, Section 2 of *The Chronicle of Higher Education, 1*(10), p. B16.

St. Jean, Y., & Feagin, J. R. (1998). The family costs of white racism: The case of African American families. *Journal of Comparative Family Studies, 29*, 297–312.

Stoddard, S., Jans, L., Ripple, J., & Kraus, L. (1998). *Chartbook on work and disability in the United States, 1998. An InfoUse report.* Washington, DC: U.S. National Institute on Disability and Rehabilitation Research.

Stronks, K., van de Mheen, H., van den Bos, J., & Mackenbach, J. P. (1995). Smaller socioeconomic inequalities in health among women: The role of employment status. *International Journal of Epidemiology, 24*, 559–568.

Szalda-Petree, A., Seekins, T., & Innes, B. (June, 1999). *Women with disabilities: Employment, income, and health.* Retrieved May 15, 2002, from http://ruralinstitute.umt.edu/rtcrural/RuDis/DisWomenFact.html

Thomas, K. R., & Weinrach, S. G. (2002). Racial bias in rehabilitation: Multiple interpretations of the same data. *Rehabilitation Education, 16*(1), 81–90.

Turnock, B. J. (1997). *Public health: What it is and how it works.* Gaithersburg, MD: Aspen Publishers.

Vande Kemp, H., Chen, J. S., Erickson, G. N., & Friesen, N. L. (2003). ADA accommodation of therapists with disabilities in clinical training. In M. E. Banks & E. Kaschak (Eds.), *Women with visible and invisible disabilities: Multiple intersections, multiple issues, multiple therapies* (pp. 155–168). New York: Haworth Press.

Vernon, A. (1999). The dialectics of multiple identities and the disabled people's movement. *Disability & Society, 14*, 385–398.

Williams, M., & Upadhyay, W. S. (2003). To be or not be disabled. *Women & Therapy, 26*(1/2), 145–154. [Simultaneously published in M. E.

Banks & E. Kaschak (Eds.), *Women with visible and invisible disabilities: Multiple intersections, multiple issues, multiple therapies* (pp. 145–154). New York: Haworth Press.]

Wilson, R. (2003). How babies alter careers for academics: Having children often bumps women off the tenure track, a new study shows. *The Chronicle of Higher Education, 50*(15), pp. A1, A6–A8.

Wise, T. (2003). *Whites swim in racial preference.* Retrieved August 25, 2003, from http://www.alternet.org/story.html?StoryID=15223

Wray, L. A. (1996). The role of ethnicity in the disability and work experience of pre-retirement-age Americans. *The Gerontologist, 36,* 287–298.

Yee, B. W. K., Nguyen, H. T., & Ha, M. (2003). Chronic disease health beliefs and lifestyle practices among Vietnamese adults: Influences of gender and age. In M. E. Banks & E. Kaschak (Eds.), *Women with visible and invisible disabilities: Multiple intersections, multiple issues, multiple therapies* (pp. 111–125). New York: Haworth Press.

CHAPTER 5

Coping with Prejudice and Discrimination Based on Weight

Anna M. Myers
Esther D. Rothblum

Imagine the following scenarios:

- Some friends of yours are going out for the evening. They ask you not to come, explaining that you are likely to "scare away potential dates."
- You go to the doctor's office with your spouse, only to discover that there is no seat that will accommodate her size. Your doctor admonishes her to lose weight, even though she is not his patient. Then the nurse draws you aside and asks in a kind voice, "Is it really fair to bring your wife out in public—where people can see her?"
- In a job interview, your would-be boss remarks, "My men need a pretty face and figure to look at, not a pig like you."
- A stranger comes up to you and says, "You're really gross! I can't believe how fat you are. I'd kill myself if I looked like you."

The above are actual experiences reported by people who are significantly above average weight—that is, people who are visibly "fat." At the office, on the street, and in the home, fat people are the targets of stares, rude remarks, discrimination, and ridicule. For fat people, weight-related stigmatization and discrimination are sad facts of life.

Consider the following newspaper account of a twelve-year-old Black boy who committed suicide in Florida: "Jacqueline Graham still can't bring herself to show her son's room to strangers, but you don't need to look past the photos in the living room to see who he was: He was the fat kid who didn't have any friends. The easy target. The mark. . . . In the social hierarchy of fifth grade . . . that put him squarely at the bottom" ("Life and Death," 1997).

Unlike other forms of prejudice such as racism, sexism, or ageism, prejudice against fat people is freely expressed in western nations. In a society that glorifies youth, beauty, and a narrowly defined "healthy" appearance, people stereotype and harass those whose bodies do not conform to this ideal. Body weight is seen as being controllable—and fatness, therefore, is seen as a voluntary condition. Perhaps for this reason, people feel free to express their prejudicial attitudes without fear of social censure. Negative stereotypes of fat people include the views that they are ugly, morally and emotionally impaired, asexual, discontented, weak-willed, and unlikable. Ironically, fat people are just as likely as average-weight people to hold these prejudiced attitudes (Crandall, 1994).

Individuals who share the stigma of obesity quickly find that weight-related stigmatization affects nearly every aspect of their lives. Fat people report job discrimination, social exclusion, exploitation by the diet and fitness industries, denial of health benefits, trouble finding clothing, mistreatment by doctors, and public ridicule (Allon, 1982; Hutchinson, 1994; Millman, 1980; Rand & MacGregor, 1990; Rothblum, Brand, Miller, & Oetjen, 1990). Fat people are less likely to be admitted to elite colleges (Canning & Mayer, 1966) or to have their education funded (Crandall, 1991). Fat people are also more likely to be of lower socioeconomic status (Sobal & Stunkard, 1989) and to lose socioeconomic status over time (Gortmaker, Must, Perrin, Sobol, & Dietz, 1993).

THE LANGUAGE OF WEIGHT

Terms used to describe body weight can be quite confusing. The term *overweight* is most often defined in relation to tables of desirable weight, such as those published by life insurance companies. People whose weight is above the weight range deemed "ideal" according to life insurance height and weight charts are called "overweight." The term *obesity*, on the other hand, refers to an increase in percent body fat relative to lean tissue (Bray, 1992). A common way of measuring obesity that takes into account the effects of height on weight is the body mass index, or BMI. BMI is body weight in kilograms divided by height in meters squared. Unfortunately, the United States is one of the few remaining countries that have not moved to a metric system, so this formula is difficult for the general U.S. public to use.

Because fatness is so stigmatized, words commonly used to describe it sound pejorative. *Obese, fat, hefty, overweight, massive,* and *morbidly obese* sound equally unflattering. Fat acceptance organizations, such as the National Association to Advance Fat Acceptance, or NAAFA, have therefore advocated a strategy for destigmatizing fatness. Such organizations propose to reclaim the term *fat,* making it merely descriptive rather than pejorative. This strategy is similar to the strategy of reclaiming words such as *dyke* or *queer* by gay and lesbian activists. It is thought that with increased use of these terms in positive or neutral contexts, they lose their pejorative power. Throughout this chapter, then, we will use the word *fat* to describe people with high body weights, unless we are citing a direct quote.

FACTS AND MYTHS ABOUT BODY WEIGHT

Two assumptions about body weight seem to underlie prejudice and discrimination against fat people. The first is that if fat people would just eat less and exercise more, they would lose weight and thus no longer be part of a stigmatized group. The second belief is that large body size causes health problems.

In 1958, Stunkard wrote, "Most obese persons will not stay in treatment of obesity. Of those who stay in treatment most will not lose weight, and of those who do lose weight, most will regain it" (p. 79). This statement is still true nearly half a century later. Between the 1960s and the 1980s, the rate of dieting doubled among women. In 1987, a study by Rosen and Gross (1987) found that 63 percent of high school girls were on diets, compared with 16.2 percent of boys. While dieting was becoming more prevalent, however, the average U.S. citizen's body weight was also increasing. This finding leads some researchers to believe that there is something about dieting that actually increases weight gain. In fact, dieting does seem to precede fatness, rather than the other way around. People who diet do lose some weight; however, rigorous follow-up studies find that nearly everyone regains the lost weight over the course of several months (Cogan & Rothblum, 1993). Fewer than 3 percent of people maintain weight loss over the long run, and after four to five years, many dieters weigh more than they did before they started dieting (Szwarc, 2003a).

There is a popular belief that Americans are more sedentary than ever before due to labor-saving devices, increased numbers of automobiles, and general lack of exercise. According to Szwarc (2003b), this is not true.

> Realistically, lifestyles for middle-class American adults haven't changed in line with bulging weights. Back in the 1960s, most Dads (or Grandpas, for younger readers) still drove to an office job each day and mowed the lawn on the weekend; Moms took care of the house with much the same appliances and modern conveniences we enjoy today. . . . Who remembers their parents donning sneakers (hardly ever called *athletic* shoes back then) and heading to the gym every day or putting in an hour on the treadmill? Among lower socioeconomic classes where obesity rates are the highest, manual labor remains the primary employment. (p. 2)

Data collected by the Centers for Disease Control (CDC) show that exercise activity from the mid-1960s through the 1990s did not change, while other studies have shown increasing levels of physical exercise from the 1960s to the 1980s (Szwarc, 2003b).

Regarding fatness and health risks, there are three major confounds in the studies that examine the relationship between weight and health (Rothblum, 1990, 1999). First, studies that examine whole communities for weight and health problems do not control for income. However, income is strongly related to weight in the United States. Statistics indicate that fat people are much poorer than thin people. In addition, income in the United States is strongly associated with access to good healthcare. Thus, comparing fat to thin people without controlling for income is equivalent to comparing poor to rich people. Second, health-risk studies do not control for frequency of dieting, and, as mentioned above, fat people have dieted more than thin people. Diets, even ones considered "healthy," are associated with many of the same risk factors that we associate with weight, such as cravings for fat, high blood pressure, increased heart rate, heart attacks, kidney disease, diabetes, and lower mortality. Finally, researchers do not (and could not easily) control for negative physiological effects of stress among fat people, who live as members of an oppressed minority group. In fact, stress has also been shown to cause many of the health problems associated with weight.

Even if one accepts the majority opinion that obesity is unhealthy, however, the health risk posed by high body weight is no justification for fat stigmatization, which is the main focus of this chapter. Eating "junk food" and consuming alcohol are also practices generally considered to be unhealthy, yet people drinking beer or eating hot dogs are not routinely subjected to harassment, public ridicule, and peer pressure to change these habits. Fat stigmatization therefore appears to be a problem independent of the purported health risks of body weight.

RESEARCH ON FAT STIGMA

The negative stigma of being fat has been extensively documented. Much of this research has emphasized how people perceive those who are fat, rather than on how fat people perceive and cope with discrimination. Existing studies have focused on attitudes toward fat people, the effects of obesity on other life experiences (such as going to college or getting a job), and social difficulties faced by fat people. Experimental as well as survey research supports the existence of extensive discrimination and prejudice against fat people.

For example, a study of stereotyping (Larkin & Pines, 1979) asked twenty male and twenty female undergraduates to use thirty-eight descriptive scales to "form a first impression" of three fictitious people, one "overweight," one of "average weight," and one "underweight." Participants rated these people on scales measuring traits such as "decisive versus indecisive," "neat versus untidy," "relaxed versus nervous," and so forth. On twenty-two of the thirty-eight variables, the fat person was rated negatively. Specifically, the fat person was seen as incompetent, unproductive, less industrious, disorganized, indecisive, inactive, less successful, more mentally lazy, and more lacking in self-discipline.

Negative stereotypes about fat people may lead others to dislike or ostracize those who are visibly fat. This effect has been demonstrated in several studies of children, adults, and health professionals. For instance, in a classic study of children's attitudes toward fat people (Richardson, Goodman, Hastorf, & Dornbusch, 1961), researchers asked six groups of children to rank-order six drawings according to how much they liked the child depicted in each. The drawings included a child with no handicap, a child with crutches and a brace, a child in a wheelchair, a child missing a left hand, a child with a facial distinction, and a fat child. Participants included 277 underprivileged, disabled, and non-disabled children attending a summer camp, 104 non-disabled children at a different camp, 42 low-income city schoolchildren, 113 rural schoolchildren, and 104 schoolchildren of middle to high socioeconomic status. All six groups of children rated the drawings in precisely the same order, with the fat child least preferred.

These same negative attitudes against fat people have been demonstrated by physicians, medical students (Blumberg & Mellis, 1985; Maddox & Liederman, 1969), nutritionists (Maiman, Wang, Becker, Finlay, & Simonson, 1979), and mental health professionals (Agell & Rothblum, 1991; Young & Powell, 1985)—in other words, by the very people whom fat individuals might go to for help and support. Crandall (1994) has suggested that weight bias derives in part from the belief that fat people are responsible for their weight, and that this belief leads to fewer sanctions against fat prejudice. Crandall argues that prejudicial attitudes toward obesity today are "overt, expressible, and widely-held," similar to racist attitudes fifty years ago. He suggests that anti-fat attitudes derive from a "Puritanical morality" that values self-discipline, self-control, and self-reliance—qualities that fat people are assumed to lack. He further notes that fat people are just as likely as average-weight people to hold negative attitudes about fatness.

Providing evidence in support of the above idea, Crandall and Biernat (1990) surveyed 478 male and 594 female undergraduates on anti-fat attitudes, political conservatism, symbolic racism, sexual attitudes, religiosity, self-esteem, and miscellaneous social attitudes. They found that bias toward obesity was associated with racism, conservative attitudes toward other social issues, and authoritarianism. Being fat, in and of itself, was not associated with anti-fat attitudes, suggesting that beliefs about fatness are more related to one's ideology than to one's personal weight. Predictably, fat respondents who did hold anti-fat attitudes tended to have lower self-esteem than fat respondents who did not. The authors conclude that anti-fat bias is in general associated with a conservative, authoritarian outlook on the world—an outlook that posits that "people deserve what they get." In other words, people will discriminate against fat people because of a naive perception that they choose to be fat.

Attitudes toward Fat People in Other Countries

While negative bias against fat people certainly exists in western nations, there is some evidence that such bias is "culture bound." For example, Cogan, Bhalla, Sefa-Dedeh, and Rothblum (1996) compared 219 U.S. college students to 349 college students in Ghana on measures of weight, dieting and restrained eating, disordered eating, and attitudes toward fatness. Between-group comparisons revealed that African students preferred a heavier body size, with Ghanaian males preferring the largest body size and U.S. females the smallest. Additionally, U.S. women were most likely to report that their weight interfered with social activities. The U.S. sample also rated thin people more positively than Ghanaians did, attributing to them qualities such as happiness, self-confidence, self-discipline, and attractiveness.

A study by Crandall and Martinez (1996) looked at anti-fat attitudes in 236 Mexican and 170 U.S. university students, who were also surveyed about their beliefs in a "just world" and political beliefs. Mexican students were found to be less concerned about their weight and more accepting of fat people than U.S. students. In the U.S. sample, anti-fat attitudes were associated with "just world" beliefs, political conservatism, and a tendency to blame the poor for their poverty. In contrast, among the Mexican students, there was no relation of anti-fat attitudes and social ideology.

The results of these cross-cultural studies provide support for Crandall's (1994) assertion that antipathy toward fat people is related to U.S. cultural values. Crandall and Martinez (1996) point to three reasons why fatness is particularly stigmatized in the United States. First, they argue that U.S. beliefs reflect negative stereotyping of fat people. Second, because fatness is naively associated with personal control and self-discipline, they posit that fatness will be less stigmatized in cultures that do not value these attributes highly. Finally, they say, the U.S. emphasis on self-control and self-determination serves a "central organizing function" around which citizens form opinions about issues. Thus, body weight and other traits that are believed to result from a lack of self-control will be negatively valued in the United States and not as much in cultures that do not value self-control as highly.

Fat People's Own Experiences of Stigmatizing Situations and Attempts to Cope with Fat Stigma

Little research has asked fat people directly about how they deal with fat stigma on an everyday basis. Furthermore, because body weight in the United States is inversely related to income, research that focuses on middle-class populations, such as college students or employees, is unlikely to come across many people who are extremely fat. Myers and Rosen (1999) sampled severely fat people who were trying to lose weight via clinical means (weight loss surgery or medication). They found that the heavier these people were, the more they reported stigmatizing experiences and the more they employed a variety of coping devices. A greater number of reported stigmatizing experiences were associated with more mental health symptoms, more negative body image, and more negative self-esteem. The authors also identified eleven types of stigmatizing situations and twenty-one ways of coping with stigma reported by fat people. Three of these coping strategies—negative self-talk, isolation, and avoidance—were related to poorer psychological adjustment. None were associated with better adjustment (Myers & Rosen, 1999).

In this chapter, we want to present evidence for the relation between stigmatization, coping attempts, and psychological distress in two groups of fat people—one a group of "fat acceptance" advocates, and another a group of subscribers to a weight loss magazine. Thus, we will be describing the perceptions of two non-clinical samples— NAAFA members and readers of a national publication targeting dieters. These groups are both examples of "voluntary associations" created to assist people in coping with fat stigma. Yet, their approaches differ. NAAFA members purportedly favor "fat acceptance," whereas the magazine subscribers are more likely interested in losing weight. We wanted to investigate how members of these two groups combated the effects of fat stigma, and whether their coping efforts were associated in any way with their levels of psychological distress.

As in the study with clinical samples (Myers & Rosen, 1999), we expected that for both magazine subscribers and NAAFA members, reports of stigmatization and coping attempts would increase in direct proportion to body size. Likewise, we expected that stigmatizing experiences would be related to more mental health symptoms, more negative body image, and lower self-esteem. In comparing the two groups, we expected that NAAFA members would report using more "fat acceptance" coping strategies, while magazine subscribers would more frequently report using "weight loss" strategies. Our final hypothesis was that "fat acceptance" strategies would be associated with less distress than weight loss strategies.

This final finding was expected for two reasons. First, dieting comprises only one response to stigmatization, and it is one that is slow to take effect and usually futile in the long run. Even for fat people who lose some weight, they will not move from clinical to non-clinical levels of "obesity," and so they will have to continue to cope with the stigma of their weight. In contrast, "fat acceptance" involves several discrete cognitive and behavioral responses. Thus, we believed that a wider range of approaches to the problem of fat stigmatization was likely to be associated with better psychological functioning. Second, weight loss is seldom maintained over time (Bennet & Gurin, 1982). Thus, any beneficial effects of weight loss upon body image, self-esteem, and general mental health are likely to be temporary. Dieters who use weight loss as their only strategy for coping with fat stigma likely feel disappointed and frustrated when they cannot maintain their weight loss. In contrast, "fat acceptance" is not dependent upon a person's weight. Self-acceptance coping strategies can be used at any time, in a variety of situations, and therefore might be associated with better psychological functioning.

Participants in Our Study

Respondents were solicited by a direct mailing to 450 readers of a national weight-loss magazine and to 300 members of the National Association to Advance Fat Acceptance. A total of 167 questionnaires were returned, for a response rate of 22 percent. Significantly more NAAFA members ($N = 112$, 37 percent) than magazine subscribers ($N = 55$, 12 percent) returned questionnaires ($X^2 = 65.6$, $p < .001$). Respondents were included if they met objective BMI criteria for "overweight" (BMI ≥ 27 kg/m^2) within the previous twelve months. Thirteen surveys—ten from magazine subscribers and three from NAAFA members—were thus excluded. The resulting sample included 154 respondents: 109 NAAFA members and 45 subscribers.

The overall sample was overwhelmingly female (80 percent female, 20 percent male; NAAFA: 79 percent female; subscribers: 82 percent female; difference not significant) and white (90 percent white; 3 percent black; 2 percent Latino/a; 5 percent other; NAAFA: 88 percent white; subscribers: 93 percent white, n.s.), with a mean age of 43.3 years ($SD = 11.3$, NAAFA mean $= 42.0$, subscriber mean $= 40.0$, n.s.). NAAFA respondents were more likely to be single (35 percent versus 16 percent; $X^2 = 15.02$, $p < .05$), better educated (60 percent college graduates versus 31 percent; $X^2 = 19.77$, $p < .01$), and of higher socioeconomic status (mean $= 46.2$, $SD = 13.6$; versus mean $= 31.59$, $SD = 13.7$; $F[1,142] = 5.18$, $p < .05$). Weights in the NAAFA group ranged from 160–600 pounds (median $= 285$ lbs., median BMI $= 46.0$, mean $= 46.2$, $SD = 10.4$), as compared to 134–339 pounds in the subscriber group (median $= 198$ lbs.;

median BMI = 32.0, mean = 33.3, *SD* = 6.8). NAAFA members were significantly heavier than magazine subscribers, (F [1,142] = 52.08, $p < .001$), but average weights for both groups were high and thus ideal for our study.

TYPES OF VARIABLES MEASURED

Demographic Information

Participants were asked to report gender, age, race/ethnicity, marital status, education, current occupation, partner's education and current occupation, current weight and height, highest and lowest weight in the past year, and whether they were currently trying to lose weight.

Stigmatizing Situations and Coping Responses

These questionnaires were developed by Myers and Rosen (1999) and consist of fifty stigmatizing situations divided into eleven categories, and ninety-nine coping responses divided into twenty-one categories. Instructions to the respondent for stigmatizing situations read, "Below is a list of situations that some people encounter because of their weight. Indicate whether, and how often, each of these situations happens to you." For coping responses, the instructions read, "The following are some strategies people use in order to deal with negative situations related to their weight. For example, someone who hears an insult about her appearance may make herself feel better by insulting the person back. Using the scale below, please indicate whether, and how often, you have used each of the following strategies to cope with the sorts of situations listed [in the previous inventory]." A ten-point ordinal scale with descriptive anchor points is used (0 = "never," 1 = "once in your life," 2 = "several times in your life," 3 = "about once/year," 4 = "several times/year," 5 = "about once a month," 6 = "several times/month," 7 = "about once/week," 8 = "several times/week," 9 = "daily"). Stigma and coping categories are listed in Tables 5.1 and 5.2.

Mental Health

The Brief Symptom Inventory (BSI) is a fifty-three-item self-report measure of mental health symptoms (Derogatis & Spencer, 1982).

Table 5.1
Stigmatizing Situation Categories

Category	Item	Mean (*SD*)
1. Comments from children	2.63	(1.9)
2. Others making assumptions about you	2.50	(1.9)
3. Loved ones embarrassed by your size	2.06	(2.0)
4. Physical barriers	1.95	(1.6)
5. Being stared at	1.76	(1.5)
6. Nasty comments from others	1.66	(1.1)
7. Inappropriate comments from doctors	1.58	(1.0)
8. Nasty comments from family	1.57	(1.1)
9. Being avoided, excluded, ignored	1.55	(1.5)
10. Job discrimination	0.85	(1.1)
11. Being physically attacked	0.35	(0.9)

Table 5.2
Coping Responses Categories

Category	Item	Mean (*SD*)
1. Self-love, self-acceptance	5.07	(2.2)
2. "Heading off" negative remarks	5.05	(2.5)
3. Positive self-talk	4.93	(2.0)
4. Refuse to diet	4.69	(2.1)
5. See the situation as the other person's problem	4.68	(2.4)
6. Using faith, religion, prayer	4.23	(2.6)
7. Refuse to hide; be visible	4.19	(1.7)
8. Social support from not-fat people	3.76	(2.0)
9. Humor, witty comebacks, or joking	3.30	(2.2)
10. Responding positively, being "nice"	3.11	(1.7)
11. Social support from other fat people	3.07	(1.7)
12. Ignoring situation, making no response	3.01	(1.6)
13. Eating	2.98	(2.7)
14. Educate self or others about fat stigma	2.82	(1.8)
15. Negative self-talk	2.77	(2.3)
16. Cry, isolate myself	2.36	(2.0)
17. Responding negatively, insulting back	1.54	(1.3)
18. Avoid or leave situation	1.52	(1.2)
19. Seeking therapy	1.19	(1.8)
20. Physical violence	0.86	(1.3)
21. Lose weight	0.85	(0.9)

This study used the Global Severity Index, which is the average severity of all fifty-three symptoms experienced over the past week, as an overall indication of psychological distress. Test–retest reliability for the BSI is $r = .90$, and internal consistency, as measured by Chronbach's alpha, ranges from .71 to .85.

Body Image

The Body Shape Questionnaire (BSQ) is a thirty-four-item scale measuring desire to lose weight, body dissatisfaction, feelings of low self-worth in connection with weight, feelings of fatness after eating, self-consciousness in public, and distressing thoughts about weighing too much or being too big in certain body regions. The total score on this measure serves as an index of overall body image distress, with higher scores indicating more negative body image. The BSQ has been shown to correlate with other measures of body dissatisfaction and disordered eating in clinical and non-clinical samples (Cooper, Taylor, Cooper, & Fairburn, 1987).

Self-Esteem

The Rosenberg Self-Esteem Scale (RSE) is a ten-item questionnaire measuring attitudes of general self-worth, positive self-esteem, and global self-esteem (Rosenberg, 1965). Higher scores represent higher self-esteem. Rosenberg normed this instrument on a sample of over 5,000 high school students in the Northeast and reported an alpha coefficient of .92 for this measure, indicating good internal consistency. Test–retest reliability was found to be $r = .82$. Demo has demonstrated that the RSE correlates significantly ($r = .32$) with peer ratings.

RESULTS

Frequency of Stigmatizing Situations and Coping Responses

The overall mean score for each of the fifty stigmatizing situation items was 1.75 ($SD = 1.1$), which corresponds to a reported frequency between "once" and "several times in my life." In other words, participants reported experiencing each of the fifty stigmatizing situations, on average, between once and several times in their

lives. The overall mean score for each of the ninety-nine coping responses items was 3.26 ($SD = 1.2$), which corresponds to a reported
frequency of more than "once a year." In Tables 5.1 and 5.2, the
mean score for each category of stigmatizing situation and coping
response is presented in descending order for the full sample of 154
respondents. Scores given reflect the mean score across items in each
category, thus controlling for the unequal number of items in each
category.

The most frequent stigmatizing situations respondents faced were
hurtful comments from children, other people making unflattering
assumptions, loved ones feeling embarrassed to be seen with the fat
person, and physical barriers (such as chairs that were too small). Respondents reported facing these situations between "once a year" and
"several times in my life." Being stared at and being subjected to
unsolicited negative comments also were frequent. Infrequent experiences included job discrimination and physical assault, which occurred on average less than "once in my life."

The most frequent coping responses reported by these respondents
were practicing self-acceptance, attempting to head off negative remarks by socially disarming people who might otherwise be critical,
and making positive self-statements. Respondents reported that they
used these strategies from "once a month" to "several times a year."

Relation of Demographic Variables to Stigma, Coping, and Adjustment

There was a significant correlation between stigmatizing situations
and BMI ($r = .39$, $p < .001$), indicating that the number of stigmatizing experiences reported increased with higher weights. Additionally, after controlling for the effects of weight and group membership,
the partial correlation ($r = .27$, $p < .001$) between stigmatizing situations and coping responses indicated that coping attempts also increased in direct proportion to stigmatizing experiences.

In these samples, body weight was *unrelated* to psychological distress. That is, fatter people were neither more nor less distressed than
less-fat people. Unexpectedly, however, people of lower socioeconomic status reported more distress overall. Partial correlations controlling for the confounding effects of group and stigmatizing
situations found that socioeconomic status (SES) was correlated with
scores on the BSI ($r = -.35$, $p < .001$), BSQ ($r = -.28$, $p < .001$),
and RSE ($r = .33$, $p < .001$), such that higher SES was associated

with fewer mental health symptoms, less body dissatisfaction, and higher self-esteem.

Relation of Stigma, Coping, and Psychological Distress

Stigmatizing situations were significantly correlated with each measure of psychological adjustment, independent of the confounding effects of group and weight. That is, more stigmatizing experiences were associated with increased mental health symptoms ($r = .30$, $p < .001$), more negative body image ($r = .29$, $p < .001$), and more negative self-esteem ($r = -.19$, $p < .05$).

After controlling for the confounding effects of group, SES, weight, and number of stigmatizing situations reported, the overall number of coping attempts reported was still significantly correlated with self-esteem ($r = .22$, $p < .01$), indicating that more frequent coping attempts were related to better self-esteem. There was no significant relation between coping attempts and either body image or mental health symptoms.

Examining the overall number of coping attempts people reported was not the purpose of this study, however. Rather, this study attempted to identify *specific* coping responses associated with psychological adjustment.

Partial correlations controlling for the frequency of stigmatization experiences, group membership, SES, and weight identified three types of apparently maladaptive coping strategies: "Negative self-talk," "Cry, isolate myself" and "Avoid or leave situation" (see Table 5.3). "Eating [more]" and "Losing weight" were also significantly related to body dissatisfaction and self-esteem, but not to mental health symptoms.

It was thought that adaptive coping strategies would be associated with fewer mental health symptoms, more negative body image, and more positive self-esteem. Again after controlling for group, number of stigmatizing situations reported, SES, and weight, two coping categories met this description: "Self-love/self-acceptance" and "Educating self and others about weight control and stigma." That is, people who reported using the above strategies to cope with weight stigma also reported less distress. Three other coping strategies—"Seeing the situation as the other person's problem," "Refusing to diet," and "Being visible despite stigma"—were associated with more positive self-esteem and less body dissatisfaction, with no

Table 5.3
Relation between Form of Coping and Psychological Distress

Category	Partial correlation[††] (r) with:		
	BSI	BSQ	RSE
Negative self-talk	.51***	.66***	−.63***
Cry, isolate myself	.49***	.49***	−.50***
Avoid or leave situation	.31***	.36***	−.27***
Eat	.22	.49***	−.32***
Diet	.14	.29***	−.27**
Seek therapy	.23[†]	.08	−.22
Ignore situation	.06	.05	−.06
Use faith, religion, prayer	.07	.05	.16
Humor	.12	.03	.11
Seek social support	.09	.03	.10
Seek support of fat people	.08	.04	.14
Head off negative remarks	.02	.04	.24[†]
Fight back physically	.02	−.16	.08
Respond negatively	.07	−.06	.11
Respond positively	.15	−.05	.20
Positive self-talk	−.05	−.03	.24[†]
See situation as others' problem	−.14	−.19	.30***
Refuse to diet	−.18	−.29***	.26[†]
Refuse to hide body, be visible	−.16	−.28**	.37***
Self-love, self acceptance	−.23[†]	−.23[†]	.48***
Educate others/self	−.24[†]	−.37***	.50***

[†]$p < .01$
**$p < .005$
***$p < .001$
[††]Controls for effects of stigmatizing situations, group, SES, and BMI.

relation to overall mental health symptoms. Finally, "Positive self-talk" was associated with higher self-esteem only (see Table 5.3). While one cannot infer that these forms of coping cause better adjustment, these data do indicate that certain types of coping are related to less distress overall.

Examination of group differences between NAAFA members and magazine subscribers was more difficult than expected, given the greatly unequal sample sizes. However, analyses of covariance controlling for weight, marital status, SES, and educational level found that NAAFA members were more likely to report stigmatizing experiences (see Table 5.4) than were magazine subscribers. The groups did

Table 5.4
Group Differences† between NAAFA Members and Magazine Subscribers on Stigmatizing Situations, Coping Responses, and Mental Health

Measure	NAAFA members (N = 109) Mean (SD)	Magazine subscribers (N = 45) Mean (SD)
Stigmatizing situations	2.09 (1.1)	0.94 (0.7)**
Coping responses	3.47 (1.2)	2.68 (0.9)
Brief Symptom Inventory	0.75 (0.6)	0.73 (0.6)
Body shape questionnaire	81.01 (35.3)	96.09 (38.4)*
Rosenberg Self-Esteem Scale	31.37 (6.5)	30.80 (6.1)

$*p < .05$
$**p < .01$
†ANCOVAs control for BMI, education, marital status, and SES.

not differ with regard to the number of coping attempts they made. On the clinical measures, magazine subscribers reported significantly greater body dissatisfaction. Magazine subscribers and NAAFA members had similar levels of psychological symptoms and self-esteem. These results are reported in Table 5.4.

Another difference between these samples was their approach to dieting. Predictably, magazine subscribers were about twice as likely to report being on a diet currently as were NAAFA members (62 percent versus 33 percent, respectively; $X^2 = 17.59$, $p < .001$). Analyses of covariance controlling for stigmatizing situations, BMI, SES, education, and marital status found that magazine subscribers also reported more overall attempts to lose weight (mean = 1.13, SD = 1.1) than NAAFA members (mean = 0.75, SD = 0.8). This difference was also statistically significant ($F[5, 132] = 18.59$, $p < .001$). These results are detailed in Table 5.5.

Unexpectedly, NAAFA members were not more likely to practice fat acceptance strategies as a whole. Summing the reported frequency of the eight hypothesized fat acceptance strategies yielded no overall difference between the frequency with which these strategies were reported by NAAFA members and magazine subscribers ($F[5, 132] = 3.00$, n.s.). Each of the eight fat acceptance coping strategies was

Table 5.5
Group Differences in Forms of Coping between NAAFA Members and Magazine Subscribers[††]

Measure	NAAFA members ($N = 109$) Mean (*SD*)	Magazine subscribers ($N = 45$) Mean (*SD*)
Positive self-talk	5.08 (2.0)	4.53 (2.0)
Self acceptance	5.42 (2.2)	4.13 (2.1)
Refuse to diet	5.09 (2.0)	3.62 (1.8)[†]
See situation as others' problem	3.44 (1.7)	2.10 (1.4)
Humor	5.02 (2.4)	3.79 (2.3)
Be visible	3.45 (2.3)	2.93 (2.0)
Fat support group	4.46 (1.7)	3.48 (1.6)*
Education about stigma	3.37 (1.8)	1.34 (1.1)***
Total fat acceptance	35.24 (11.7)	25.91 (9.9)
Lose weight	0.75 (0.8)	1.13 (1.1)***

[†]$p < .06$
*$p < .05$
***$p < .001$
[††]ANCOVAs control for BMI, education, marital status, and SES.

therefore analyzed individually. The resulting analyses of covariance controlling for weight, SES, educational level, marital status, and number of stigmatizing situations found that NAAFA members were more likely to report attempts to educate themselves and others about fat stigma and weight control and were also more likely to seek social support from other fat people (see Table 5.5).

IMPLICATIONS OF STIGMATIZING SITUATIONS AND COPING RESPONSES FOR FAT PEOPLE

The purpose of this study was to examine the relationships among stigmatization, coping efforts, and mental health in two non-clinical samples. This study also investigated whether "fat acceptance"—an approach that has been gaining popularity as a way to combat fat stigma, is associated with better psychological adjustment. We found that stigmatization is a nearly universal experience among people who are visibly fat. As in our prior study with clinical samples (Myers & Rosen, 1999), increased stigmatization was associated with more symptoms, more body dissatisfaction, and lower self-esteem.

As with fat clinical samples, stigmatization among fat people in non-clinical settings apparently triggers a great deal of coping effort, with certain coping strategies being associated with worse adjustment. Coping strategies that appear to be particularly maladaptive include self-deprecation, isolation, avoidance of stigmatizing situations, overeating, and—somewhat paradoxically—dieting. The first three of these strategies were significantly associated with more mental health symptoms, more body dissatisfaction, and lower self-esteem. Overeating and dieting in response to fat stigmatization were both associated with more body dissatisfaction and lower self-esteem.

The findings of this research mirror those of coping studies (Tobin, Holroyd, Reynolds, & Wigal, 1989), which found that self-criticism, avoidance, and social withdrawal are associated with worse psychological adjustment. Surprisingly, the current study also found that dieting was associated with worse adjustment. Given that dieting is the most common approach to dealing with weight stigmatization, this finding is particularly important.

This study also found that certain coping strategies were associated with better psychological adjustment, particularly with regard to body image and self-esteem. Of eight strategies recommended by fat acceptance proponents, five were found to be associated with less body dissatisfaction and more positive self-esteem. Two of these eight strategies were also associated with fewer mental health symptoms. As in prior research on coping (Tobin et al., 1989), the forms of coping associated with the best adjustment involved cognitive restructuring, active problem-solving (such as educating oneself about stigma and weight control), and eschewing isolation and avoidance as a means of coping (such as refusing to hide one's body).

It is unclear why this study of fat people in non-clinical samples found coping strategies associated with better adjustment while a study of patients (Myers & Rosen, 1999) did not. One explanation is that patients in the clinical sample were so fat and so frequently stigmatized that their coping strategies were relatively less effective. This hypothesis seems unlikely, however, since a high number of respondents in the current, non-clinical sample weighed just as much as the patients in our prior study. Another explanation, then, is that non-patients do not present for treatment because they are not as distressed by their weight. Presumably, they are not as distressed because their coping attempts are more effective.

The most likely explanation for why this sample reported coping strategies associated with better adjustment, though, has to do with the particular population sampled. In this study, the overwhelming majority of respondents were members of NAAFA, an organization that espouses and teaches fat acceptance. In this select group, members may be particularly adept at countering social stigma because they have been taught and have had the opportunity to practice particular stigma-management techniques. Additionally, this is a population composed in large part of non-dieters, who by definition have had to adopt other strategies for coping with fat stigma. Finally, NAAFA members may benefit from the self-esteem-buffering properties of group affiliation (Crocker & Major, 1989).

This study thus lends credence to fat activists' assertion that acceptance of one's body protects self-image against the negative effects of weight stigma. Surprisingly, though, members of NAAFA were no more likely to employ these strategies than were readers of a national weight-loss publication. Interestingly, NAAFA members also reported significantly more stigmatization than subscribers, even after controlling for their higher weight. This finding could be due to NAAFA members being more sensitized to stigma and therefore noticing more prejudice. This hypothesis may also explain why more NAAFA members were willing to participate in this study.

An unexpected finding of this research was that higher socioeconomic status appears to protect against psychological distress. It may be that fat people who are better educated and who have higher-paying jobs have more resources to draw from as they combat the negative internal effects of stigmatization. Conversely, poorer people with less education may have fewer resources with which to buffer self-image. In fact, it appears that SES has more of an impact on psychological adjustment than weight, which has not been shown to negatively impact mental health (Stunkard & Wadden, 1992). Thus, despite popular belief, there is no evidence to suggest that fatness is either caused by or leads to unhappiness. In fact, this study provides some support for the reverse idea: that *weight loss attempts* are either caused by or contribute to unhappiness.

It is important to note that due to the cross-sectional, correlational method of this study, no conclusions can be made about the direction of the relation between these variables. For instance, more stigmatization may lead to more distress, but it is just as likely that more distressed people report more stigmatization. Similarly, more distressed persons might be more likely to report certain (maladaptive) coping responses. This research is further limited by the fact that participants were overwhelmingly members of NAAFA. While attempts were made to obtain equal samples of subscribers and NAAFA members, the response rate was much greater in the NAAFA group. This finding probably illustrates that the study was of more interest to NAAFA members, and their reports thus bias the results in their favor. It is therefore inappropriate to generalize the findings of this research to other, less-specialized populations of fat people.

Limitations notwithstanding, this study provides a useful extension of previous research. Clearly, weight-related stigmatization is a frequent and distressing experience that requires considerable coping effort, even in non-patient samples. Verbal harassment and abuse, public ridicule, intrusive remarks, and geographic barriers such as seats and clothing that are too small are among the various types of events frequently reported by fat respondents in our study. Additionally, while it has often been assumed that weight stigma contributes to low self-esteem and poor body image among fat people, this is the first empirical study to provide support for this conclusion. Our findings suggest that more frequent reports of stigmatizing experiences are associated with more mental health symptoms, more negative body image, and lower self-esteem. In contrast, weight alone was unrelated to psychological adjustment.

Sadly, although we read almost daily about the health risks and social problems associated with "obesity," never are we provided with effective ways of losing weight. In the absence of effective methods for weight reduction, millions of people are left to cope with health and social problems on their own. Too often, these people engage in repeated, fruitless attempts to diet—diets that most often result in no weight loss and, perhaps, in a decrease in self-esteem and body image. Our research adds to the body of evidence that suggests that weight loss—this culture's traditional remedy for stigmatization—is ineffective and associated with worse psychological adjustment among fat people.

Fortunately, our findings also suggest that at least one population of fat people has discovered ways of coping with stigmatization that are associated with lower levels of distress—among them the same forms of coping associated with better adjustment to other stressors. "Fat acceptance" as an approach to weight stigmatization therefore appears to have at least some validity and is worth further study. In the absence of a way to make fat people's bodies conform to socially acceptable norms, these findings are welcome news, indeed.

Suggestions for combating prejudice and discrimination against fat people appear in the Toolbox for Change below.

Toolbox for Change

For	Images/perceptions	Strategies for change
Individuals	Fat people are stereotyped and harassed. People believe that fatness is easily remedied by dieting or exercise. Fat people are socially excluded. Fat people are blamed for their weight. As a result, fat people (as well as everyone who feels fat) have poor self-esteem and poor psychological adjustment.	Stop dieting. Join fat-affirmative group or form one. Protest dieting posters, companies, and media. Teach children to love their bodies in all sizes. State fat-affirmative views. Inform people about the risks and failures of diets. Model self-acceptance of body weight. Correct disparaging remarks about weight in all people. Seek out people with similar views for social support. Regardless of your size, make friends with fat people.
Community/ society	Beauty is narrowly defined as thinness. All people are exploited by the diet and fitness industries. Fat people are believed to lack self-discipline and willpower.	Protest dieting posters, companies, and media. Teach children to love their bodies in all sizes. Add size discrimination to non-discrimination policies. Encourage physical activity in all people, and do not link it to weight loss. Profile community leaders of all sizes.
Practitioners/ educators	Fat people are not hired or are denied benefits. Fat people are told to lose weight. Fat people are mistreated by health and mental health practitioners.	State fat-affirmative views. Inform people about the risks and failures of diets. Model self-acceptance of body weight.

continued

Toolbox for Change (continued)

For	Images/perceptions	Strategies for change
	Educators do not protect children from harassment based on weight in schools.	Correct disparaging remarks about weight in all people. Have office chairs that fit all sizes. Distribute resources of fat-affirmative books, magazines, children's books, videos, web sites, etc. Refer people to fat-affirmative healthcare providers, therapists, etc.

REFERENCES

Agell, G., & Rothblum, E. D. (1991). Effects of clients' obesity and gender on the therapy judgments of psychologists. *Professional Psychology: Theory and Practice, 22*, 223–229.

Allon, N. (1982). The stigma of overweight in everyday life. In B. B. Wolman (Ed.), *Psychological aspects of obesity: A handbook.* New York: Van Nostrand Reinhold Co.

Bennet, W., & Gurin, J. (1982). *The dieter's dilemma.* New York: Basic Books.

Blumberg, P., & Mellis, L. P. (1985). Medical students' attitudes toward the obese and the morbidly obese. *International Journal of Eating Disorders, 4*, 169–175.

Bray, G. A. (1992). Pathophysiology of obesity. *American Journal of Clinical Nutrition, 55* (Supplement), 488S–494S.

Canning, H., & Mayer, J. (1966). Obesity—its possible effect on college admissions. *New England Journal of Medicine, 275*, 1172–1174.

Cogan, J. C., Bhalla, S. K., Sefa-Dedeh, A., & Rothblum, E. D. (1996). A comparison study of United States and African students on perceptions of obesity and thinness. *Journal of Cross-Cultural Psychology, 27*, 98–113.

Cogan, J. C., & Rothblum, E. D. (1993). Outcomes of weight-loss programs. *Genetic, Social, and General Psychology Monographs, 118*, 385–415.

Cooper, P., Taylor, M. J., Cooper, Z., & Fairburn, C. G. (1987). The development and validation of the Body Shape Questionnaire. *International Journal of Eating Disorders, 6*, 485–494.

Crandall, C. S. (1991). Do heavy-weight students have more difficulty paying for college? *Personality and Social Psychology Bulletin, 17*, 606–611.

Crandall, C. S. (1994). Prejudice against fat people: Ideology and self-interest. *Journal of Personality and Social Psychology, 66*, 882–894.

Crandall, C. S., & Biernat, M. (1990). The ideology of anti-fat attitudes. *Journal of Applied Social Psychology, 20*, 227–243.

Crandall, C. S., & Martinez, R. (1996). Culture, ideology and antifat attitudes. *Personality and Social Psychology Bulletin, 22*, 1165–1176.

Crocker, J., & Major, N. (1989). Social stigma and self-esteem: The self-protective properties of stigma. *Psychological Review, 96*, 608–630.

Derogatis, L. R., & Spencer, P. M. (1982). *The Brief Symptom Inventory (BSI): Administration, scoring and procedures manual—I.* Boston: Johns Hopkins University School of Medicine.

Gortmaker, S. L., Must, A., Perrin, J. M., Sobol, A. M., & Dietz, W. H. (1993). Social and economic consequences of overweight in adolescence and young adulthood. *New England Journal of Medicine, 329*, 1008–1012.

Hutchinson, M.G. (1994). Imagining ourselves whole: A feminist approach to treating body image disorders. In P. Fallon, M. A. Katzman, & S. C. Wooley (Eds.), *Feminist perspectives on eating disorders* (pp. 152–168). New York: Guilford Press.

Larkin, J. C., & Pines, H. A. (1979). No fat persons need apply. *Sociology of Work and Occupations, 6*, 312–327.

Life and death of "miracle boy" leave scars. (1997, March 23). *The Burlington Free Press*, p. 6A.

Maddox, G. L., & Liederman, V. (1969). Overweight as social desirability with medical implications. *Journal of Medical Education, 44*, 214–220.

Maiman, L. A., Wang, V. L., Becker, M. H., Finlay, J., & Simonson, M. (1979). Attitudes toward obesity and the obese among professionals. *Journal of the American Dietetic Association, 74*, 331–336.

Millman, M. (1980). *Such a pretty face.* New York: W. W. Norton & Co.

Myers, A. M., & Rosen, J. (1999). Obesity stigmatization and coping: Relation to mental health symptoms, body image, and self-esteem. *International Journal of Obesity, 23*, 221–230.

Rand, C. W., & MacGregor, A. M. C. (1990). Morbidly obese patients' perceptions of social discrimination before and after surgery for obesity. *Southern Medical Journal, 83*, 1391–1395.

Richardson, S. A., Goodman, N., Hastorf, A. H., & Dornbusch, S. M. (1961). Cultural uniformity in reaction to physical disabilities. *American Sociological Review, 26*, 241–247.

Rosen, J. C., & Gross, J. (1987). Prevalence of weight reducing and weight gaining in adolescent girls and boys. *Health Psychology, 6*, 131–147.

Rosenberg, M. (1965). *Society and the adolescent self-image.* Princeton, NJ: Princeton University Press.

Rothblum, E. D. (1990). Women and weight: Fad and fiction. *Journal of Psychology, 124*(1), 5–24.

Rothblum, E. D. (1999). Contradictions and confounds in coverage of obesity: Psychology journals, textbooks, and the media. *Journal of Social Issues, 55*(2), 355–369.

Rothblum, E. D., Brand, P. A., Miller, C. T., & Oetjen, H. A. (1990). The relationship between obesity, employment discrimination, and employment-related victimization. *Journal of Vocational Behavior, 37*, 251–266.

Sobal, J., & Stunkard, A. J. (1989). Socioeconomic status and obesity: A review of the literature. *Psychological Bulletin, 105*, 260–275.

Stunkard, A. J. (1958). The results of treatment for obesity. *New York State Journal of Medicine, 58*, 79–87.

Stunkard, A. J., & Wadden, T. A. (1992). Psychological aspects of severe obesity. *American Journal of Clinical Nutrition, 55* (Supplement), 524S–532S.

Szwarc, S. (2003a, July 31). *The diet problem.* Retrieved on November 1, 2003, from www.techcentralstation.com

Szwarc, S. (2003b, July 31). *The truth about obesity.* Retrieved on November 1, 2003, from www.techcentralstation.com

Tobin, D. L., Holroyd, K. A., Reynolds, R. V., & Wigal, J. K. (1989). The hierarchical factor structure of the Coping Strategies Inventory. *Cognitive Therapy and Research, 13*, 343–361.

Young, L. M., & Powell, B. (1985). The effects of obesity on the clinical judgments of mental health professionals. *Journal of Health and Social Behavior, 26*, 233–246.

CHAPTER 6

Prejudice in an Era of Economic Globalization and International Interdependence

Teru L. Morton

The world is getting smaller. Internet communication allows all parts of the planet access to the other parts. Transportation advances permit cross-border travel for an ever-growing portion of the planet's population.

Business is going global. Now the United States has declared a war on terrorism worldwide. The explosion in contacts with different "others" exponentially heightens the likelihood of prejudice and discrimination. In addition, our interdependencies are increasing in complex ways as we and the institutions we support are no longer just "here" but "there" in countries around the world. This chapter will focus on the deleterious effects of economic globalization and its backlash and the need for addressing prejudices that contribute to mounting tensions globally. Then it will discuss core prejudice clusters and perceptions and strategies that individuals, communities, and practitioners/educators can use to provide checks and balances, help avert wars, and guide us safely through this era of globalization toward a more harmonious and peaceful coexistence on this small planet. Because the chapter topic is relatively new, it is important first to note what it does and does not presume with respect to perspectives it builds on.

This chapter is written from the U.S. perspective, in the expectation that most readers will be fellow Americans. "America(n)" where used in this chapter means the United States, although the term most properly refers to countries in all of the Americas, as their citizens rightfully point out.

The literature on prejudice is rich. Much has already been written about prejudice, its relationship to behavior, and how it develops and changes. It is generally agreed that personal and institutionalized prejudice and discrimination are linked in a mutually causative manner. Remedial action on one front furthers synergistic remediation on the other, although institutionalized prejudice may be more evasive and difficult to change. It is also generally agreed that changing prejudicial attitudes and beliefs can change behavior, and also that changing behavior can change attitudes and beliefs. The value of laws in guiding behavior and subsequently attitude change is noted accordingly. Finally, it is generally agreed that prejudice functions to distort perceptions and limit the reception of information that might loosen the prejudice, so that prejudice can create self-fulfilling prophecies and be quite resistant to change. The dynamics of prejudice will not be further covered here, except at the margin, that is, as they apply in international and global issues.

The literature on multiculturalism is likewise quite rich, with most of our attention to date focused on addressing prejudice and discrimination and restoring social justice within our own rapidly diversifying society. Markedly less attention has been paid to prejudice and discrimination internationally. This is in part due to our desire to tend to business at home first. It is also attributable in part to the generally deep well of ignorance and unfamiliarity about other countries that most U.S. citizens have. We as a nation are isolated in the main from the rest of the world by vast oceans, so relatively few of us have spent much time outside our borders or interacted extensively with international sojourners here, who typically operate from enclaves. We are a relatively young country still absorbed in self-definition. Our land mass is vast with marked regional and ethnocultural variegation, so we are still preoccupied with discovering and experiencing our own heterogeneity, which may be a larger task than for other countries. We have also been, in recent times, the most financially healthy and militarily mighty country in the world. While less rich and powerful nations could not afford to know about us, we have felt we could afford our relative ignorance about them. In many ways, then, an international or global perspective is quite a new proposition for many Americans.

Area studies, foreign language programs, and study abroad experiences were more prevalent in American higher education a quarter of a century ago than they are now. As we grew richer, more complacent with the end of the Cold War, and more absorbed in fueling our booming economy and attending to our unfinished domestic business in social justice and diversification, we abandoned earlier efforts to globalize education and the American mind-set. A relatively recent series of staccato wakeup calls such as the rioting protestors at the 1999 World Trade Organization meetings in Seattle, the 9/11 attacks on New York City's World Trade Center towers, and sporadic reports of backlashes against globalization occurring around the world, have rekindled internationalization efforts, particularly in higher education. As we as a country ran to atlases to learn where Afghanistan was and scrambled for crash courses to understand Islam, as our president concluded a domestic speech with the plea for anyone knowing Arabic to step forth and help out, our country recognized with alarm that it had been quite asleep at the wheel. Presently there is urgent consensus that we must extend our attention to the larger world arena and accept the responsibilities as well as rights of being citizens of the world.

For some years the multiculturalism movement in this country has gained strength in the counseling and health professions, in academia at all levels, and in private and public sector organizations striving to become inclusive and user-friendly for the diverse members of the American population. The multicultural and international perspectives are complementary and synergistic, with the multicultural perspective necessary but not sufficient for a properly internationalized or global perspective. Multiculturalism is generally addressed within national boundaries, as in discussion of diversity and social justice issues within this or some other country or a given organization within a given country. Many key parameters or common grounds of the field are fixed and taken for granted, such as citizenship and shared laws. Internationalism assumes these fields but adds the dimension of boundary sets, such as different nations, trading blocks, and environmental systems. An internationalized perspective thus recognizes the importance of population heterogeneity and the degree, type, and distribution of social justice within any given nation but also entails understanding the laws, policies and practices, and economic and geophysical environments, etc., in each country. It also recognizes issues of international law and commerce, shared environments, shared institutions such as the United Nations and the World Bank, and breaches of justice in nation-to-nation interfaces and in multinational organizations of commerce and government. In that sense, the international perspective described here requires a broader and deeper knowledge base—multiculturalism's values and content and then some. This relationship is reflected in the substantial presence of multicultural perspectives and material in international courses and the relative paucity of international content and perspectives in multicultural ones. If global thinking were an edifice, then, multiculturalism would be one of its supporting pillars. This chapter presumes the multicultural perspective covered elsewhere and will only add at the margin to emphasize extension to the international arena.

ECONOMIC GLOBALIZATION AND ITS BACKLASH

Economic globalization is the competitive extension of commerce from the local to the global arena, the emergence of global megacorporations, and the redistribution and consolidation of power it brings on the world stage—within countries and between countries, in commerce, and between governments and commerce. Global corporations can throw their weight around in imperialistic fashion, colonizing new territories worldwide for cheaper goods and labor and for new consumers. Economic globalization promotes hegemonic domination and interchangeability at the cultural and psychological levels—the economic, cultural, and psychological subjugation of less-powerful groups and organizations. The United States has spawned a disproportionate share of the global corporations, has led the global effort to nurture them by tearing down trade barriers, and has spearheaded the unfettered free market capitalism sweeping the planet in an inexorable march toward what Hardt and Negri (2001) call "Empire." It is an era of accelerating economic globalization and of "manic" expansion of free market capitalism (Greider, 1996), with the United States at the forefront. Momentum is intense, and stockholders in the extraordinarily powerful global corporations are celebrating.

But not everyone else is. In this country, we are seeing increasingly vehement protests against the effects of economic globalization from an amalgam of organizations representing labor, environmentalism, nativism, feminism, isolationism, and human rights. Elsewhere in countries around the world, there are even more fervent, passionate, and violent responses to economic globalization and its cultural subjugation—ethno-nationalist, pan-nationalist, regionalist, environmentalist, feminist, and religious movements that assume emphatically anti-imperialist positions. These are likely to assume the form of "indigenization"—puzzling and threatening to those accepting of hegemonic globalization—but they have been occurring and are expected to continue in this new era (Huntington, 1996; Jameson & Miyoshi, 1999). Al Qaida, a Muslim fundamentalist religious group, has resorted to aggressive terrorism against what it perceives as imperialistic capitalism dead-set on wiping out its core values and beliefs. The Sendero Luminoso activists of Peru also resorted to terrorism, their Maoism appealing to indigenous peoples deprived of their agrarian, subsistence-based lives by global economic forces. The Zapatistas, a long-deprived group in southern Mexico, used a mix of guerilla warfare and peaceful negotiation to protest their treatment by the wealthier classes, made worse by the press of globalization. Nativist movements in this country and around the world continue despite centuries of subjugation, in some cases gaining strength in the face of the new pressures for hegemony. Nationalism breeds nationalism, regionalism breeds regionalism, religious organization breeds heightened organizational activity in alternative religions, and various value and belief systems fiercely resistant to subjugation by economic globalism seek broader and broader world networks. The currently inexorable march of economic globalization will be met with continued backlashes as tensions mount. Dangers of erupting conflict with disastrous human tolls will build until we have reached a new balance of power at the global level.

In the last decade, respectable futurists from a wide range of persuasions have warned of the mounting tension, conflict, and indeed clash of civilizations being driven by economic globalization. Economic empire-building has been portrayed as a competitive colonization of the world market, bringing with it a major threat to the basic values of an open society (Soros, 1997). The exploitation of the planet's natural resources by global corporations is unprecedented and threatens the future of human life (McKibben, 1998). Indeed, participants in the snare of economic globalization, irrespective of their witting or unwitting role, are increasingly unable to access the accurate and reliable information needed to guide an appropriately alarmed but also informed response, since global communication corporations are managing opinions of the world's masses and threatening free thought with orchestrated information control and packaging (Vidal, 1996). Breakdowns in the old sovereign nation-based world order brought about by such unprecedented and massive changes are predicted to lead to world anarchy (Kaplan, 1994) or to a clash of civilizations and their values and worldviews. Indeed, Huntington (1996) predicts a congealing and head-on collision of eastern, western, and Arabic cultures and organizations. Either hegemonic domination or multilateral agreements and multicultural understandings will result.

As the world gets ever smaller, our global village (McLuhan, 1989) becomes more interdependent and complex. It becomes interdependent in that an event on one political, social, economic, and environmental level's causes and effects are increasingly played out at worldwide levels. It becomes complex in that the massive migrations of groups, consequent diversification of once relatively homogenous groups, and the hybridizing of races, cultures, and value/belief systems makes this world multiethnic, multicultural, multinational, and multireligious. One country may be composed of many ethnic and cultural groups. Individuals may have more than one race, nationality, ethnicity, culture, and spiritual system.

Effective response to global trends will require successful multicultural understandings and multilateral agreements rather than simple hegemonic domination and brute unilateral reaction. In the United States, the melting pot metaphor has been replaced with those of quilt, mosaic, smorgasbord, and chop suey to acknowledge the differences in the whole.

Global adoption of multilateral agreements and multicultural understandings has been slower because of the historical precedents of imperialism and colonialism worldwide and the current implicit and widespread acceptance of free market capitalism. The United Nations and its evolving scope of activities are our best collective attempt so far at a vehicle for mediating multilateral, multicultural understanding at the global foreign affairs level. In global business, truly successful multicultural and multilateral understandings occur only in partnerships and conglomerate organizations where power is shared as evenly and widely as possible, ample occasions are taken to solicit feedback from all parties affected, and stakes in possible outcomes are equitably shared in win–win agreements. At present, the tensions between empire and isolationism, unilateralism and multilateralism, and hegemony and diversity in our new global interdependence intertwine in international commerce and foreign affairs. Resolution comes only through the setting aside of prejudice and immediate self-interest in order to gain, in the longer term, a better world for all involved.

If our own corporations have been contributing to the growing hostility and chaos on the global stage, enabled by our own government, why have we not yet as a people moved in an orchestrated and expedited manner to weigh in? Because we have not fully comprehended the problems the world is struggling with, recognized our role in them, and accepted our responsibility for working collaboratively in the world community to solve them. In equal parts, this is a function of rank ignorance, self-absorption, and self-protective dysfunctional prejudices that prevent us from receiving the ample information available to us all along, a topic we turn to next.

PREJUDICE CLUSTERS THAT INHIBIT PROBLEM IDENTIFICATION

Prejudice truncates information received from the environment and prevents accurate assessment of the situation and one's relationship to it. On the global playing field, the United States has been a major player in creating world problems and will of necessity be a major player in solving them. Until some key prejudice clusters are acknowledged and diminished, however, it will be difficult to engage in optimal public discourse regarding the nature of any problems, our relationship to them, and the best approaches to their solutions. Four clusters of self-serving and limiting prejudices—ethnocentrism, nationalism, xenophobia, and noble-savage myths—will be commented on briefly here.

Ethnocentrism

For Americans, and "Americentrism," this involves the tacit assumption that our American values and beliefs are universal, rather than probably quite unique to the United States. It is the single most limiting blind spot in our thinking, pervading many of the disciplines and professions spawned in this country, and manifesting in our international business and governmental foreign affairs with regularity. It is manifest in thoughtless presumptions that ours is the only form— or if not, the best form—of democracy, feminism, freedom, family values, work ethic, leisure, etc. Our national leaders and the rarity of information sources in this country without an Americentric bent perpetuate it. Ethnocentrism is reflected in the insular claim that we don't need to leave this country to experience the world, since it comes to us. It is closely related to a more specific prejudicial belief that we are the world's ideal, a topic taken up later in this chapter.

Nationalism

Nationalism for Americans—or patriotism—is in need of redefinition if we are to love our country without unnecessary prejudice against others. The "love it or leave it" mentality by which we signal devoted patriotism and deny dissension in effect forces a blind prejudice for the United States and against anything or anyone alleged to be against it. We must reframe nationalism and patriotism in ways that allow continued pride and commitment to our country and also a healthy scrutiny of alternative policies and practices domestically and internationally. This prejudice cluster was in part responsible for the internment of Japanese Americans during World War II and also for McCarthyism, for example. Correctly framed national pride would allow us to love our country and appreciate our military personnel while still allowing disagreement with our foreign affairs policies to be expressed. It would support multiperspective discourse and not just the dominant "party line"—because it strengthens, not diminishes, us.

Xenophobia

Xenophobia, or fear of strangers, may be in part responsible for our obsession with classifying and categorizing people, as if a label makes them more known. It can contribute to the difficulties in distinguishing race, culture, and nationality that many Americans experience. It also feeds discomfort about multiracial, multicultural, and multinational individuals and institutions. The xenophobe's obsession with distinguishing "us" versus "them" is taxed when the world is complex and highly interdependent, and xenophobia may undergird the mix of nihilistic and white supremacist thinking of some of our population who opt for "head for the hills " isolationism.

Noble-Savage Myths

These myths presume that people are either an endangered species of untainted aboriginals, residual from an earlier epoch, or they are just like us, or at least "wannabes." Superficially appreciative of culturally different peoples, these myths assume that culture is static and not changing, they idealize the native group while dismissing or

demonizing their surrounding "conquering" group, and they promote patronizing protectionism that handicaps the groups' viability in
their larger society. Many countries have indigenous peoples. In
transnational exchanges, the population heterogeneity and issues
of social justice within that country may well involve issues of environmental and economic sustainability and careful attention to the
proposals and plans indigenous leaders have for restoring financial self-
sufficiency, developing culturally appropriate forms of education, law,
social services, etc., and other culture-centered mechanisms for building
community empowerment and collective self-respect. In dealing with
multicultural complexities of other countries we engage with, it is important to recognize indigenous and other minority groups and their
specific needs with respect to their surrounding environments, without
dismissing the rest of that nation as "just like us" except poorer.

PREJUDICE OF THE "HAVES" AND "HAVE NOTS"

In the battle against prejudice and discrimination, we have focused
most on the prejudice of the powerful and dominant hegemony, the
"haves," who oppress and discriminate against the disenfranchised
and underprivileged "have nots." But "have not" minority groups
hold reciprocally negative views of their oppressors. Post-colonial
scarification and emergent anti-imperialist positions reflect their own
share of prejudices held by the "have nots." Many subjugated people
on this planet harbor quite negative opinions about the selfish and
self-serving United States, in that Americans are (in their view) hypo-
crites and imperialistic capitalist pigs, cultural invaders, enemies of
traditional values, environment destroyers, self-proclaimed but unin-
vited world police, etc. In the same way, many members of exploited
minority groups have biases against the dominant group in any country. However, in a socially unjust and economically inequitable world,
it is up to the "haves" and not the "have nots" to make the big
changes—not out of philanthropic motive but because a short-term
loss of power permits long-term gain and because the "haves" indeed
have more resources to bear in establishing a socially just balance of
power and harmonious coexistence.

Just as the citizens of a rich and powerful nation like the United
States can afford their prejudice and ignorance of circumstances in
other countries—for at least the short term—so can the United States
as a nation, with its reserves of money and military might, mount

unilateral and aggressive interventions without first seeking world approval—but again only for the short term. At a larger, longer-term level, the dense interdependencies the United States has with all other countries of the world make unilateralism nonviable. The United States needs the support of the world community on both economic and military fronts. Short-term concessions to consult world opinion and develop more widespread consensus afford the United States more viable solutions in the long term. Similarly, the historically dominant institutions of this country are finally now striving to be more inclusive—again, not out of charity but because the burgeoning diverse groups constitute significant voting and buying power, and it is prudent and in the best interests of our institutions' long-term viability that they be courted and power shared with them.

An example of a dominant group willing to share power with a less-empowered one is occurring in Hawaii. Native Hawaiians, heavily outnumbered by newcomers and relegated to the bottom tier of society since the illegal overthrow of their monarchy, are seeking restoration of their sovereign rights. The "Akaka Bill," at the time of this writing before the U.S. Congress, calls for the U.S. government to recognize the Hawaiian race as an indigenous Native American group, and for the United States to develop a political relationship with this group—one sovereign entity to another—that is, a political and not judicial remedy. Importantly, the non-Hawaiian dominant population is in very strong support. The majority "haves" recognize that rectifying past injustice and restoring morality to the life of the land are in the long-term interests of the interdependent island residents and the visitors they host—"It wouldn't be Hawaii without the Hawaiians."

Because of the breadth, depth, and complexities of our global interdependencies, the social and economic inequities extant on this planet are likely to be addressed by the richer and most powerful nations—for sheer self-preservation. Remediation of prejudice and discrimination at the international or global level will require the same recognition of interdependence, commitment to social justice, and significant personal and institutional action that it does and has at the more parochial level.

IMPORTANCE OF ENLIGHTENED LEADERS AND MULTIPERSPECTIVE DISCOURSE

The influence of enlightened leaders in this regard cannot be overstated. Just as the malevolent prejudices and malicious discriminatory aggressions of leaders like Adolf Hitler and Slobodan Milosevic ignited and fueled horrendous genocidal campaigns, so can leaders like Martin Luther King Jr. and Mahatma Gandhi ignite a collective vision of a world without prejudice, discrimination, and violence. Bigotry in any form can be transformed majestically by charismatic leaders focused on its eradication. It is important that only politicians demonstrating enlightened plans to move us toward a world without prejudice be elected, and that only enlightened corporate boards and executives be granted the funds and power to conduct our business.

Equally important in identifying and eliminating prejudice and discrimination at the national or global level is ample and ongoing dialogue, discourse, and debate in the public arena. This optimizes input from all possible perspectives and participative engagement and "buy in" by all possible parties, and reminds all involved of the diversity of viewpoints and values. Decision-making teams are slower to get going when they comprise heterogeneous members rather than homogenous teams, because they face more points of potential conflict and impass and cannot resort to simple "groupthink" processes. Once they get going, however, they can be markedly more creative in their problem solving (Adler, 1991; Maznevski, 1994; McLeod & Lobel, 1992). At the interdependent world level, it is at the surface much easier for a country or corporation to operate at a unilateral level, but the multilateral form of agreement maximizes the long-term gains for all involved and minimizes unforeseen and costly backlashes of many kinds.

IMAGES AND PERCEPTIONS THAT FUEL PREJUDICE

In today's environment of rapid globalization and escalating imbalance and danger, full and accurate information and precise communication that have their intended effect and no more become crucial. But prejudice blocks information transfer and distorts accuracy of information that is both sent and received in communication. More, and more complex, interdependence makes prejudices more actively dangerous, and efforts to identify and eliminate destructive prejudices and use engagement and change strategies better suited to our multicultural and shrinking world become increasingly important. Four fallacious and damaging core images or perceptions sustaining prejudice at the international level are identified here.

We Are the Ideal

"We are the ideal" is a core ethnocentric belief that pervades our society. Our freedoms, wealth, luxuries, form of democracy, morality, style of marriage and family, knowledge—this is as good as it gets, we tell ourselves. All the rest of the world is to be judged against us as an ideal and will always be found wanting. When we encounter anti-American sentiment, we dismiss it as pure jealousy: the rest of the world covets what we have, we are sure. They are motivated by the same things we are, but we simply have more of what all of them value.

This perception is shaken when we review our cross-border missteps in hindsight. In the United States, overtime pay is a great incentive, but when American managers offer much more pay to Mexican maquilladora workers to work more hours, they walk off the job—family time is valued much more than money there. Similarly, creating friendly competition spurs productivity in American factories, but it is offensive in a maquilladora, where competing against peers to benefit American management violates friendships (Lane, DiStefano, & Maznevski, 2000). The initial attempt to replicate Disneyland in Paris was a near-fatal failure because of the marked offense the French took at such Americanisms as the "snaking roped line" method of crowd control, the constant-smile requirement for park attendants, and the ban on wine (Hodgett & Luthans, 2001). Americans seem puzzled by the rationing of American films and television shows in France, and by the recent concerns expressed in Mexico that an overload of U.S.-made movies would erode their culture with unwanted values and perspectives. Current problems in Iraq have shaken the "we are the ideal" prejudice, and there is a rash of public discussion regarding whether or not there is more than one kind of democracy, whether democracy can exist without Judeo-Christianity, and whether ours is not surely the best.

A particularly blinding iteration of this ethnocentric belief is that "they see us as we see us." This reflects what Lane et al. (2000) call lack of cultural empathy. Cultural empathy is the recognition that other groups have their own values and ideals, and may likely see us in a different light.

One way to counteract this ethnocentric narcissism is immersion in the literature of comparative values on the global stage. Trompenaars and Hampden-Turner (1998), Hall and Hall (1995), Hofstede (1980), Kluckhohn and Strodtbeck (1961), and Ronen and Shenkar

(1985) are among those who have modeled cultural differences in values based on extensive empirical investigations. Examining issues of collectivism, power distance, materialism, contextual communication, tolerance for uncertainty, and so forth, as these issues differentiate cultures around the world, can help loosen the "we are the ideal" or "they see us as we see ourselves" beliefs to sufficiently allow better information processing and problem solving. The more accurately we can assess their perceptions of us, the more effective and mutually beneficial our actions will become.

Another approach to counteracting this ethnocentricity is to review some of the ways in which we are not the best (for example, gun-related deaths, abuse of children and elderly, vacation days or retirement security, workaholism and workplace violence, health insurance or mental health profiles, safety nets for the poor, academic achievement of children) and question why. A complementary approach is to review some of the ways in which the worldviews and lifestyles of people in other countries may set higher standards in certain areas (for example, Chinese elders get more respect, Europeans walk more than we do and have a wider selection of cheeses, family relationships are stronger in Latin countries) and again ask why. This usually leads to a more balanced and suitably modest self-assessment.

Probably the best approach to counteracting ethnocentricity is seeing Americans as people from other countries might. Glimpses are possible in living abroad or travel abroad immersion experiences, through coverage of the United States by the news media of other nations, and in some of the American culture books designed for sojourners and students of English as a second language (Nussbaum, 1998), or those sources for Americans that poke fun at us (Moore, 2001). It is endlessly entertaining and instructive to see the different "takes" people in other countries may have of our foreign policy, lifestyle, management of diversity, approach to religion, business management, and folksy ways.

Might Is Right

The view that "might is right" and the corresponding perception that "it's a dog eat dog world" also fuel prejudice and discrimination at the global level. They suggest threat and the need for reflexive, pre-emptive aggression—pressures allowing little room for contemplative analysis and extended information-getting. As such, they reflect a primitive approach founded in uninformed prejudice that creates a self-fulfilling prophecy—the more a country throws its weight around, the more offended groups fight back, leading to renewed aggression and further confirmation that it is indeed a zero sum field of conflict, with only winners and losers. These dynamics can be seen in the current unilateral interventions of the United States in its war on terrorism. The economic, cultural, and psychological imperialisms associated with economic globalization are more insidious, but the core premise of imperialism is "might is right," and the fiercely competitive "dog eat dog world" of international business at present can have wide ripple effects.

The World Is Quite Simple

Another primitive cluster of perceptions is that "the world is quite simple—it's just us and them." Such simplicity permits ample prejudice development because it presumes there is only one version of "us" and one version of "them." Every country has some diversity in terms of demographics, politics, religion, values, wealth and power, etc., and most of its citizens may well be quite multicultural. Furthermore, religions, races, ethnicities, political leanings, and other values frameworks are generally distributed across numerous countries and even continents. On certain issues, the world's women, Catholics, indigenous peoples, or teenagers may find more in common with one another than they do with fellow citizens of their countries. In short, it is not so easy to determine who is "us" and who is "them."

Prejudices based in this perception are often seen in isolationist perspectives, which can tend toward xenophobia. They are also typically a part of genocidal fascism, as was seen in the Nazi Party, and of racial supremacy movements, like the Aryan Brotherhood. They were manifest in improper actions against Arab Americans—many of whom were third-generation Americans—subsequent to 9/11. They are often found when a country's leader and its citizens are seen as the same, when generalizations about national character are overblown, and when ethnicity and nationality are equated.

Another version of this perceptual system is "the world is quite simple—people are the same everywhere." The more insulated and less worldly the individual or group, the more its universal model will tilt toward its own uniqueness. The assumption that the world is quite simple permits rampant prejudice development because it tilts the perceiver away from close observation and information seeking and forces premature closure of ambiguity. With a paucity of information and premature judgment, prejudice can bloom unfettered. Antidotes for both versions involve delving for more complexity and heterogeneity in oneself, one's country, and the world; recognizing that there are not many pure types in this hybridized, morphing multicultural world; and that increasingly people can and will hold allegiances to previously separate identities and groups.

The World Is Just Too Complicated

Another core perception feeding prejudice at the global level is that "the world is just too complicated for me to understand and improve." Like not exercising one's voting rights, this functions as a "cop out" from social responsibilities and perpetuates ignorance and complacency. It is a dangerous premise that permits the surmise that others are more qualified to operate on the world, and it permits the abdication of responsibility to monitor the efficacy and moral good of those others, allowing a vacuum that could be filled by unenlightened or even detrimental leadership.

While most of us take at least some responsibility for understanding and acting to improve things within our own country, fewer Americans pay as much attention to foreign affairs. The canvas seems so much broader and more irrelevant to our well-being. It is commonly observed that many people in other countries follow U.S. politics more than U.S. citizens do; that Americans' knowledge of basic geography is lower and its insularity and self-absorption higher than that of its trading partners; that Americans mistake their own diversity for that of the world; and that while American government and business interests have a major presence and aggressive impact around the world, Americans as a people are not very worldly.

Yes, the world is indeed complicated, but not so much that we should avoid the responsibility of learning about its issues and acting to protect or improve it. As the world shrinks and we become increasingly interdependent, we also become increasingly citizens of the world. Just as we teach our children about our nation's history and government and urge each other onward toward social and political activism in our home country, we will be wanting to teach our children about the world and its issues and move ourselves toward increased agency in addressing prejudice and social injustice on the world stage.

STRATEGIES FOR CHANGE

In significant ways, prevalent unconscious and unquestioned prejudices hinder the development of an informed international or global perspective. As with the early days of feminism and multiculturalism, we must focus on making the unconscious conscious and the unquestioned questioned; on reworking relevant language as needed; on leaning into the discomfort that confronting prejudice in oneself or others brings; on accepting the responsibility of changing dangerous prejudices at the international level proactively; and on building bench strength in organizers and "bridge people" who are able to bring disparate groups together for common aims. Just as developing awareness, knowledge, and skill is necessary to the development of multicultural competence (Sue & Sue, 1999), so too is it necessary to the development of international competence.

Awareness

Awareness can be heightened in many ways at the individual level and later at the larger community and institutional levels. International news reporting of current events via the Internet, *Manchester Guardian, Le Monde*, BBC, and so on can be obtained, and international students or sojourners can be interviewed to give a different perspective on ourselves than we hold. Instances of "we are the ideal" ethnocentrism are everywhere in our classrooms, news media, and casual discussion. We can ask ourselves how news could be delivered without this implicit bias, and what difference that would make in its effect. We can identify the "might is right" and "dog eat dog world" motifs in nearly all discussions having to do with economic inequity and political power, and ask what other values and approaches might be introduced in counterpoint. We can engage colleagues and friends in discussion of world events, identify the "world is quite simple" and "it's just too complicated" themes, and take delight in the insights and "aha" experiences that growing awareness and consciousness-raising provide.

Some of our biases are contained unwittingly in our language itself, and over time some language changes may occur as vested parties work through their assorted attributions and meanings and arrive at more precise and less offensive terminology. In the history of race relations in this country, we have witnessed the progression of labels, for example, Negro to black to African American, etc. Similar grappling for different terminology occurred with the women's movement and the evolution of other oppressed groups as the objects of labels protested the pejorative baggage of words and proposed their own terms. This will undoubtedly occur for some time to come as global thinking capacity is expanded. We have already discussed the problems attached to U.S. citizens appropriating the term *American* when it belongs technically to people throughout the Americas. Another currently contentious term in some circles is *global*. For some, this has a positive valence—as in joining the world family, having a cosmopolitan perspective, or business strength and health—but for others it reeks of imperialistic exploitation of the weak and poor and needs alternative language. The terms *alien* and *illegal alien* have a pejorative ring and may at some time be up for revisiting. *Foreign* and *foreigner* sound negative and distancing to some who prefer terms like *international* or *visiting*. *Pre-emptive strike* and *developing countries* may be up for future review. Examining our labels and terms and clarifying our meanings will be time- and effort-intensive and frustrating, but will help raise consciousness as the different attributions and aspirations of disparate stakeholders are recognized.

Knowledge

Knowledge is a major need for moving us from a position of ignorance and complacency to one of informed and effective agency in global issues. The vast majority of American parents want their children to receive a globalized education, and most college entrants in this country want a study abroad experience, although both remain extremely rare for U.S. higher education students. Basic requirements for international competence would be some understanding of geography; the ways in which geophysical environment, economy, religion, government, law, social structure, and culture vary worldwide; some unbiased understanding of how one's own country is the same and different from other countries; and objective perspectives on our country's foreign policies and on how our country and its policies are perceived by various scrutineers outside our borders.

To become proactive about aggregating tensions and misunderstandings occurring worldwide in this era of economic globalization, special emphasis should be given to new information regarding the effects of our country's actions on others around the world, and from their perspective and not ours—to receive accurate and sufficient feedback in communication or general systems terms. This lack of self-awareness at the national level may be almost a national characteristic

at this point for the United States, but it can be corrected, and relatively quickly, with concerted effort and vigilance—provided it is not
simply delegated to a government branch or service, such as the State
Department or the Central Intelligence Agency, but rather monitored by enlightened and vigilant citizens at large. Among other
things, this calls for us to demand more and better from our press—
which can be quite nationalistic and parochial as it selects and spins
its stories. In the main, we hear much more about what is happening
to "us" than to "them," more about how "we" feel than how "they"
do. Our news is also from a very Americentric perspective that rein-
forces already existent biases. We must insist on answers to questions
like, "What are they like, what do they want, how do they see it, and
how do we know?" It is this kind of knowledge that will best help
build more cultural empathy, understanding, and responsiveness as a
more internationally competent people.

Our country's insufficient sense of its effect on the world around it
is supported by all of the core prejudicial perceptions. If we are the
ideal, we don't need to worry about how we're coming across. It is
treason to question our foreign policy, particularly in a time of war,
and in any case might is right—the rest of the world just has to go
along with us. Things are quite simple, and our papers and television
channels tell it just like it is. It would be too complicated to process
multiple views—that's someone else's job. Information about the
ways in which people, cultures, and governments are linked through
resource transfer, the finiteness of environmental and human resources, and pathways to long-term global sustainability is particularly
needed at this time.

Skill

Skill, or measurable outcome behavior, is the necessary goal of any
efforts to change prejudice or increase awareness and knowledge. If
we are to develop greater global competence in our citizens and institutions, if we are to become better citizens of the world at the individual and national levels, there are a number of competencies we
might focus on.

Effectively soliciting, interpreting, and responding to feedback are
perhaps the most important skill sets. In general, these skills are
better developed in those low in power than in those high in power
for obvious reasons—they are critical for survival of the vulnerable
and less necessary for the powerful and well defended, who can afford

to throw their weight around less cautiously. Because conditions change, however, even the most powerful will want to have antennae out as they interact with the larger environment. Particularly when awareness and knowledge are low, feedback about one's impact on the environment helps improve competence, that is, it furthers awareness, knowledge, and other skill development.

Other skills particularly valuable in reducing individual and group prejudice at the international level include those associated with changing public opinion on a large scale, for example, through use of media campaigns, influential advocates, artful educational venues, etc. Another related skill set uses the political system, such as community development and empowerment, advocacy, and activism regarding policies and practices from the local to the federal and international levels (United Nations, World Health Organization, the Catholic Church, global corporations, etc.). Still another skill set involves abilities to effectively lead change in teams and larger organizations in all respects—mission and goals, strategic planning, climate and culture, structure and process, etc. "Bridge person" skills are critically needed as globalization's march demands increasing numbers of effective liaising, coordinating, mediating, negotiating and brokering agents to manage or solve conflict, and facilitating partnerships and increasingly complex multilateral, multinational agreements. Because cultures and nations can vary quite dramatically in approaches to conflict and consensus, such bridge persons will require cross-culturally effective skill repertoires.

Reducing prejudices that hinder optimized peacemaking and harmonious coexistence on this shrinking planet will then require large-scale efforts to increase awareness, knowledge, and skills. These efforts can and must be made at the individual, community, and educator/practitioner levels as we work to increase our bench strength in international competence.

Individual Change

Individual change is needed whether the individual seeks to be an enlightened leader or enlightened community member, stockholder, worker, consumer, or voter. Given the historical newness of globalism, consciousness-raising for individuals in any roles must and will occur to increase awareness of the ways in which we are increasingly interconnected, the ways in which we unintentionally choose the less desirable course of action, and the ways in which we blindly ignore or misread our feedback regarding international and global involvements. Individuals' knowledge bases can and should be expanded regarding ways that action or practice by their government, the corporation in which they own stock, the company they work for, the company whose shoes or food they buy, and the religious organization they affiliate with have social, economic, and moral consequences for people outside our borders. Individuals armed with sufficient awareness and knowledge can and should boycott corporations behaving in socially irresponsible ways, lobby for improved social justice on the world stage, and protest stridently against socially irresponsible actions of their employers, churches, and elected and appointed government officials.

Community

Community changes are also much needed in changing collective prejudices and their pernicious and damaging consequences. At the local level, developing a sister relationship with a school, parish, city, or company overseas facilitates mutual learning about differences and common grounds. Groups with established internationalist issues and agendas can affiliate around specific projects with shared concerns and attendant strategies to increase their influence. New groups can be created. Witness the Internet-based burgeoning of virtual penpals, chatrooms, news reporting, and special interest organizations allowing people around the world to exchange information and perspectives, and find common grounds and concerns. The speed of virtual community development cannot be underestimated, nor can its powers for either good or bad.

People are organizational, and organizations are nested within other organizations and families of organizations. So, in most cases people find they have, through such organizational chaining, an international interface, a world affairs task force, or a global strategy unit of their employer, investment company, church, etc. This group, or an independently established one, can be organized and charged as an international watchdog to monitor and publicize social responsibilities of the organization worldwide, so that affiliated individuals can take informed ownership, supporting social responsibility or sanctioning bad practice and leveraging change where needed. While there are periodic and sporadic disclosures of graft and corruption, child labor, unhealthy workplaces, sexual harassment and coercion, and so forth in some arm or another of our government or corporate organizations, much of their overseas behavior is still largely unmonitored and un-regulated by the public, contributing to our widespread and continu-ing complacency, ignorance, and prejudices. Standards are still quite low, with the United Nations not yet very evolved and international business law and ethics still embryonic, uneven, and biased. The bars for social responsibility in the global arena must thus be ever reset at higher levels if economic globalization is to have the appropriate checks and balances. When the United States passed the Foreign Cor-rupt Powers Act (Graham, 1983) that made it illegal for our compa-nies to use bribery in their overseas dealings, the companies protested that it would make them noncompetitive because bribery was how international business was conducted. In fact, host country govern-ments worldwide were grateful—the Act helped their own anti-corruption efforts—and our companies actually prospered more. In short, the individual person, community, or nation can, and should, strive to make a positive difference in business and government affairs at the global level.

Educators/Practitioners

Educators and practitioners are, of course, individuals and mem-bers and leaders of groups and communities, but they also have areas of specialty that they can internationalize and direct toward pressing global concerns. Educators have the critical task of preparing in-formed and responsible citizens of the world and of grooming the much-needed "bridge persons" who will have special roles in guiding us safely through this era of globalization. Globalizing higher educa-tion in the post-9/11 United States has been declared urgent, with more languages, area studies, study abroad, and exchange programs being called for. At least as importantly, consensually, is meeting the marked need of our students for more information about countries other than ours and frameworks that permit them to make compara-tive and informed analyses about the wide range of physical, political, and socioeconomic conditions elsewhere. Most existing educational material has been developed by American writers, showing some-times-alarming levels of Americentrism and perpetuating blissful lack of self-awareness and related prejudices. Educators must then make a point of presenting information from alternative perspectives to the Americentric one. Use of texts and other materials written by non-American authors can challenge Americentrism with alternative voices. Use of sojourning international faculty more routinely can help our students understand and accept alternative perspectives. Confronting unacknowledged prejudices and misconceptions, and exposure to sometimes unflattering views of ourselves, can produce emotional reactions and resistance. Instructors also need additional skills to manage the painful dialogues associated with meaningful attitude change and enlightenment. In addition, as more international student and faculty visitors join our classrooms and bring with them their assets of divergent perspectives, learning styles, and knowledge bases, instructors will need training and support in optimizing their priceless contributions to their classrooms, as well as in providing them with an education optimally useful to them in returning to their very different home countries.

The United States has a great comparative resource in its higher education. Given the phenomenal educational needs in developing countries, the greatest market for our higher education is outside our borders, and U.S. educational institutions are competing for shares of the world market and the privilege of training leaders and professionals necessary for world development. The speed of economic globalization has exponentially increased this worldwide need for an educated technical, professional, and managerial workforce. The sheer economic practicalities indicate that the training must and will occur overseas and in those countries, via new arrangements and partnerships supported by virtual distance learning. Education has long been held as a vehicle for economic, social, political, and even moral enlightenment around the world, so this is a case where U.S. educators may perchance do well by doing good. It is vitally important, however, that the export of American-style education be culturally appropriate, requiring considerable overhaul and the need to develop more information about the host country or region and from that perspective. Incenting research and scholarship in less-developed countries, partnering with overseas educators in new and mutually rewarding approaches, and reworking both the content and delivery format (language included) poses an important challenge if we are to avoid cultural imperialism and respond effectively to the task of developing "bridge persons" for the new environment.

Finally, some of our disciplines and professions are distinctly western or American, and therefore culturally encapsulated in ways unseen to Americentric scholars, teachers, and students. If they are to be adopted and utilized in nations around the world, their content and form may need major overhaul. Marsella (1998) has described the need to overhaul western psychology and develop a meta-discipline of "global community psychology" if the field is to be relevant and useful in addressing the needs of our changing world.

Practitioners of all stripes can work on remedying issues of prejudice, ignorance, and incompetence at the global level. They can partner with colleagues or sponsors outside our borders to develop and disseminate knowledge about needs, best solutions, and practices for particular countries and regions, providing culturally appropriate and needed services in host countries while helping to expand and globalize the knowledge base of their discipline, profession, or trade. Physicians can investigate indigenous healing methods and delivery systems while offering their services as needed to effect bilateral and mutually rewarding exchanges. Managers can seek ways to improve short-and long-term business yields through multinational teams, multilateral agreements about workforce issues, and corporate responsibilities. They can host communities and develop and broadcast improved forms of feedback mechanisms for globalizing entities. Researchers can participate in internationally collaborative research and demonstration projects for the problems facing impoverished countries around the world—water treatment, urban planning, agricultural productivity, worker health, etc., and thereby extend our existing knowledge base for solving problems in living. Information technology and communications specialists can sponsor developed forms of global communication and information transfer, attending to the wide range of data sources and heterogeneity of communication environments worldwide. They can also possibly do well by doing good if they remain conscious (and conscientious) that in today's world, information and control of communication are power. Lawyers have an almost open field in terms of international law. Behavioral health practitioners can expand their targets, addressing with overseas partners the many problems of economically developing countries, such as illiteracy, poverty, civil war, minority group disenfranchisement, workforce development, and child exploitation. In addition, they can apply their understanding of prejudice, attitude change, group decision-making, cooperative conflict resolution, and social justice dynamics to social groups larger than individuals and families and in culturally different contexts, seeking approaches to change in more collectivist environments as increasing interdependence makes all problem solutions increasingly multilateral.

Individuals, groups, and educators/practitioners face enormous challenges in overcoming prejudices and developing our international competence—but also the prospects of exciting new solutions and

Toolbox for Change

Images/ perceptions	Strategies for change*		
	Individual	Community	Practitioners/ educators
We are ideal	Use values/ perspectives of other groups to frame how others perceive Americans.	Create true reciprocity in a transnational activity, avoiding power imbalance and ensuring a mutually satisfactory feedback system.	Import/apply collectivist problem-solving tactics/skill sets learned elsewhere, for example, high-context communication, face-saving strategies, and consensual decision-making.
Might is right	Reframe patriotism, seek enlightened leadership, and engage with social responsibility, not imperialism issues.	Develop/enforce international standards of social responsibility for global corporations to follow within the local communities in which they operate.	Participate in solving a problem of another country's disenfranchised group with a focus on a process to better share power.
Simple world	Practice cultural relativism, cultural empathy, understanding and acceptance of differences.	Appropriately compose multinational teams, optimize input from all possible perspectives, and use a process of consensual problem-solving.	Address cultural heterogeneity within individuals, communities, and countries, and address the complex interdependencies on a worldwide level.

Toolbox for Change

Image/ perception	Strategies for change*		
	Individual	Community	Educators/ practitioners
Complex world	Study economic and environmental sustainability.	Participate actively in an international organization concerned with social justice abuse.	Utilize systemic, ecological, and contextual models of organizational change.

*This is only one set of examples from a very large number of possible ones.

the satisfactions of addressing problems in living worldwide. Economic globalization and increasing international interdependence heighten danger but afford new opportunities. Expanding our battle against prejudice and discrimination to the world stage is critical if we are to contribute to helping solve world problems in meaningful ways. It is a moral call, and a practical one, too. If not us, who? If not now, when? As we begin to make the unconscious conscious and the unquestioned questioned, we will find creative and proactive ways as an enlightened and empowered population to make our contributions conscientiously and collaboratively with the rest of the world community toward our shared goals of achieving peace, prosperity, and balance globally.

REFERENCES

Adler, N. J. (1991). *International dimensions of organizational behavior.* Boston: PWS-Kent Publishing.

Graham, J. (1983, Fall). Foreign corruption practices act: A manager's guide. *Columbia Journal of World Business, 93.*

Greider, W. (1996). *One world, ready or not: The manic logic of global capitalism.* New York: Simon and Schuster.

Hall, E. T., & Hall, M. R. (1995). *Understanding cultural differences.* Yarmouth, ME: Intercultural Press.

Hardt, M., & Negri, A. (2001). *Empire.* Cambridge, MA: Harvard University Press.

Hodgett, R., & Luthans, F. (2001). *International management.* New York: McGraw-Hill.

Hofstede, G. (1980). *Culture's consequences: International differences in work related values.* Beverly Hills, CA: SAGE Publications, Inc.

Huntington, S. (1996). *The clash of civilizations.* Cambridge, MA: Harvard University Press.

Jameson, F., & Miyoshi, M. (1999). *The cultures of globalization.* Durham, NC: Duke University Press.

Kaplan, R. (1994, February). The coming anarchy. *The Atlantic Monthly, 273,* 44–76.

Kluckhohn, F. R., & Strodtbeck, F. L. (1961). *Variations in value orientations.* New York: Row, Peterson, and Co.

Lane, H. W., DiStefano, J. J., & Maznevski, M. L. (2000). *International management behavior.* Malden, MA: Blackwell.

Marsella, A. J. (1998). Towards a "global-community psychology." *American Psychologist, 53,* 1282–1291.

Maznevski, M. L. (1994). Understanding our differences: Performance in decision-making groups with diverse members. *Human Relations, 47,* 531–552.

McKibben, B. (1998, May). The future of population: A special moment in history. *The Atlantic Monthly, 281,* 55–78.

McLeod, P. L., & Lobel, S. A. (1992). *The effects of ethnic diversity on idea generation in small groups* (pp. 227–231). Academy of Management Annual Meeting Best Papers Proceeding.

McLuhan, M. (1989). *The global village: Transformation in world life and media in the 21st century.* New York: Oxford Press.

Moore, M. (2001). *Stupid white men.* New York: HarperCollins.

Nussbaum, S. (1998). *The ABCs of American culture.* Colorado Springs, CO: Global Mapping International.

Ronen, S., & Shenkar, O. (1985). Clustering countries on attitudinal dimensions: A review and synthesis. *Academy of Management Journal, 9,* 435–454.

Soros, G. (1997, February). The capitalist threat. *The Atlantic Monthly, 279,* 45–58.

Sue, D. W., & Sue, D. (1999). *Counseling the culturally different.* New York: John Wiley & Sons.

Trompenaars, F., & Hampden-Turner, C. (1998). *Riding the waves of culture.* New York: McGraw-Hill.

Vidal, G. (1996, September). The end of history. *The Nation,* 11–18.

CHAPTER 7

The Sociocultural Abuse of Power: A Model for Shared Power

BraVada Garrett-Akinsanya

When I dare to be powerful, to use my strength in the service of my vision, then it becomes less and less important whether I am afraid.
—Audre Lorde, 1934–1992 (as quoted in Lloyd, 1997)

The constructs of prejudice and discrimination are not only interpersonal but sociocultural in nature. It is through sociocultural practices that institutional prejudices are erected and maintained. Systems, by nature, are therefore designed to perpetuate themselves and maintain homeostasis (Bowen, 1978; Minuchin & Fishman, 1990). When those systems have an inequitable distribution of power, the tendency to abuse power is inexplicably enhanced (McIntosh, 1988; Heylighen, 1992). Prejudicial attitudes and beliefs develop and can negatively impact behaviors and create pain for those who are its targets (L. Comas-Diaz, as quoted in McGuire, 1999). An extreme example of this negative behavior is hate crimes. In an FBI report (2001), it was noted that blacks were the largest group targeted for hate crimes and experienced a level that was over three times higher than that of other groups.

This chapter explores abuses of power by utilizing a model of sociocultural abuse of power/control that identifies eight elements of abuse that occur within a social context. A discussion will ensue regarding how abusive systems contribute to the development of what the author calls "oppression reactive syndromes." The chapter will conclude with the introduction of a model of shared power and control that leads to the healing of individuals and systems. The model will be contrasted against incidences of power abuse and will provide an exploration of how power can be shared when eight core aspects of empowerment are present.

Throughout this chapter, the author will illustrate principles and elements of each aspect of the models discussed (abuse of power versus shared power) by referring to research, data, and/or case examples derived from her twenty-four years of clinical experience in providing consultation, training, supervision, and clinical services to diverse individuals. While many references will be made to blacks, the reader is challenged to consider how these incidences apply to other groups as well.

THE SOCIOCULTURAL MODEL OF ABUSE
OF POWER AND CONTROL

The current model of sociocultural abuse of power and control originated one day during a therapy session with a black female who had left a physically abusive relationship one year earlier. During the session, the client began to describe problems at her worksite, including experiences of isolation, sexual harassment, and lack of economic opportunities. During the previous course of therapy, the therapist had introduced the client to the power and control wheel created through the Domestic Containment Program in Duluth, Minnesota (Pense & Paymar, 1993). In that model, the power and control wheel describes eight forms of psychological abuse consisting of specific behaviors associated with domestic violence. It then occurred to the author that people of color who live in America have also experienced domestic (as compared to international) violence. Consequently, America, as the domicile of many "minority" groups, has resulted in sociocultural disparities in the ways in which majority versus minority cultures are treated. Over the course of time, the treatment endured by many groups of minority status can be easily described as violent and abusive in nature.

Lenore Walker (1994) has highlighted the similarities that exist between sociocultural abuse and domestic violence. She suggests that domestic violence researchers and practitioners incorporate the definitions of psychological violence or terrorism endorsed by Amnesty

International, as they closely resemble the ways that male batterers control and intimidate their female partners. Thus, in order to capture the constructs of psychological violence, the current sociocultural model of abuse of power and control is characterized by eight oppressive elements that contribute to the development and maintenance of discrimination and prejudice: (1) isolation; (2) emotional abuse; (3) economic abuse; (4) sexual abuse; (5) using children; (6) using threats; (7) using intimidation; and (8) using white, male, or American privilege.

Because oppression is institutionalized in our society, members of marginalized groups often believe and internalize the oppressive messages created about them. Thus, oppression incorporates the development of multiple "isms," including externalized and internalized biases such as homophobia, able-ism, classism, sexism, racism, size-ism, ageism, and religious oppression (Public Agenda, 2004b). In the face of marginalization, subjugated groups develop oppressive reactive syndromes.

Oppression Reactive Syndromes

Authors have defined the nature of oppression (Winters, 1996; Wendell, 1990). Kammer (2002), for example, contends that the major source of oppression and sickness in our society is unresolved, unhealed personal trauma. He surmises that it is unresolved individual trauma that becomes institutionalized as oppressive forces that propagate more personal trauma. Van der Kolk (1987) also attests to the deleterious social impact of personal trauma. Miller (1990) attempts to address the formation of the oppressive reactive syndromes by her reference to the "cultural relational paradox." In her model, the cultural relational paradox is applied to marginalized groups within the dominant culture. Specifically, she posits that people from non-dominant groups long to be in connection to the dominant culture but experience repeated violations and disconnections within the dominant culture. In response, members of the non-dominant group consciously keep parts of their experience "away from" their interactions with the dominant group, or unconsciously distance themselves from their own cultural and ethnic experiences.

Within each perspective from which it is explained, oppression is distilled to a definition that incorporates the systematic abuse of power by one group over another in order to maintain social benefits, power, and control. Oppression, by definition, also includes a systematic mistreatment of one group by another group within a context of "socially oppressive" imbalances that must be expressed through the governmental and societal systems that sustain them.

An oppressive reactive syndrome is operationalized as a group of signs and symptoms that occur concurrently to characterize a particular reaction to an oppressive condition or state. Oppressive reactive syndromes comprise identifiable patterns of symptoms including the following:

Lowered self-esteem

Lowered sense of self-worth

Loss of own self-identity

Reduced self-confidence in abilities

Decreased sense of competence

Restricted sense of possible life options

Increased self-doubt

Lack of trust in others

Hyper-vigilance

Feelings of loneliness and social isolation

Feelings of helplessness and hopelessness

Embarrassment, humiliation, shame

Guilt

Depression

Anxiety

Rage, anger

Blocking (or difficulty concentrating or processing information)

Fear of abandonment

Fear of serious physical, economic, or social harm to oneself, one's children, or other family members

Emotional paralysis

Poverty of spirit and spiritual depletion

The "fly in the buttermilk" syndrome comes from an exposure to discriminatory and oppressive behaviors by the mainstream culture that overmagnifies the presence of the "minority group" members. This is evidenced by the experience of being "singled out" by practices such as racial profiling at airports, in cars, and in other venues of import. It is also seen in the workplace, where people of color report that their employers and white peers overemphasize and magnify their mistakes or differences, while minimizing their successes or similarities.

The fly in the buttermilk syndrome is the opposite of the invisibility syndrome. The "invisibility syndrome" (Franklin, 1993) was originally used to describe the experience of blacks in reaction to the dominant culture ignoring, minimizing, or marginalizing the existence, contributions, and needs of blacks in America. The phenomenon of invisibility is also evident when individuals go shopping and are ignored by clerks who "did not see them." It is also noted in employment situations where many organizations find it much easier to hire or promote white employees than to recognize the talent or contributions of culturally different individuals.

People with the "dangerous minds" syndrome complain that they are perceived as being "too hostile, too outspoken, too confident, too aggressive, too knowledgeable, and too intimidating with their knowledge." Because of the ethnic belief that being "twice as good" will lead to getting "half as much," many individuals who are not affiliated with mainstream cultures believe mainstream authority figures perceive them as threats. Within this realm of logic, if one wishes to "get ahead" (as opposed to simply "getting half as much"), then it is necessary not only to be "twice as good" but to be "three or four" times as good. For this reason, it is not unusual for individuals who have characteristics of the "dangerous mind" syndrome to seek extra degrees, training/experience, or expertise as a means of leveling the playing field or seizing new opportunities. They also tend to assess the goal of others as "bringing them down a notch or two and keeping them in their places."

Similar to people with the dangerous minds syndrome, individuals with the "man enough" or "woman enough" syndrome have an element of super-achievement and pressure to perform. This syndrome is a direct reaction to economic abuse, sexual abuse, and emotional abuse. The individuals' behavior is self-destructive, and they become addicted to drugs, alcohol, sex, shopping, eating, gambling, or other means of achieving immediate gratification. Children have impulse control problems and are belligerent and susceptible to gang activity. The primary aspect of this syndrome is that the person becomes excessive, fights a lot (either physically or verbally), and seeks material wealth to compensate for internal feelings of inadequacy. In essence, people who experience the syndrome feel as if they are never good enough and often mistake who they are with what they do or how much they possess.

"Stereotyped threat syndrome" is described by the research of Claude Steele (1997) and is a reaction to circumstances involving a negative cultural bias about one's group. Individuals with the syndrome internalize those biases and modify their behavior because of them. Specifically, individuals may "live up to what is expected" of them and do less well because they are "being viewed through the lens of a negative stereotype."

Successful inclusion in a predominately white society may often translate into the practice of "culture swapping," during which a culturally different person perceives that she is expected to discard her cultural values, practices, and identity. Some members of ethnic minority groups complain that they are asked to "sell themselves out" by relinquishing their cultural integrity in order to assimilate—until they are no longer recognizable to themselves or others. This practice results in alienation or disconnection from their cultural communities, and it leads to what Na'aim Akbar (1981) calls an "alien self disorder." Lillian Comas-Diaz (McGuire, 1999) offers a similar framework in her reference to the identity formation of immigrants, called the "post-colonization stress disorder." The process of developing post-colonization stress disorder is one in which individuals are relegated to enduring the stress of moving into a mainstream culture that does not embrace their cultural values or practices, but instead attempts to erase their systems of existence in order to force the new immigrant to fit into the mainstream.

Finally, "aversive racism reaction" syndrome is based on the work of John Dovidio, who studied a process of modern-day pro-racist behaviors, which suggests that negative attitudes toward minority groups are acquired early in life, resulting from immersion in a society with a long history of racial bias (Dovidio & Gaertner, 1991). Yet, because pressures exist against overt expression of negative attitudes toward minority group members, dominant culture members only demonstrate their racist attitudes covertly when acting on their biases can be attributed to factors other than race. People of color who experience aversive racism reactions tend to question their competence and worth. They demonstrate self-doubt, lack of trust, and a restricted sense of possible life options. They also complain that the "rules keep changing or shifting" and they eventually experience feelings of helplessness, hopelessness, and shame (about never being accepted).

Survivors of power abuses face numerous barriers that may leave them believing that their minority group status implies that they must be long-suffering. Despite their experiences, however, many marginalized groups are resilient; and their stories, songs, and poems often speak to their strengths. Within the cultural fabric of these communities are messages that they must "hold on," "wait and/or fight for change," and "keep hope alive." Hope can only be realized when there is a context of shared power.

THE SOCIOCULTURAL MODEL OF SHARED POWER AND CONTROL

Power is often addressed in the context of its abuse, and few studies actually evaluate the impact of sharing power (Ng, 1980; Bourhis, Sachdev, & Gagnon, 1994). Yet, when power is shared, sociocultural barriers are minimized, avenues for solving problems are enhanced, and outcomes improve (Wilson, 1996; Speer & Hughey, 1995). The distribution of power is often up to those who hold it. For example, Tajfel and Turner (1986) proposed that unstable intergroup situations contributed to insecure social identity and could trigger group members' attempts to change their positions in the social structure. Other studies looking at power differentials between groups concluded that "dominant group" members discriminated more than "subordinate group members" while "no power" group members did not discriminate at all against people placed in "outgroups" (Bourhis, 1994; Sachdev & Bourhis, 1985, 1991).

Proponents of social dominance theory (Sidanius and Pratto, 1999) hold that societies are inherently hierarchical such that some groups control the majority of power and resources to the exclusion of other social groups. The maintenance of this inequality is achieved, at least in part, by system-legitimizing beliefs that serve to intellectually and morally justify the relative differences in group status. Legitimizing beliefs such as racism and sexism casts ethnic minorities and women as less capable and therefore less apt for high-status positions in society. Thus, the dominant group has a general sense of superiority associated with a proprietary claim over material as well as immaterial resources in the society. The bottom line is that those in power often have difficulty giving it up.

Sharing power requires that those who are in power recognize and become receptive to those who are not. In other words, within the sociocultural model of shared power and control, being connected is the key to wellness, and wellness is a fundamental right of each individual. Finally, a tenet of this model is that healthy connections yield healthy individuals, families, and societies. Thus, from this perspective, it is unnatural for people to be disconnected because, biologically, we are similar in more ways than not. Mutuality and equality are our natural states. Therefore, when we discover the gift of cultural differences in each other, those gifts are to be celebrated, and our common human conditions are to be honored through processes that nurture and sustain mutually healthy connections.

Jean Baker Miller (1986), in her relational cultural model, agrees that mutuality is a core condition for healthy human connections. She contends that healthy relationships must be characterized by mutual influences and mutual responsiveness within a context of empathy. Empathy is the highly developed, complex ability to join with another at a cognitive and affective level without losing connection to one's own self. Thus, one needs to have the capacity to be authentic in relationships while also being able to see and understand the needs of others. Mutuality and empathy result in a growth-fostering relationship, which in turn, both facilitates and relies on the ability of each party to connect.

Therefore, healthy connections are mutual, empathic, creative, energy-releasing, and empowering in nature. Miller (1986) describes the impact of healthy connections as yielding (1) an increased zest and vitality, (2) empowerment to act, (3) knowledge of self and others, (4) value for self/self-worth, and (5) a desire to create and sustain connections. Conversely, unhealthy connections (Miller, 1990) yield abusive relationships that result in a "depressive spiral" characterized by (1) diminished zest or vitality, (2) disempowerment, (3) confusion and lack of clarity, (4) decreased sense of self-worth, and (5) withdrawal and turning away from other relationships.

The remainder of this chapter will use the sociocultural model of shared power and control to explore disconnections within the context of power abuse and how they could have been remedied if power had been shared. Likewise, oppressive reactive syndromes will be highlighted as the natural responses of diverse people to the unnatural condition of experiencing prejudice and discrimination. The components to be discussed in the context of this model include the following:

- Community inclusion (versus isolation)
- Emotional affirmation/respect for diversity (versus emotional abuse)
- Economic empowerment (versus economic abuse)
- Honesty and accountability/restorative justice and restitution (versus intimidation)
- Respect for physical health/sexuality (versus physical/sexual abuse)
- Shared value and responsibility for all children (versus using children)

- Non-threatening behavior/creating safety for challenge and risks (versus use of threats)
- Equal opportunity/dismantling privilege through fairness (versus using white, male, or American privilege)

Community Inclusion (versus Isolation) as an Element of Shared Power

Isolation as an efficacious strategy for gaining dominance is not a new one to man or beast. We have all seen the multiple animal documentaries narrating the plight of some lone gazelle (with a limp) that falls victim to a predatory cheetah. Once the lone or weak animal is separated from the pack, it is doomed. Likewise, in human conditions, it is not uncommon for people who are different to describe being "singled out" in multiple settings. Creating a victim requires isolation (whether real or imagined) in order for that individual to lose power, while group affiliations and attachments create power, facilitate problem-solving, enhance resource availability, and provide buffers in the face of potential adversity (Bowlby, 1988).

In contrast to community connections/inclusion, social isolation serves as a stressor (House, 2001). Isolation is difficult to manage because it is not only physical in nature but intellectual. In abusive relationships, perpetrators control what victims do, whom they see and to whom they speak, where they go, and what they read. Such relationships are characterized by the abuser's tendency to limit or cut off the victim's access to friends or relatives and by stalking the victim and assuring that the victim does not go anywhere that she/he does not have permission to go. Thus, for culturally different groups in our society, being "the only one" or the "first one" is not always a positive experience; these factors represent isolation and vulnerability—as the story of Janice illustrates.

Case Example: Janice

Prominent Syndromes: Dangerous Minds, Fly in the Buttermilk, Invisibility Syndrome, Stereotyped Threat

Janice was the first black female to be hired at a Fortune 500 company as an executive vice president of corporate finance. She had also been in the top of her class at a prestigious MBA program, had over fifteen years of experience, and was known in the industry as "someone who could get the job done." As a new corporate executive,

Janice found herself being not just the only woman, but the only black. During meetings, Janice's colleagues made negative comments about the competence of other black or female employees. Janice stated that she experienced the difficulties alone until a white woman, Margaret, joined the management team. It was not long, however, until she and Margaret were treated with the same level of disrespect. For example, the men would go to lunch and exclude both Margaret and her. One day the company president gave Margaret a highly visible project and advised her to select her work team. Janice said that Margaret selected "everyone" except her for the team. When Janice questioned Margaret, she was told that upper management had "advised" Margaret that it would be in her best interest to "avoid" using Janice for the project. It was on that day that Janice said that she felt the most isolated.

A shared model of power would have included numerous safeguards to protect Janice from isolation. For example, Margaret would have been empowered to defray the "divide and conquer" move put on her by the system in which she worked. She would have been able to engage honestly with Janice and create with her the best strategy to confront systems issues in a way that reframed the project as inclusive of all team members. Also, the work environment may have invested in mentoring programs for women or minorities. On her own, Janice may have affiliated with identity-specific professional organizations such as the National Black MBA Association or groups for women, such as the National Association for Female Executives. The key to building community is to recognize that the individual is part of a larger system that can be nurtured to sustain the connections necessary to facilitate growth. Other community-inclusion ideas could comprise social and professional functions such as book clubs, networking groups, seminars, or forums.

Emotional Affirmation and Respect for Diversity (versus Emotional Abuse) as Elements of Shared Power

Perpetrators who abuse emotionally tend to make light of their abuse or do not take the victims' concerns about it seriously. They also shift responsibility for their abusive behavior to the victim or other situations. Emotional abuse also entails demeaning, devaluing, marginalizing, or putting a person down. Individuals who experience emotional abuse often state that they feel "spiritually depleted."

On a sociocultural level, emotional abuse also includes negative stereotyping, or name-calling, and dates back to the origination of ethnic/racial slurs. Other abusive practices include blaming individuals for things outside their control, creating systems in which they do not gain power, questioning the competence or intelligence of ethnic minorities, and/or making them think that they are "crazy" or that they are "imagining things."

Moreover, sociocultural forms of emotional abuse include a lack of cultural competence and forcing individuals and/or communities to follow mainstream rules of behavior, dress, and conduct. Perpetrators perceive victims' cultural practices and beliefs as barbaric, sinful, inadequate, or flawed. Basically, emotional abuse means leaving individuals with a sense of systemic disfavor of their cultural, racial, and/or ethnic group. An example of an emotionally abusive situation is the case of Tomas.

Case Example: Tomas

Prominent Syndromes: Stereotyped Threat,
Alien Self Disorder

Tomas was an attractive, athletically built, conservative, brilliant gay Latino who was finding it difficult to "come out" because he realized that those around him assumed that a Latino male would be "macho" and heterosexual. Because he enjoyed playing sports of all types (including football, baseball, tennis, and hockey), he was often called a "man's man" and was subjected to hearing "gay jokes." His visit to counseling was precipitated by a company party to which he invited his partner, Bill (a local sportscaster), to attend. Throughout the evening, Tomas related that he needed to "find a woman and get laid!" After the party, Tomas found himself withdrawing from Bill and his colleagues. He also noted that he would tell "off the cuff" gay jokes himself. He even made sexually inappropriate statements about having sex with women.

One day in a meeting, Tomas stated that the work environment was perpetuating both ethnic and sexual orientation stereotypes. As he spoke, he began to tear. Afterward, rather than matters getting better, Tomas related that they got worse. People began to question his sexuality and make jokes about him being "sensitive." Others made racist/sexist remarks by calling him a "Latina." From those experiences, Tomas described an emotionally unsafe environment in which he was free neither to be gay nor Latino.

In an emotionally affirming environment, Tomas would have experienced value for his opinions, his sexuality, and his race/ethnicity. In reaction to Tomas' statements, colleagues would have seized an opportunity to reflect and make appropriate adjustments in the stereotypes and biases that were being supported by the environment. Some companies utilize staff retreats, set aside times to engage in difficult dialogues around issues of diversity, and offer "you're your mind" forums, which are open forums for staff to complain and co-create solutions to organizational problems. These are strategies for respectful dialogues about diversity. Affirming environments are defined by mutual appreciation and respect for diversity in all areas—including opinions. Finally, boundary-setting within a cultural context is taught (and accepted) while assertiveness and openness are encouraged and rewarded.

Economic Empowerment (versus Economic Abuse) as an Element of Shared Power

Economic abuse as a source of disempowerment and victimization involves placing the less-powerful partner in the position of having to ask for money, obtaining a set allowance, or having resources taken away. Partners may use money for personal pleasure or gain rather than for necessary expenses and may put the less-powerful partner in financial risk (running up large debts, not paying taxes, etc.). Finally, perpetrators try to keep the victims from getting or keeping jobs.

Economic abuse within the sociocultural context is characterized by a tendency of systems to victimize by forming economic dependencies; failing to create equitable access to wealth, opportunity, and education; and by making decisions that may not be in the best interests of minority populations. For example, for every dollar earned by a white man, white women earned 71.9 cents, black men earned 75.1 cents, black women earned 62.6 cents, Latino men earned 61.4 cents, and Latinas earned 53.9 cents, comparatively (U.S. Bureau of Labor Statistics, 1997). At that time, the median income of full-time male workers with a professional degree was approximately $70,284, while for women with the same credentials, it was only $42,602. There is also a disproportionate impact of poverty on ethnic minorities (U.S. Census Bureau, 2001b).

The most blatant examples of economic abuse occur within the workplace. Despite stereotypes of blacks, who are often depicted as "shiftless and lazy," a recent study (Economic Policy Institute, 2002) revealed that black employees spent more time at work than did white employees. From 1989 to 1998, black middle-class families logged an average of 4,278 hours of work per year—almost 500 more hours per year than white families. Although they are spending more time at work, the report noted that blacks were still finding it difficult to catch up to their white counterparts in earnings. The story of Kunle highlights these disparities.

Case Example: Kunle

Prominent Syndromes: Dangerous Minds, Aversive Racism Reaction, Fly in the Buttermilk, Invisibility Syndrome, Post-Colonization Stress Disorder

Kunle was an African immigrant with three master's degrees, who taught at the local college. He came to the United States with the dream of starting his own development company. He had an American mentor, Marcus, who advised him to change his name to "Ken" and exposed him to the process of getting subsidies and bidding for government land and grants. Eventually, Kunle obtained a contractor's license, a real estate license, and a broker's license and had amassed enough money from his savings at the university to start his own business.

Despite his attempts to "learn the ropes," Kunle stated that building specifications and requirements would be inexplicably changed for his projects and were often based on ambiguously and subjectively determined criteria. He reported that it felt as if the "rules kept changing," and he threatened to sue the development council if they continued to subject him to "double standards." Immediately, the development council voted to create a new policy of "not doing business" with people who *threatened* to sue—which automatically blocked him from building homes in one particular neighborhood.

In turn, Kunle became even more tenacious about building homes in other communities, and as business picked up, city inspectors began dropping in to take photographs of any mistakes that his construction crew made. The last straw for Kunle was when he went before the city council to finalize a subsidized land purchase only to discover that the development council had recommended that the city give the land to another company headed by a white person. After much debate, the city council approved the sale of land to Kunle, stating that they needed to support a minority-owned builder (he was the only one in the community).

Within two months, the development council told Kunle that they were not going to give the $30,000 subsidy to him (despite an affirmative city council vote) because the appraiser he had used was not a "city approved" appraiser. Consequently, the council gave the subsidy to the white builder to whom they had originally wanted to render support. Although legally Kunle had the basis for a lawsuit, he quickly discovered that "you can't fight City Hall"—especially when he didn't have the money or energy to sue and there loomed the possibility that he might not be able to "do business again" if he sued them.

Economic empowerment would translate into the building of supports rather than barriers for people like Kunle. His belief in the American dream of education and hard work was met with deleterious systemic processes designed to maintain an abuse of economic power. Kunle demonstrated personal empowerment by setting a financial goal for himself and following through with the course of action. While shared economic power existed through the support of his American mentor, cultural disempowerment simultaneously occurred in the mentor's advice to change his name to Ken.

Also, a viable model of sociocultural power-sharing would have meant that government agencies would equitably apply rules and go the extra mile to provide mentorship/support in nurturing the development of new minority-owned businesses. Other elements of economic empowerment include having incentives and economic packages that attract and retain diverse participants in projects and on staffs. The creation of economic empowerment also includes developing strategies such as cooperatives, which help groups pool resources to obtain common goals. Minimally, systems should invest in the creation of clearly defined processes that provide fair and equal opportunities for communities of color to compete for resources.

Honesty and Accountability (Restorative Justice and Restitution) (versus Intimidation) as Elements of Shared Power

Within the context of domestic violence, intimidation involves making one's partner frightened or fearful by the perpetrator's behaviors or words. Intimidation does not necessarily require the direct use of threat but instead relies on the historical threat/abuse experiences of the individual or group being threatened. Within the sociocultural context, intimidation takes the form of racial profiling (such as "driving while black"); following individuals in stores; and publicly mistreating, firing, laying off, or demeaning others who come from a specific group. The purpose of this profiling is to instill fear in them and to "keep them in their places."

Historically, multicultural communities have experienced intimidation as an abuse of power by organized groups such as children's protection services, education systems, law enforcement, the U.S. immigration department, and renegade groups such as the Ku Klux Klan. Today, "driving while black" and "shopping while black" in stores have replaced previously socially sanctioned acts of intimidation. Because abusive relationships are often characterized by stalking, it is not surprising that people of color may feel intimidated when they are followed by police officers or followed in department stores. They may also feel intimidated when they are being "watched" in the work environment so that any error will be monitored and magnified (fly in the buttermilk syndrome). As an example, perpetrators of socially based abused frequently create a lack of safety by "making an example" of someone who is vulnerable. Blacks are considered ready targets. A survey conducted by researchers at the Public Agenda Institute suggests that blacks are more likely than whites or Latinos to say they have been treated like potential shoplifters. About 44 percent of the blacks surveyed stated that they had been followed around in a store by an employee because they were suspected of shoplifting. Conversely, 30 percent of the whites who participated in the study stated that they had been followed. Interestingly, only 10 percent of the Latinos related that they had been exposed to similar circumstances (Public Agenda, 2004a).

Comparable trends were also noted in a poll conducted by the Gallup Organization (1999a, 1999b), in which 40 percent of the white Americans thought that there was police brutality in their areas, while 66 percent of the blacks thought that brutality existed in their areas. Similarly, only 6 percent of the white Americans stated that they felt police had stopped them just because of their race or ethnic backgrounds, while 42 percent of blacks said that they felt they had been stopped just because of their race or ethnic backgrounds.

The subtle nature of intimidation is not only in the behavior of the oppressor but also in the oppressor's past actions. For example, victims of sociocultural abuse of power note that intimidation works best when, by history, reputation, or previously witnessed deeds, the behaviors of the perpetrator are known. The case of Lisa illustrates this phenomenon.

Case Example: Lisa

Prominent Syndromes: Dangerous Minds, Aversive Racism Reaction, Fly in the Buttermilk, Invisibility Syndrome, Stereotyped Threat Reaction

Lisa was one of five managers at a local training institute and was one of only two blacks until an organizational restructuring process changed the team from five managers to nine. Throughout the course of the year, the newer managers formed alliances and asked Lisa to go along without inviting the other black peer, John, to join them. It was not long before the white team members tried to get Lisa to "help" John because he was not as "competent" as she. The white team members created rumors that John was not qualified to do his job and, during meetings, the managers became increasingly confrontational and disrespectful to John. Lisa reported that she felt paralyzed with fear at work and experienced symptoms of anxiety and depression. She related that after John endured months of emotional abuse, he quit. Thereafter, they began to collude against her and question her competence. In response, she started to work later and harder in order to avoid appearing incompetent or inept. She even enrolled in additional training courses so that she could "stay ahead of the game." She lost so much sleep that inevitably her work did begin to falter.

The others expressed a desire to do a team-building retreat (in an isolated wooded area) where they could engage in a "ropes" challenge course activity. Lisa said that she had an immediate negative and visceral reaction to the plan and admitted she was afraid to go on the retreat because of the vicious nature of her colleagues. She feared that she could be physically harmed (she might be pushed or even hung) while doing the "team building activity." Lisa jokingly conveyed that if something happened to her, her peers would tell the world that she "fell down." Lisa concluded by highlighting that as a southern-raised black female, she was always taught to "never go to the woods with a bunch of white people carrying rope!"

In Lisa's case, shared power would have required mutuality with all group members, even John. For example, including some group members and not others promoted distrust. One strategy for sharing power in the situation of intimidation is to first recognize that the intimidation exists. Then those in power must focus on the need for honesty and accountability. If John honestly were having problems on the job, being accountable to him (rather than getting someone to "help him out") would have been the optimal solution. Honesty and accountability also mean that when systems (or individuals) are intimidating, the organization takes the necessary action to make reparations for any damage done. Thus, to regain balance and mutuality in their relationships, the treatments of Lisa and John would have possibly required that team members (and especially management staff) offer an apology in front of the group and/or financial reparations to them.

Sharing power also dictates that consensus-based, outcome-driven strategies for shared communication and decision-making be used. Using shared governance and consensus-driven models requires that an agreement (at least in principle) be shared by each group member, or the decision does not pass. Also, systems could purport the use of management "safe zones." Safe zones allow staff an opportunity to identify problems and seek solutions with managers who are skilled in conflict negotiations and bias-reduction strategies. Such models empower each person to comment in a safe manner (without fear of retaliation). Shared power solutions dictate responsive systems that will allow their members to honestly and safely complain about the intimidating and hurtful outcomes of discriminatory behaviors. Another institutional strategy for sharing power and reducing intimidation is to create evaluations and complaint-investigatory systems that do not leave individuals and groups vulnerable. Following these suggested techniques will give oppressed groups a chance to be heard without fear of retaliation.

Respect for Physical Health and Sexuality (versus Physical/Sexual Abuse) as an Element of Shared Power

Many relationships involve acts of physical harm, such as using weapons, denying access to health/medical care resources, or forcing the individual to use drugs or alcohol. Physical abuse also includes violence perpetrated on vulnerable communities via disparate treatment by society or its agents, such as law enforcement, courts, or healthcare systems. Within the context of physical health, health disparities are an example of systemic abuse. A health disparity is a population-specific difference in the presence of disease, health outcomes, or access to care (U.S. Department of Health and Human Services, 2000). One example is the variance in the life expectancies between blacks and whites. Specifically, black men live an average of 7.4 years less than white men (64.9 years to 72.3 years), black women live an average of 5.5

years less than white women (73.4 years to 78.9 years), and the black infant mortality rate is double that of whites.

Also, the U.S. Census Bureau (2001a) reported that of those without public or private health insurance, Latinos represented the highest group (32 percent). This figure was followed by blacks (18.5 percent) and Asian/Pacific Islanders (18 percent). Comparatively, only 12.9 percent of whites were without public or private health insurance. This disparate access to medical care/insurance is a core indicator of discrimination in sociocultural health practices.

Additional concerns are noted in the area of mental health. Data (U.S. Department of Health and Human Services, 2001) suggest that people of color are disproportionately impacted by disparities in the diagnosis and treatment of mental health concerns. Specifically, these populations wait until their conditions are more severe before seeking treatment. Yet, when they do access treatment, the treatment quality and procedures that they receive are poor compared to the services provided to the dominant culture. Another issue involves barriers faced by ethnically diverse clients in locating providers from culturally similar backgrounds. This area is impacted by industry barriers (such as low graduate school/internship admissions of minority candidates) as well as managed care barriers, such as requiring practitioners to be licensed for five years before they are eligible to apply for reimbursement of services as network providers.

Finally, the recidivism associated with drug-related crimes (due to limited treatment options) suggests that society is economically invested in the "prison industrial complex" as a means of obtaining financial gain through the continued perpetration of drug-related criminal behavior. Likewise, unchecked violence results in higher rates of homicide and crime victimization among black and other multicultural communities (Bachman, 1994).

Sexual abuse also constitutes a problem and involves acts of harassment, assault, and even practices around reproductive rights. According to a study conducted by the National Victim Center (1992), 1.3 women (age eighteen and over) in the United States are forcibly raped each minute. Vulnerable populations such as developmentally disabled adults and youth are the most frequent victims of sexual assault (Disabled Women's Network, 1991). Women of color are disproportionately impacted by sexual assault and other violent crimes (U.S. Bureau of Justice Statistics, 2001). Most important, when women report crimes of sexual assault, the veracity of their claims is often questioned and victims are portrayed as "asking for it."

In turn, sexual harassment is the experience of unwelcome sexual advances, requests for sexual favors, and other verbal or physical conduct of a sexual nature when submission to or rejection of this conduct explicitly or implicitly affects an individual's employment, performance, or safety within a specified environment. Studies (U.S. Bureau of Labor Statistics, 1994) suggest anywhere between 40 and 70 percent of women have experienced sexual harassment in the workplace. Finally, the incidence of sexual harassment appears to be impacting children at younger ages (U.S. Department of Justice, 1998), such that four out of five students (81 percent) have experienced some form of sexual harassment during their school years, with teachers being the primary perpetrators (Timmerman, 2003). Thus, women (and especially young women of color) grow up with an experience of marginalization of their bodies, physical health, and a minimization of their sexual vulnerabilities within a sociocultural context that is patriarchal, race-biased, and often predatory in nature. Sexual harassment is highlighted in the case of Brandi, whose organizational culture "set up" its female employees by emphasizing that "the customer is always right."

Case Example: Brandi

Prominent Syndromes: Stereotyped Threat, Alien Self Disorder

Brandi was a young, attractive, ambitious, and married black female claims adjuster at a leading insurance company. Brandi prided herself on being a "customer focused" insurance adjuster and, in fact, was often commended for her expertise and company loyalty. She worked at a "conservative company" and consequently went through multiple gyrations to make sure that she "fit in." For example, when some of the black employees wanted to celebrate Black History Month by wearing African clothes and wearing braids, Brandi was among the first to say that the company would "frown" on their efforts. She even refused to eat fried chicken or watermelon (her favorite food) at work for fear of being stereotyped.

Brandi's visit to counseling was precipitated by an incident that involved one of her customers, a middle-aged white male, who had been in a serious car accident. Brandi related that she had visited the customer at the hospital and had rendered an estimate of damages for his automobile, but because of the physical nature of his injuries, the claim could not be settled. Meanwhile, the customer called her several times a day asking her to meet him for "lunch or dinner" in order to discuss the processing of his claim.

Brandi approached her supervisor and requested permission to give the claim to someone else, although she had already completed a majority of the work. Her male supervisor defined her request as an attempt to "pass the buck" to someone else. After a few days, Brandi completed processing the claim and invited the man into the office to pick up his check early the next morning. When he arrived, however, it was close to noon and there were only a few employees in the work area. Brandi related that the office had open cubicles, so she invited him to sit at her desk to complete the paperwork. When she turned around, he grabbed her, said "I've always liked brown sugar," pinned her against the wall, and kissed her on the mouth. Brandi stated that she immediately pushed him away and told him that if he wanted his check, he would have to wait for it in the lobby.

Brandi described feeling shocked, disgusted, angry, and terrified at the same time. She described feeling betrayed by her company—which gave its clients more power than its employees. Brandi informed her supervisor about the incident, but nothing was done. Her supervisor told her that he was sorry that such a thing had happened to her, but suggested that she should not have met "the insured" at the lunch hour. Brandi felt that she was being blamed for the incident and believed that if she were to pursue any further discussion of the matter, she might run the risk of losing her job or receiving a poor rating on her annual evaluation. After the incident, she missed several days of work with symptoms of insomnia, anxiety attacks, depression, and flashbacks of the situation.

Brandi's story is not an isolated one. The U.S. Bureau of Labor (1997) has estimated that American business loses about $1 billion annually from absenteeism, low morale, and new employee training and replacement costs due to sexual harassment. This figure does not include judgments in civil court cases. These statistics also reveal that 31 percent of the female workers claimed to have been harassed at work, yet 62 percent of those women, like Brandi, took no action.

Shared power assures that people, especially women, do not have to endure sexual harassment/abuse/assault. In situations such as Brandi's, organizations should have policies that protect employees and assist them (rather than blaming them) in seeking legal remedies for sexual harassment by *clients* as well as co-workers or supervisory staff. In an environment that respected sexuality and physical health, it would be demonstrated through policies and practices that provided individuals and groups with equal access to safety and physical/mental health services, especially culturally competent and culturally specific services, if requested.

Shared social power would also promote physical and sexual health through system-based incentives for creating wellness and safety. For example, a strategy for shared power may be for tax incentives to be given to any agency or system that provides reduced insurance premiums for persons who participate in safety and wellness programs (such as self-defense, HIV awareness programs, assertiveness training, weight loss/stress management, exercise club memberships, etc.).

Shared Value and Responsibility for All Children (versus Using Children) as an Element of Shared Power

Children are among the most vulnerable of populations when it comes to abusive relationships. The National Clearinghouse on Child Abuse and Neglect Information (2003) revealed that approximately 903,000 children were found to be victims of child maltreatment, including various forms of neglect, physical abuse, sexual abuse, and psychological maltreatment. Half of all victims were white (50 percent), one quarter (25 percent) were black, and 15 percent were Latino. Native Americans and Alaska Natives accounted for 2 percent of victims, and Asian/Pacific Islanders accounted for 1 percent of victims—a majority of whom were abused by their parents.

Evidence (U.S. Census Bureau, 2002) supports the contention that our society is simply not taking care of its children in the manner that it once did. A larger group of our children are being raised by others (such as grandparents, relatives, or social service systems, including foster care or residential facilities). In 1960, only 3.2 percent of children were being raised by "others"; by 2000, an alarming 22.4 percent of children were. Children of color are particularly vulnerable, as they are also disproportionately represented in special education, juvenile justice, and foster care systems (U.S. Department of Health and Human Services, 2001). Specifically, they spend longer times in those systems with the least amount of support. The author refers to this course of failure as the "jail track" and views it as a sociocultural conditioning process to prepare children, especially black males, to be institutionalized. Other scholars agree (Kunjufu, 1990; Akbar, 1981). On a sociocultural level, children of color are marginalized and devalued. Their risks, worth, and needs become invisible to the systems around them, and consequently they become vulnerable to predatory adults. This was the case of Justin and Latisha.

Case Example: Justin and Latisha

Prominent Syndromes: Invisibility Syndrome, (Young) Man Enough

The story of nine-year-old Justin and his seven-year-old sister Latisha describes the process of systemically using children for the service of financial gain. The black children got into the foster care system because their mother's parental rights had been terminated due to her continued use of drugs. Their father was incarcerated for possession of crack cocaine. Justin was belligerent, depressed, and often uncontrollable. His sister had been sexually abused on at least three occasions at two different foster care placements and was prone to acting out sexually. After going through many residential treatment and placement facilities, Justin and Latisha were placed together in the home of white foster parents and their children.

During the initial months after the children had been placed with the foster parents, numerous incidents of impulsive outbursts, violence, and sexual acting out were heaped upon the biological children of the foster parents. This supports the notion that foster care can have not only a negative impact on the children being placed, but it can also have a deleterious effect on the children already in the home. Nonetheless, after almost one year in the residence, the foster children began to display decreased incidents of misbehavior. Problems were noted when, despite the fact that the children had been *improving* in their display of problems, the parents approached the mental health provider to seek documentation that the foster children had developed "higher needs than expected" so that the family could receive additional funding for their care. When the provider questioned their request, the family terminated therapy and went to see another therapist, who gave them the documentation. Within two months of receiving the increased funds, the family (without the foster children) took a two-week trip to Disneyland and placed Justin and Latisha in respite care.

Within a model of shared power, the foster parents would have treated the foster children as if they were their own children. Reasonably, respite may have been needed for the family, but to go to Disneyland and leave a seven-year-old and a nine-year-old in a respite facility was indicative of emotional abuse. Co-perpetrators were the mental health workers, who supported the abuse of power without argument. In the case of children, suggestions for sharing power would include support groups, training, and guidelines for biological and foster parents as well as forming advisory boards of parents, foster parents, and children who are/were formerly "products" of those systems. Asking these individuals to participate in focus groups, form advisory boards, and set new policies can create opportunities for system improvement and client empowerment. Also, children like Justin and Latisha could have benefited from community engagement, such as the use of community elders through church programs, mentor programs, and black community connections that would facilitate the development of cultural influences and values for cross-cultural families.

Further, shared-power models would see the mutual value of all children, and adult participants and systems of care would commit equally to outcomes that would benefit them. Strategies such as family group conferencing models would be used to empower families in formulating their own solutions (Robinson, 1996).

Non-Threatening Behavior and Creating Safety for Challenge and Risks (versus Using Coercion and Threats) as an Element of Shared Power

Threats always contain an element of psychological violence and are characterized as implying intent to inflict harm and fear in order to control the other person (Burman, Margolin, & John, 1993). Abusive dominance in domestic violence situations can also involve forcing the subordinate party to drop legal charges or perform illegal acts, stalking, threatening to stop economic support, leaving, taking the children, threatening to commit suicide, and reporting the person to an authority whom they may fear (such as a children's protection agency, or a welfare or immigration bureau). Threats often involve "if-then" contingencies, ultimatums, and sanctions. They may also involve the physical removal of a valued item, person, resource, or opportunity.

On a sociocultural level, groups of individuals may experience similar oppressive acts by the society in which they live. Oppressive systems are designed to sustain socially sanctioned threats. Often these systems are devoted to controlling the availability of resources (such as student financial aid, Social Security, or welfare-to-work programs) or persons (such as the criminal justice system or child protection/foster care). For example, an if-then contingency statement may work as follows: "If you are drug-addicted and get caught using drugs, your children will be removed and placed in foster care—and you may never see them again." As an example, Minnesota parents with children under six years old have only six months to get their children back before parental rights are terminated and the children are put up by the state for adoption. Therefore, if an isolated parent is drug-addicted and treatment takes more than six months (and it usually does), then she/he is bound to lose custody of a child.

Other sociocultural sectors (such as schools, police, social services, medical, and mental health) appear threatening to children and their parents because of their legal mandates to report to an authority whom the parent or child may fear. As an example, immigrants become afraid of deportation when they hear questions such as, "How many people live in the house and what are their names?" This question appears on most forms and elicits apprehension when clients are unsure of the legal status of their friends or family members. The contingency statement for this issue is, "If I, as a provider, even suspect that you have an illegal immigrant in your home, then I will have to report you." Therefore, it is important to know that *there is a high potential for abuse among institutions that provide support to persons from vulnerable populations.* When describing the use of threats and coercion, few case illustrations can be as clearly articulated as the case of Jackie, her husband Jonathan, and her son, Darius.

Case Example: Darius

Prominent Syndromes: Invisibility Syndrome, (Young) Man Enough, Post-Traumatic Stress Disorder

Darius was an eleven-year-old black boy with a contagious laughter and beautiful smile. He had a younger brother, Michael, who was eight. Darius's schoolteachers often commented on how mannerly, soft-spoken, and hardworking he was. Jonathan, his father, had recently secured a job as a mail handler. His wife, Jackie, worked (at $18 per hour) as a personal care attendant for an elderly woman who lived down the street from the family's home.

One day, Darius and his father were driving to the mall when two men started shooting at each other (in an apparent a gang fight).

Darius's father reached over to grab his son to press him lower into the seat. About that time, a gunshot hit Jonathan in the head and he died instantly. Within three to six months after his father's death, Darius began to show marked behavior changes in school, including poor concentration, angry outbursts, and "talking back." He rarely completed his homework, began to get into fights, and was even expelled one day for carrying a sharpened potato peeler to school.

While school authorities seemed to be concerned, at no point did anyone refer Darius for therapy or counseling. It was not until one night when the police picked him up (because he was in the park after curfew) that Darius and his family were even approached about getting mental health support. The evening the officers took Darius home, they informed his mother that if they caught him that late in the park again, he would be arrested. She brought Darius to therapy immediately, but within two weeks, he had slipped out of the house through the window and was at the park again. The police picked him up, called children's protective services, and Darius's mother was placed on a "case plan."

Part of the case plan was for the case manager to make home visits. Consequently, Jackie asked the case manager to schedule the visits after she got home from or work (she worked from 7 a.m. until 3 p.m. each day). Yet, the case manager repeatedly scheduled appointments during the times that Jackie was supposed to be at work, and when the case manager did come to the house, she was consistently one to two hours late. Eventually, Jackie began to leave for work even if she knew that she had an appointment with the caseworker. The case manager told Jackie that if she missed another appointment, then she would remove Darius and Michael (her other son) from the home. Jackie then began to call in "late" at her job in order to wait for the social worker—instead of risking the loss of her children. This pattern of calling in late continued until Jackie was fired. Afterward, she couldn't find another job, went on welfare, and never missed another appointment with the caseworker.

Shared social power in this instance would have consisted of creating a non-threatening environment that was safe for challenge and risk. Shared power would have meant that Jackie was in a partnership with the social worker for the benefit of the parent. There would have been no need for threats, and there would have been a mutual respect for the client's time as well as the empathic awareness of the family's trauma around the death of the father. Further, school personnel, police, and social service agencies would have worked collaboratively when the crime was committed to proactively set up culturally competent trauma support and follow-up services for the family. Finally, shared power in this case would have meant that participants in each system rallied around supporting Darius and his family.

Equal Opportunity (Dismantling Privilege through Fairness versus Using White, Male, or American Privilege) as an Element of Shared Power

In an abusive intimate relationship, male privilege involves treating the female partner like a servant. In these situations, the male partner makes all the big decisions without respect for input from the female partner. Such relationships are characterized by communication patterns of commands and directives. Women who participate in these relationships often state that their partners tell them what they must do and that they are expected to comply without question. Within these contexts, the dominant partner has the authority to define the balance of power in the relationship as well as the roles that each partner will assume.

On a more systemic level, however, the use of privilege both includes and supersedes gender. From a sociocultural perspective, the impact of privilege is extended to gender (male dominated), race (white dominated), and nationality (American dominated). In her article "White Privilege: Unpacking the Invisible Knapsack" (1988), Peggy McIntosh eloquently describes her experience of white privilege by saying that "white skin in the United States opens many doors for whites whether or not we approve of the way dominance has been conferred on us." White privileges exist in many systems and are most notable in the ways in which individuals and groups access those systems for support or inclusion.

An excellent example of the continued existence of white and male privilege is eloquently presented in an analysis conducted by University of Cincinnati sociologist David J. Maume (1999). Maume confirmed in his study that white males enjoyed the benefits of a so-called "glass escalator" that enhanced their career mobility in female-dominated professions. David J. Maume Jr. (Maume, 1999) analyzed work histories in female-dominated fields (1981–1987) and found that 44 percent of men had been promoted after twelve years on the job, in contrast to just 15 percent of white women, 7 percent of black women, and 17 percent of black men.

While most Americans are familiar with "white" and "male" privilege as sources of power abuses, being able to recognize the sociocultural component of power abuse in terms of "American privilege" requires a paradigm shift for most Americans. Americans rarely recognize how they abuse power internationally through their practices and assumptions. Take, for example, the tendency of Americans to travel abroad and boldly ask (in any country) whether anybody speaks English. We take for granted that the rest of the world has to learn our language, our customs, and our geography in order to conduct business with us. We also make the assumption that people will accommodate our tastes in food, clothing, and other commercial products. As an illustration, note that it is highly unlikely that an American will visit France, Germany, Italy, or Hong Kong and not be able to locate a McDonald's in order to get a "decent burger and some fries."

Some individuals, such as Senator Joseph Biden (Preston, 2003), contend that American privilege is demonstrated by our government's policy of "pre-emption" when it comes to invading a country that "could" have had weapons of mass destruction. America has had the privilege of possessing the most resources and largest military arsenal in the world. Consequently, when world events that impact our national interests are out of kilter, we have the "privilege" of doing something about them.

American privilege is also seen in our responses to immigrants who come to our country. Besides expecting immigrants to engage in "culture swapping," we also expect them to speak without "foreign accents," and we become frustrated with people whose primary language is not English. At times, Americans do not even attempt to pronounce foreign names, and they probably feel much more comfortable when immigrants change their names from Juan to Joe, Po-Chu to Polly, etc.

In a report titled *Now That I'm Here: What America's Immigrants Have to Say about Life in the U.S. Today* (Farkas, Duffett, Johnson, Moye, & Vine, 2003), the authors describe the sentiments of American immigrants based on a survey funded by the Carnegie Corporation of New York. In the survey, about 60 percent of the immigrants said that there was at least some anti-immigrant discrimination in the United States, while approximately 30 percent of the immigrants conveyed that they had personally experienced discrimination themselves.

Moreover, all Americans share American privilege—a construct that is especially notable for people of color. As an example, this

Toolbox for Change I

For	Images/perceptions	Strategies for change
Individuals	Isolation	*Develop shared power through community inclusion processes:* Avoid "divide and conquer" tactics. Focus on team-based projects. Get mentors. Join professional organizations. Use family, friends, and colleagues outside the office. Join social and professional organizations (book clubs, and so forth).
Community	Isolation	*Develop shared power through community inclusion processes:* Sewing circles. Elder boards. Mentoring programs. Professional networking meetings (first Fridays). Community seminars of corporate survival.
Practitioners/ educators	Isolation	*Develop shared power through community inclusion processes:* Support groups. Relationship-building skills. Corporate support and team building. Minority professionals support group. Self-care groups/workshops.
Individuals	Emotional abuse	*Develop shared power through emotional affirmation and respect for diversity:* Learn boundary-setting skills. Use assertiveness skills. Keep journals (work and personal).
Community	Emotional abuse	*Develop shared power through emotional affirmation and respect for diversity:* Show respect for diversity in all areas including opinions.

		Celebrate culture-awareness days.
		Offer "free your mind" forums.
		Offer "Set-aside" times to discuss cultural issues.
		Provide cultural sensitivity training and policy development support through community based agencies.
Practitioners/ educators	Emotional abuse	*Develop shared power through emotional affirmation and respect for diversity:*
		Teach affirmation skills.
		Perform affirmation rituals.
		Offer seminars on personal talents/gifts.
		Provide anger management support.
		Provide stress management support.
		Assertiveness skills support.
		Conflict management support.
Individuals	Intimidation	*Develop shared power through*
		Honesty and accountability (restorative justice and restitution):
		Don't buy into "divide and conquer" strategies.
		Be prepared to be "cautiously optimistic" when attempts are made at reconciliation.
		Seek support from counselors or others who have lived through similar circumstances.
		Be assertive.
Community	Intimidation	*Develop shared power through*
		Honesty and accountability (restorative justice and restitution):
		Do *not* leave individuals vulnerable.
		Restorative justice (apologize, pay restitution and reparations).
		Evaluation systems that share feedback.
		Oversight committees.
		Be honest and accountable for past and perpetuation of abuses.

continued

Toolbox for Change I (continued)

For	Images/perceptions	Strategies for change
Practitioners/ educators	Intimidation	Establish "safe zones."
		Use shared governance and consensus.
		Create evaluation and complaint systems.
		Develop shared power through
		Honesty and accountability (restorative justice and restitution):
		Teach communication skills.
		Teach consensus-building skills.
		Provide anger management support.
Individuals	Sexual and physical abuse	*Develop shared power through*
		Respect for physical health and respect for sexuality:
		Get educated on sexuality and disease prevention.
		Educate on self-defense and crime prevention.
		Learn assertiveness and communication skills.
		Learn stress management.
		Create a healthy lifestyle for yourself.
		Get counseling if victimized or to assist with physical management of diseases.
Community	Sexual and physical abuse	*Develop shared power through*
		Respect for physical health and respect for sexuality:
		Provide women's support groups.
		Rites of passage for girls and boys.
		Sexual harassment/abuse prevention services.
		Public service announcements on wellness.
		Provide system-based incentives for wellness.
		Provide forums on health and wellness.
		Provide forums on sexuality and gender issues.

Practitioners/ educators	Sexual and physical abuse	*Develop shared power through* Respect for physical health and respect for sexuality: Groups and workshops on sexuality and sexual health. Sexual harassment/abuse counseling. Counseling for families (married or not, straight or not). Provide support for physical illnesses and behavior change.
Individuals	Threats	*Develop shared power through* Non-threatening environments and creating safety for challenge and risks. Learn communication skills (especially assertiveness skills). Learn conflict mediation and negotiation skills. Engage in self-care. Join social support groups. Volunteer to advocate for systems change. Don't be afraid to be political. Learn stress-management skills.
Community	Threats	*Develop shared power through* Non-threatening environments and creating safety for challenge and risks. Create non-threatening environments safe for challenge and risks. Be aware of high potential for power abuses. Partner with non-dominant community members through a mutually determined agenda. Proactively support communities in cross-cultural ways. Create community-run oversight committees and advisory boards. Keep data on offenses by group (race, gender, ethnicity, and so forth). Provide community issues forums. Create administrative safe zones for complaints. Reward courage by acknowledging risks.

continued

191

Toolbox for Change I (continued)

For	Images/perceptions	Strategies for change
		Resolve issues and provide feedback openly to the individual, community, or group offended.
Practitioners/ educators	Threats	Rally around victims.
		Develop shared power through
		Non-threatening environments and creating safety for challenge and risks.
		Teach alliance-building skills.
		Teach cultural competence.
		Teach cultural sensitivity.
		Develop trauma response teams to assist children and families when deaths or injuries occur due to violence.
Individuals	Economic abuse	*Develop shared power through economic empowerment:*
		Set financial and business goals (that is, getting rid of debts).
		Seek money management and financial planning support.
		Seek mentorship; don't give up.
		Set aside funds for legal and technical assistance.
		Seek strategies to support your business (grants, subsidies, loans, and fellowships).
		Partner with others to pool resources.
Community	Economic abuse	*Develop shared power through economic empowerment:*
		Small business mentorship programs.
		Provide legal services and seminars for individuals and groups on advocacy and fair wage support issues.
		Provide legal support to small businesses.
		Establish clear, consistently applied rules for engagement.
		Financial/business planning courses.

	Community oversight and accountability groups for business processes/contracts.
	Economic packages to attract and retain minority staff and program participants.
	Development of cooperatives.
	Pay people the same for the same work offended.
	Rally around victims.
	Provide free credit and debt counseling to community members.
	Provide free money management semiars and support services to families seeking support.
Practitioners/ educators	Economic abuse	*Develop shared power through economic empowerment by providing therapeutic support and training in the following areas:*
	Business etiquette and social skills.
	Negotiations.
	Money management.
	Stress/anger management skills.
	Emotional support for economically abused individuals and communities.
Individuals	Using children	*Develop shared power through shared value and responsibility for children:*
	Participate in mentor programs.
	Focus on the development of pro-social, character-based skills.
	Develop coping and self-responsibility skills.
	Develop hobbies (arts, sciences, and so forth).
	Focus on school success.
	Learn about wellness and safety.
	Become a peer counselor.
	Join local activities (rites of passage, drumming, dance, scouts, and so forth).
	Learn refusal skills.

continued

Toolbox for Change I (continued)

For	Images/perceptions	Strategies for change
Community	Using children	*Partner with others to pool resources:* Develop shared power through shared value and responsibility for children. Adopt community values for placing children within the cultural contexts of families and relations. Use community-based supports such as respite and family group conferencing, church elders, and so forth. Treat all children as if they were *your* children. Provide respite support and counseling services for families impacted by foster care. Create user-based advisory boards and oversight committees. Offer community focus groups on child-based needs. Provide support for foster parents. Create safe zones for children.
Practitioners/ educators	Using children	*Develop shared power through shared value and responsibility for children:* Provide in-school counseling and life skill education/support. Address grief/loss issues. Provide culturally competent interventions in outreach and therapeutic support. Provide outreach to systems to assure developmentally appropriate interventions. Teach emotional regulation. Teach children and caregivers about safety. Teach conflict mediation.
Individuals	Using white, male, or American privilege	*Develop shared power by dismantling privilege through fairness and equal access to opportunity:*

		Make a commitment to be an advocate for change.
		Personally invest in looking at personal (and changing) biases and behaviors.
		Speak against abuses of power when you can (be assertive).
		Do the right thing; become aware of privilege and its abuses in your environment.
		Seek cultural guides to assist you in navigating through the issues of white, male, or American privilege.
Community	Using white, male, or American privilege	*Develop shared power by dismantling privilege through fairness and equal access to opportunity:*
		Establish ways to share power on domestic and international levels (through such common agendas as the universal rights of children).
		Increase accountability and access by looking at systemic disparities in health, education, arrests, service delivery, and so forth.
		Share power by within-group methods such as consensus and shared governance.
		Advertise job openings and avoid promotions based on "rearrangements of existing staff."
		Create an affirmative hiring and promotions plan to prepare under-represented staff for leadership.
		Address issues of political advocacy and systems change.
		Dismantle privilege through fair and equal access.
Practitioners/ educators	Using white, male, or American privilege	Teach individuals and groups how to "undo racism."
		Teach cultural diversity and sensitivity.
		Teach and practice culturally competent strategies of intervention, including empowerment strategies, positive self-talk, and problem-solving skill-building.

Toolbox for Change II

Abuse of power	Shared power strategies for	Individual strategies	Community-based strategies	Practitioner/educator strategies
Isolation	Community inclusion	Avoid "divide and conquer" tactics. Focus on team-based projects. Get mentors. Join professional organizations. Use family, friends, and colleagues outside the office. Join social and professional organizations (book clubs, and so forth).	Sewing circles. Elder boards. Mentoring programs. Professional networking meetings (first Fridays). Community seminars of corporate survival.	Support groups. Relationship-building skills. Corporate support and team building. Minority professionals support group. Self-care groups/ workshops.
Emotional abuse	Emotional affirmation and respect for diversity	Learn boundary-setting skills. Use assertiveness skills. Keep journals (work and personal).	Respect for diversity in all areas including opinions. Celebrate culture-awareness days. Free your mind forums. Set-aside times. Cultural sensitivity training and policies.	Teaching affirmation skills. Affirmation rituals. Seminars on personal talents/gifts. Anger management. Stress management. Assertiveness skills. Conflict management.

Intimidation Honesty and accountability (restorative justice and restitution)	Don't buy into "divide and conquer" strategies. Be prepared to be "cautiously optimistic" when attempts are made at reconciliation. Seek support from counselors or others who have lived through similar circumstances. Be assertive.	Do *not* leave individuals vulnerable. Restorative justice (apologize, pay restitution and reparations). Evaluation systems that share feedback. Oversight committees. Be honest and accountable for past and perpetuation of abuses. Establish "safe zones." Use shared governance and consensus. Create evaluation and complaint systems.	Teach communication skills. Teach consensus-building skills. Provide anger management support.
Sexual abuses Respect for physical health and respect for sexuality	Get educated on sexuality and disease prevention. Educate on self-defense and crime prevention. Learn assertiveness and communication skills. Learn stress management. Create a healthy lifestyle for yourself. Get counseling if victimized or to assist with physical management of diseases.	Women's groups. Rites of passage for girls and boys Sexual harassment/abuse. Public service announcements on wellness. Provide system-based incentives for wellness. Provide forums on health and wellness. Provide forums on sexuality and gender issues.	Groups and workshops on sexuality and sexual health. Sexual harassment/abuse counseling. Counseling for families (married or not, straight or not). Provide support for physical illnesses and behavior change.

continued

Toolbox for Change II (continued)

Abuse of power	Shared power strategies for	Individual strategies	Community-based strategies	Practitioner/educator strategies
Threats	Non-threatening environments Creating safety for challenge and risks	Learn communication skills (especially assertiveness skills). Learn conflict mediation and negotiation skills. Engage in self-care. Join social support groups. Volunteer to advocate for systems change. Don't be afraid to be political. Learn stress-management skills.	Create non-threatening environments safe for challenge and risks. Be aware of high potential for power abuses. Partner with non-dominant community members through a mutually determined agenda. Proactively support communities in cross-cultural ways. Create community-run oversight committees and advisory boards. Keep data on offenses by group (race, gender, ethnicity, and so forth). Provide community issues forums. Create administrative safe zones for complaints. Reward courage by acknowledging risks. Resolve issues and provide feedback openly to the individual, community, or group offended. Rally around victims.	Teach alliance-building skills. Teach cultural competence. Teach cultural sensitivity. Develop trauma response teams to assist children and families when deaths or injuries occur due to violence.

Economic abuse	Economic empowerment	Set financial and business goals. Seek money management and financial planning support. Seek mentorship. Don't give up. Set aside funds for legal and technical assistance. Seek strategies to support your business (grants, subsidies, loans, and fellowships). Partner with others to pool resources.	Small business mentorship programs. Legal services for small businesses. Establish clear, consistently applied rules for engagement. Financial/business planning courses. Community oversight and accountability groups for business processes/contracts. Economic packages to attract and retain minority staff and program participants. Development of cooperatives. Pay people the same for the same work.	Business etiquette and social skills. Negotiations. Money management Provide stress/anger management skills. Provide emotional support for economically abused individuals and communities.

continued

Toolbox for Change II (continued)

Abuse of power	Shared power strategies for	Individual strategies	Community-based strategies	Practitioner/educator strategies
Using children	Shared value and responsibility for children	Participate in mentor programs.	Adopt community values for placing children within the cultural contexts of families and relations.	Provide in-school counseling and life skill education/support.
		Focus on the development of pro-social, character-based skills.	Use community-based supports such as respite and family group conferencing, church elders, and so forth.	Address grief/loss issues.
		Develop coping and self-responsibility skills.	Treat all children as if they were *your* children.	Provide culturally competent interventions in outreach and therapeutic support.
		Develop hobbies (arts, sciences, and so forth).	Provide respite support and counseling services for families impacted by foster care.	Provide outreach to systems to assure developmentally appropriate interventions.
		Focus on school success.	Create user-based advisory boards and oversight committees.	
		Learn about wellness and safety.	Offer community focus groups on child-based needs.	Teach emotional regulation.
		Become a peer counselor.	Provide support for foster parents.	Teach children and caregivers about safety.
		Join local activities (rites of passage, drumming, dance, scouts, etc.).	Create safe zones for children.	Teach conflict mediation.
		Learn refusal skills.		

Using white, male, or American privilege	Dismantling privilege through fairness			
		Make a commitment to be an advocate for change. Personally invest in looking at personal (and changing) biases and behaviors. Speak against abuses of power when you can (be assertive). Do the right thing. Become aware of privilege and its abuses in your environment. Seek cultural guides to assist you in navigating through the issues of white, male, or American privilege.	Establish ways to share power on domestic and international levels (through such common agendas as the universal rights of children). Increase accountability and access by looking at systemic disparities in health, education, arrests, service delivery, and so forth. Share power by within-group methods such as consensus and shared governance. Advertise job openings and avoid promotions based on "rearrangements of existing staff." Create an affirmative hiring and promotions plan to prepare under-represented staff for leadership. Address issues of political advocacy and systems change. Dismantle privilege through fair and equal access.	Teach individuals and groups how to "undo racism." Teach cultural diversity and sensitivity. Teach and practice culturally competent strategies of intervention, including empowerment strategies, positive self-talk, and problem-solving skill-building.

author never thought of herself as "American" in terms of her primary identity until the September 11 bombing of the World Trade Center towers. It was after that event that the author realized that privilege was an experience of power that was unconscious and un-earned, yet bestowed upon an individual or group of individuals simply because of their group affiliation. More important, privilege is not recognized until it is lost or threatened. The construct of American privilege firmly places people of color who have traditionally been outside the group (on a domestic level) in a position within the group when the perspective is an international/global one. It was not until 9/11 that it became clear to most individuals who possessed American passports that regardless of one's race, creed, color, religion, sexual orientation, or gender, it is now primarily one's nationality and place of residence that can elicit worldwide biases—an experience to which we had never been subjected in modern times. Americans can no longer enjoy the privilege of traveling or living without fear.

Therefore, efforts to share power must occur both in domestic and international policymaking arenas. We are challenged to eradicate racist, sexist, self-serving policies in exchange for mutuality, empathy, courage, and connection. Sharing power on an international level will require that we first learn to share power with each other as individu-als, as communities, and as a nation. Models of sharing on a national level may dictate that groups assure that they have equal access to policymakers via campaign finance reform.

Other power-sharing strategies on national and international levels will require the creation and maintenance of common national and international agendas such as signing (and adhering to) practices that limit the exploitation of children (such as the document on the uni-versal rights of children). Power-sharing requires responsibility. It also requires that individuals have equal access to opportunities so that rates of promotion, pay, arrests, etc. do not disproportionately impact specific groups. Thus, whether we are white, male, or American, "doing the right thing" requires that we open systems up so that ev-eryone has access and opportunity to participate. Systems such as ed-ucation, health care, child care, etc. will require that we dismantle privilege through fairness.

CONCLUSION

This chapter compared domestic violence/abuse to the experience of people of color in terms of the sociocultural abuse that they have experienced in the United States of America. Using a sociocultural model of abuse of power and control to illustrate systems-based abuses, the chapter introduced readers to eight elements of abuse of power within a social context (isolation; emotional abuse; economic abuse; intimidation; sexual abuse; using children; use of threats; and using white, male, or American privilege). Further, this chapter explored multiple models of "oppressive reactive syndromes." It introduced the concept of developing a model of shared power and control that relied upon mutuality, empathy, and empowerment through the implementation of eight core elements (community inclusion; emotional affirmation and respect for diversity; economic empowerment; honesty and accountability/restorative justice and restitution; respect for physical health and sexuality; shared value and responsibility for children; creating safety for challenge and risks; and equal opportunity/dismantling privilege through fairness and access). It is hoped that through the practice of shared power and control, connections can be strengthened and the harmful impacts of discrimination and prejudice can be minimized.

REFERENCES

Akbar, N. (1981). Mental disorder among African-Americans. *Black Books Bulletin, 7*(2), 18–25.

Bachman, R. (1994). *Violence against women: A national crime victimization survey report.* Publication no. NCJ-145325. Washington, DC: Department of Justice.

Bourhis, R. Y. (1994). Power, gender, and intergroup discrimination: Some minimal group experiments. In M. P. Zanna & J. M. Olson (Eds.), *The psychology of prejudice: The Ontario symposium* (Vol. 7). Mahwah, NJ: Lawrence Erlbaum Associates, Inc.

Bourhis, R. Y., Sachdev, I., & Gagnon, A. (1994). Intergroup research with the Tajfel matrices: Methodological notes. In M. P. Zanna & J. M. Olson (Eds.), *The psychology of prejudice: The Ontario symposium* (Vol. 7). Mahwah, NJ: Lawrence Erlbaum Associates, Inc.

Bowen, M. (1978). *Family therapy in clinical practice.* New York: Jason Aronson.

Bowlby, J. (1988). Developmental psychiatry comes of age. *American Journal of Psychiatry, 145,* 1–10.

Burman, B., Margolin, G., & John, R. S. (1993). America's angriest home videos: Behavioral contingencies observed in home reenactments of marital conflict (Special section: Couples and couple therapy). *Journal of Consulting & Clinical Psychology, 61*(1), 28–39.

Disabled Women's Network. (1991). *Sexual assault against women with disabilities.* Disabled Women's Network.

Dovidio, J. F., & Gaertner, S. L. (1991). Changes in the expression and assessment of racial prejudice. In H. J. Knopke, R. J. Norrell, & R. W. Rogers (Eds.), *Opening doors: Perspectives on race relations in contemporary America* (pp. 119–148). Tuscaloosa, AL: University of Alabama Press.

Economic Policy Institute. (2002). *The state of working America 2000–2001.* Washington, DC: Economic Policy Institute.

Farkas, S., Duffett, A., Johnson, J., Moye, L., & Vine, J. (2003). *Now that I'm here: What America's immigrants have to say about life in the U.S. today.* New York: Public Agenda.

Federal Bureau of Investigation. (2001). Hate crimes statistics 2000. In *Uniform crime reports.* Washington, DC: Federal Bureau of Investigation.

Franklin, A. J. (1993). The invisibility syndrome. *Networker, 17*(4), 33–39.

Gallup Organization. (1999a). *Police brutality.* Princeton, NJ: The Gallup Organization.

Gallup Organization. (1999b). *Racial profiling.* Princeton, NJ: The Gallup Organization.

Heylighen, F. (1992). Evolution, selfishness and cooperation: Selfish memes and the evolution of cooperation. *Journal of Ideas, 2*(4), 70–84.

House, J. (2001). Social isolation kills, but how and why? *Psychosomatic Medicine, 63,* 273–274.

Kammer, B. J. (2002). *The cycle of devolution: A psychological inquiry into the relationship between personal trauma & social oppression.* Montpelier, VT: The Union Institute and University, Vermont College.

Kunjufu, J. (1990). *Countering the conspiracy to destroy black boys.* Chicago: African Images.

Lloyd, C. (1997). *Creating a life worth living.* New York: HarperCollins Publishers.

Maume, D. J. (1999). Glass ceilings and glass escalators: Occupational segregation and race and sex differences in managerial promotions. *Work and Occupations, 26,* 483–509.

McGuire, P. A. (1999). Multicultural summit cheers packed house: The two-day dialogue aimed to foster creative strategies of inclusion. *APA Monitor Online, 30*(3). Retrieved from http://www.apa.org/monitor/mar99/foster.html

McIntosh, P. (1988). *Unpacking the knapsack: White privilege and male privilege: A personal account of coming to see correspondences through work in women's studies* (Working Paper No. 189). Wellesley, MA: Wellesley College Center for Research on Women.

Miller, J. B. (1986). *What do we mean by relationships?* (Working Paper Series, Work in Progress No. 22). Wellesley, MA: Stone Center.

Miller, J. B. (1990). *Connections, disconnections, and violations.* (Working Paper Series, Work in Progress No. 33). Wellesley, MA: Stone Center.

Minuchin, S., & Fishman, H. C. (1990). *Family therapy techniques.* Cambridge, MA: Harvard University Press.

National Clearinghouse on Child Abuse and Neglect Information. (2003). Gateways to information: Protecting children and strengthening families. *Foster care national statistics report.* Retrieved on March 6, 2004, from http://nccanch.acf.hhs.gov/pubs/factsheets/foster. cfm

National Victim Center and Crime Victims Research and Treatment Center. (1992). *Rape in America: A report to the nation.* Charleston: National Victim Center and Crime Victims Research and Treatment Center, University of South Carolina.

Ng, S. H. (1980). *The social psychology of power.* New York: Academic Press.

Pense, E., & Paymar, M. (1993). *Education groups for men who batter: The Duluth model.* New York: Springer Publications.

Preston, C. (2003, August 1). *Biden advocates for new UN Iraq resolution, challenges preemption.* UN Wire. Retrieved from http://www.unwire. org/UNWire/20030801/449_7154.asp

Public Agenda. (2004a). *Race: People's chief concerns. Percentage of Americans saying they have been treated like potential shoplifters.* New York: Public Agenda.

Public Agenda. (2004b). *The issues.* Retrieved on March 1, 2004. http:// www.publicagenda.org/issues/issuehome.cfm

Robinson, J. (1996). Research on family group conferencing in child welfare in New Zealand. In J. Hudson et al. (Eds.), *Family group conferences: Perspectives on policy and practice* (pp. 49–64). Monsey, NY: Criminal Justice Press.

Sachdev, I., & Bourhis, R. Y. (1985). Social categorization and power differentials in group relations. *European Journal of Social Psychology, 15,* 415–434.

Sachdev, I., & Bourhis, R. Y. (1991). Power and status differentials in minority and majority group relations. *European Journal of Social Psychology, 21,* 1–24.

Sidanius, J., & Pratto, F. (1999). *Social dominance: An intergroup theory of social hierarchy and oppression.* New York: Cambridge University Press.

Speer, P. W., & Hughey, J. (1995). Community organizing: An ecological route to empowerment and power. *American Journal of Community Psychology, 23*(5), 729–748.

Steele, C. M. (1997). A threat in the air: How stereotypes shape intellectual identity and performance. *American Psychologist, 52,* 613–619.

Tajfel, H., & Turner, J. C. (1986). The social identity theory of intergroup behavior. In S. Worchel & W. G. Austin (Eds.), *Psychology of intergroup relations.* Chicago: Nelson-Hall.

Timmerman, G. (2003, March). Sexual harassment of adolescents perpetrated by teachers and by peers: An exploration of the dynamics of power, culture, and gender in secondary school. *Sex Roles: A Journal of Research.*

U.S. Bureau of Justice Statistics. (2001). *Serious violent crime victimization rates by race, 1973–2000.* Washington, DC: Bureau of Justice Statistics, U.S. Department of Justice.

U.S. Bureau of Labor Statistics. (1994). Violence in the workplace comes under closer scrutiny. *Issues in Labor Statistics. Summary 94*(10). Washington, DC: U.S. Department of Labor.

U.S. Bureau of Labor Statistics. (1997). *Division of Labor Force statistics.* Washington, DC: Author.

U.S. Census Bureau. (2001a). *Health insurance report 2000.* Washington, DC: U.S. Census Bureau.

U.S. Census Bureau. (2001b). *Poverty in the United States 2000, June 2001.* Washington, DC: U.S. Census Bureau.

U.S. Census Bureau. (2002). *America's family and living arrangements.* Washington, DC: U.S. Census Bureau.

U.S. Department of Health and Human Services. (2000). *Eliminating health disparities in the United States.* Rockville, MD: Author, Health Resources and Services Administration.

U.S. Department of Health and Human Services. (2001). *Mental health: Culture, race and ethnicity. A supplement to mental health: A report of the surgeon general.* Rockville, MD: Public Health Service, Office of the Surgeon General.

U.S. Department of Justice. (1998). *Prevalence, incidence and consequences of violence against women: Findings from the national violence against women survey.* Washington, DC: Office of Justice Programs.

Van der Kolk, B. (1987). *Psychological trauma.* Washington, DC: American Psychiatric Press.

Walker, L. E. A. (1994). *Abused women and survivor therapy: A practical guide for the psychotherapist.* Washington, DC: APA Press.

Wendell, S. (1990). Oppression and victimization: Choice and responsibility. *Hypatia, 5*(3), 15–45.

Wilson, P. (1996). Empowerment, community economic development from the inside out. *Urban Studies, 33*(4–5), 617–630.

Winters, P. A. (1996). *Hate crimes.* San Diego: Greenhaven Press.

CHAPTER 8

From Prejudice and Discrimination to Awareness and Acceptance

Marie L. Miville
Jill M. Rohrbacker
Angela B. Kim

Beginning with Allport (1954), scholars have written extensively on the nature of prejudice and discrimination. For many decades, psychologists have studied social attitudes resulting from the harsh realities of the social world, concluding that prejudice is almost inevitable for most people, particularly in social settings that promote and reward these attitudes. Once developed, prejudice seems to become psychologically entrenched and difficult to change. Indeed, as Allport (1954) wrote many years ago, "It is easier . . . to smash an atom than a prejudice" (as quoted in Tal-Or, Boninger, & Gleicher, 2002, p. xvii).

So, what are the possibilities of developing positive social attitudes that focus on awareness, understanding, and acceptance of others? Can such attitudes realistically be fostered in children and adults across a variety of settings? What mechanisms, psychological and otherwise, need to be involved in the successful development of positive social attitudes? What conditions are necessary to create successful interventions that reduce prejudice and foster more accepting social attitudes?

Miville et al. (1999) recently defined the construct of *universal-diverse orientation* (UDO) as "an attitude toward other persons that is inclusive yet differentiating in that similarities and differences are both recognized and accepted . . . [T]he shared experience of being human results in a sense of connectedness with people and is associated with a plurality or diversity of interactions with others" (p. 292). UDO represents a social attitude marked by awareness and acceptance of how people are *both* similar and different. Similarities (that is, universal) are those aspects of being human that are perceived as common between oneself and others, while differences (i.e., diverse) refer to aspects that are meaningfully unique among people, as based on social group memberships (such as race, gender, age, sexual orientation) and individual/personal factors (such as personality traits). UDO is a social attitude that is a hopeful alternative to prejudice and is characterized by a unique understanding of the important ways in which people are similar and different at the same time.

FOSTERING UDO: IMPORTANT INGREDIENTS

How can UDO be fostered or developed? What are important ingredients? Anderson and Miville (2002a) examined developmental aspects of UDO, using Dabrowski's (1967, in Anderson & Miville, 2002b) theory of positive disintegration. The theory states that people develop across a number of levels, the most sophisticated being group-oriented (communionistic) levels that emphasize common or universal qualities among people. Movement across levels is necessarily accompanied by anxiety and the "disintegration" of the previous developmental level. This translates into shifting away from old thoughts and feelings about oneself and others, perhaps marked by fear and/or hostility, into new, and qualitatively different, ways of thinking and feeling about oneself and others, marked by openness and acceptance. As important, previous identities based, for example, on family, race, or religion may not necessarily be at odds with identifying with an ever-widening group (that is, humanity). Indeed, Anderson and Miville (2002b) propose that as people develop a more group-oriented perspective, social group boundaries become more permeable. For example, people may become more comfortable interacting with others from different racial/cultural backgrounds because they also perceive a larger group boundary based on common humanity. A limitation of Dabrowski's framework appears to be the western presumption of an individualistic worldview; those with collectivistic worldviews might be presumed to begin at a more advanced level developmentally. Anderson and Miville (2002b) found that spirituality, openness, and emotional intelligence were significant predictors of UDO attitudes. In short, people with a spiritual outlook, a personality characterized by openness, and the ability to accurately sense one's and others' feelings were more likely to express UDO attitudes.

Recent social psychology theory also has suggested ways of reducing prejudice and developing UDO. For example, the cognitive process of *social categorization* has driven much research on prejudice, particularly among different social groups (Brown, 1995; Dovidio & Gaertner, 1986). Social categorization occurs in people's attempt to understand, order, and simplify the social world. People place themselves and others in a variety of categories, for example, based on social group features (race, gender, size, etc.). Resulting favorable attitudes toward one's own group (ingroup) and negative attitudes toward other groups (outgroups) thus are believed to be a major cause of prejudice.

Social psychologists have begun to ask how inevitable or entrenched social categorization is. Can people *decategorize* (minimize the importance of social categories) or *recategorize* (create new inclusive categories) both themselves and others? Research now suggests that under certain conditions, people can develop a common ingroup identity (Dovidio & Gaertner, 1999; Gaertner, Dovidio, Anastasio, Bachman, & Rust, 1993). This identity "involves change [to] people's conceptions of groups, so that they think of membership not in terms of several different groups, but in terms of one, more inclusive group" (1999, p. 103). In doing so, negative attitudes toward outgroups become more positive, ideally because outgroup members become ingroup members ("they" become "we"). Dovidio and Gaertner also proposed the possibility of "dual identities" in which people simultaneously see themselves as members of a smaller ingroup (as based on race or gender) as well as a superordinate group (see Figure 8.1).

Brewer (2000) has alternately suggested that prejudice reduction occurs in conditions where people *cross-categorize* themselves and others. That is, people come to perceive that they and others belong to several social groups at the same time; thus people are placed in multiple, simultaneous categories. Research suggests that cross-categorization reduces prejudice (and potentially increases UDO), because other people can be seen as similar to oneself in one dimension (universal) while being different in other dimensions (diverse). Pettigrew (1998) and others have written about how cognitive processes might work together, building upon each other to reduce prejudice and foster UDO (Tal-Or et al., 2002). For example, a first step

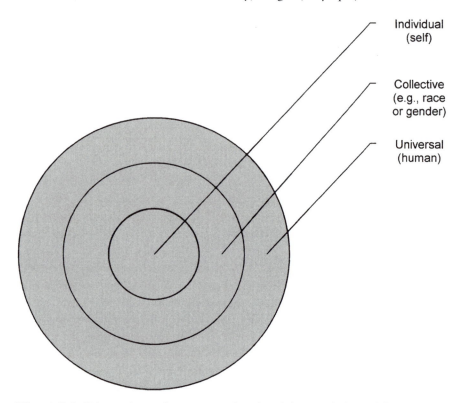

Figure 8.1. Dimensions of group membership/identity (adapted from Sue & Sue, 2003; Turner, 1987)

toward reducing prejudice and developing UDO might be to de-categorize other people (de-emphasize the outgroup to which others presumably belong). The next step is to recategorize others as members of one's own group (presumably a larger superordinate group). A third step is marked by cross-categorization and developing a more complex perception of oneself and others within social categories. That is, one comes to perceive the simultaneous and multiple groups to which each person belongs (Sue & Sue, 2003; Turner, 1987); for example, as Figure 8.1 shows, a person is seen as an individual as well as both a racial being and a human being. Steps two and three lay the groundwork for developing UDO by creating the cognitive complexity necessary for perceiving that both similarities and differences exist among oneself and others. Similarities are perceived because of common group membership (being human or, perhaps for younger people, being in the same grade), while differences are perceived based either on membership in a different group or acceptance of the diversity of one's own ingroup (current evidence appears to better support the former) (Brown, 1995).

Social psychology processes described above likely affect one's *social identity*, thoughts, feelings, and attitudes one has toward one's group memberships (Tajfel & Turner, 2001). Social identity is another variable that has received much attention in research on prejudice, providing motivation to favor one's own group, often at the cost of viewing other groups negatively, as a means of feeling good about one's own groups. The construct of social or collective identity also has been a focus of much research in multicultural psychology, resulting in the development of identity models based on social group memberships, such as race (Cross, 1971; Cross & Phagen-Smith, 1995), gender (Downing & Roush, 1985; Ossana, Helms, & Leonard, 1992), and sexual orientation (Cass, 1979). Social/collective identities, particularly for oppressed groups, are believed to be a critical aspect of one's self-concept, providing essential grounding and buffering in the face of prejudice and discrimination (Helms, 1990). More sophisticated social/collective identity attitudes have been linked to low prejudice and high UDO for both white and black participants (Miville et al., 1999). Thus, a critical aspect of fostering UDO and reducing prejudice is developing more sophisticated or mature social or collective identities; such maturity would parallel the sophisticated understanding of the social world that underlies UDO, "in which existing social group boundaries are viewed, depending on the time and circumstances, as potentially permeable and traversable" (Miville et al., 1999, p. 305).

The social context in which people interact is critical in changing how they think about themselves and others. Simply put, the social context can reinforce how people perceive themselves and others as individuals, as social group members, and as members of a larger superordinate group. Allport (1954) noted four key ingredients needed for the social context to enable positive intergroup contact: equal status, common goals, cooperative relations, and institutional support. Pettigrew (1998) recently updated the intergroup contact theory originally proposed by Allport (1954) by describing processes that help bring about more positive attitudes toward others. These include learning about the outgroup (getting more accurate information), changing behavior to approach and interact with diverse others (leading to dissonance that must be reduced by creating more positive attitudes), generating emotional attachments (particularly through friendship), and reappraising one's ingroup (as not having the *only* acceptable worldview). The essence of successful intergroup contact is that it must be *repeated and sustained in ultimately positive ways*. One-shot interventions thus are not as likely to be successful as those that are ongoing.

FOSTERING UDO: CRITICAL CONDITIONS, ESSENTIAL CHARACTERISTICS

From the previous section, it is possible to outline important conditions necessary to reduce prejudice and develop UDO. Settings or interventions with these goals in mind need to incorporate the following:

- Sustained and positive contact among demographically diverse participants characterized by
  - Equal status.
  - Common goals.
  - Cooperative relations.
  - Institutional support.
- Accurate knowledge of social groups
- An increase in the psychological complexity of perceptions of self and others such that participants
  - Develop common ingroup or universal identity.
  - Perceive multiple social group memberships/identities.
- Being emotionally evocative. This will
  - Allow for anxiety, dissonance, and/or emotional discomfort to be felt and openly expressed.
  - Allow for friendships/positive emotional attachments to develop.
- Emphasis/recognition of both group and individual factors/processes
  - Change can occur collectively through group processes and experiences.
  - Change can be facilitated or hindered by individual factors (such as different levels of openness, emotional intelligence, ability to process information, right-wing authoritarianism). (Levy, 1999)

To be sure, it is doubtful that many settings that might foster UDO actually do so, because the above conditions do not exist in consistent and sustained ways. Nevertheless, there is tremendous potential that UDO can be fostered in a variety of settings and for many different people if resources and political will are directed toward this goal. The first step toward making the potential of UDO a reality is to think about creating interventions that include the above conditions. Of course, it is hoped that many settings will eventually take on these conditions without a need for specialized programs.

The goals of interventions designed to help participants develop UDO might focus on enhancing the following characteristics in people:

- willingness to tolerate and learn from ambiguity and anxiety,
- openness to and experience with interacting with diverse others,
- feelings of connectedness with others,
- accurate knowledge of social groups,
- cognitive flexibility and complexity,
- more sophisticated social identities based on existing social groups, as based on race and gender, and
- social identity based on membership in the human race.

These characteristics might be thought of as important precursors or correlates of UDO that foster UDO's dual components: attitudes that acknowledge and accept the common or shared aspects of people (universal), and attitudes that understand and accept people's unique aspects as based on group membership or individual characteristics (diverse). These dual aspects of UDO are believed to be orthogonal (see Figure 8.2). That is, they may not necessarily be believed or expressed simultaneously. For example, a person may believe that people share common qualities, but the person may not recognize important differences (that is, people are people and differences do not matter); or a person may believe that people are very different from each other, indeed so different that it is impossible to perceive important or meaningful commonalities. However, in order to achieve a genuine reduction of prejudice and to develop a universal-diverse orientation, people must have accepting attitudes about both universal and diverse qualities of others. The characteristics listed above support the adoption of the dual aspects of UDO, rather than one or another component.

Given that individual differences might exist in the above characteristics within a group of potential program participants, it is important to look at both individual and group needs for fostering UDO. It is also reasonable to expect that differing levels of success will be achieved within the same program among the participants. Thus, it

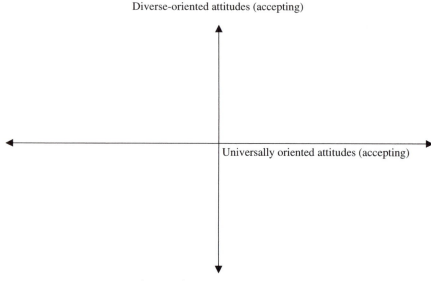

Figure 8.2. Orthogonal components of universal-diverse orientation. Universal-diverse orientation is located in the quadrant made of accepting attitudes of both universally oriented attitudes and diverse-oriented attitudes.

is important to consider assessing the needs and abilities of potential participants in order to establish minimum conditions leading to UDO for all participants.

FOSTERING UDO: EFFECTIVE INTERVENTIONS

Interventions aimed at reducing prejudice and increasing positive social attitudes have existed for some time (Brown, 1995; Khmelkov & Hallinan, 1999). Multicultural education or diversity programming also may be placed into this category, given the general aim of increasing knowledge and more positive relations among various social groups (Banks, 1995). A number of settings already have initiated these interventions, including schools, universities/college, and the workplace. As well, clinical settings have been a recent area targeted for reducing bias, increasing understanding, and creating more effective strategies among mental health practitioners for the diverse clientele they serve. With some adjustments, it is possible for these existing interventions to focus not only on reducing prejudice but also on replacing these negative attitudes with UDO (akin to the "positive disintegration" mentioned earlier that replaces fear and hostility among participants with openness and understanding). Unfortunately, due to space concerns, it is not possible to fully review here applications of the conditions described above for each setting. Instead, the following sections will describe specific considerations for interventions centered on fostering UDO for each specific setting.

School Settings

Without a doubt, many scholars view childhood and adolescence as key time periods in which prejudice develops (Brown, 1995). Given a different set of circumstances or conditions, childhood is a period during which more positive social attitudes instead might develop. According to Carter and Rice (1997), a child begins to understand that she or he belongs to a particular group by as early as age five and to distinguish differences between groups by age ten. A primary socializing agent for children in shaping and influencing social attitudes are schools (Byrnes, 1988; Wotorson, 2001). Children are required to spend much of the day in school, and it is likely their main social milieu. In addition, school experiences occur at a time in children's lives when they begin to understand social group membership and develop attitudes regarding these memberships. School experiences also occur when children are most open to new information and experiences, socialization, character development, and attitude change (Khmelkov & Hallinan, 1999). Schools can thus play a critical role in shaping how children think and feel about the world and their social reality, and it represents a critical time and space for promoting the development of UDO and systemically reducing prejudice and discrimination.

When thinking about how to intervene in reducing prejudice and foster UDO, it is important to have a sense of how a child's development might affect his or her beliefs and actions. Byrnes (1988) states that the elementary school years constitute a developmental period during which children's attitudes toward various social groups and their distinguishing characteristics are elaborated upon and crystallized. In addition, experiences (group and otherwise) children have and do not have during these years are important determinants of later attitudes and feelings. Byrnes suggests that unless children are placed in situations in which they are required to rethink their beliefs about group differences, it is unlikely they will do so of their own accord. Wotorson (2001) further states that elementary school years are a time of great transition for children and are marked by the following shifts:

- There is a shift in focus from family to peers.

- Friendships and finding a place in a group become increasingly more important.

- There is an increased ability to consider someone else's point of view.

- Older siblings and acquaintances become more influential in their lives.

- Television and other media become a strong influence, especially in the very early grades when children tend to believe what they see.

- Abstractions are difficult to comprehend for the early elementary age child; older elementary age children begin to develop the ability to move from the concrete to the abstract.

- Children in kindergarten or first grade may still believe in the power of wishes and magical thinking; by second and third grades, children understand the difference between fantasy and reality.

- Differences among people are apparent, and children are beginning to absorb societal judgments about these differences. (p. 86)

In considering the above, it is critical that schools realize the tremendous impact they have on children's development of their identities, attitudes, beliefs, and behavior. Schools, thus, have the responsibility to provide a safe, nurturing environment with teachers and peers of diverse social group memberships with whom the children can share, learn, model, and gain appreciation and respect for similarities and differences among each other (Bigler, 1999; Stephan, 1999). In this way, schools can effectively facilitate the conditions for reducing prejudice and promoting UDO with children.

The following are suggestions for classroom activities that help children focus cognitively, affectively, and behaviorally on developing and displaying an awareness and appreciation of similarities (universal) and differences (diverse) among themselves and others (Aboud & Fenwick, 1999; Bigler, 1999; Byrnes, 1988; Lynch, 1987; Pate, 1995; Schofield, 1995; Slavin, 1995; Stephan, 1999; Wotorson, 2001):

- Provide an opportunity for children/students to appreciate and identify with the ethnic/cultural similarities and differences of their classmates by role-playing. Have the students actively participate in the dance, music, and crafts of, for example, Korean culture and have them discuss the meanings and significance of activities performed in these situations. In addition, discuss how the values reflected in the customs and traditions of a particular culture might be related to similar values in the students' own culture and in other parts of the world.

- Whenever teaching the topics related to various group memberships/ identities (racial, ethnic, gender, age, sexual orientation, religious, socio-economic), discuss the common or universal elements shared by all the groups as well as acknowledging and discussing unique differences. Programs for older children and adolescents might also include discussion of resulting social experiences based on differences (both positive and negative).

- Provide students the opportunity to interact with members of other social groups in academic learning teams. Assign a project in which they have to band together in completing the task. Working together toward a collective goal promotes a greater sense of identification with one another and realization of their similarities as students despite their differences in their social, cultural, and personal traits.

- To increase their dialogue, awareness, and empathy for members of other groups, have the children/students write and act out their own plays, skits, or short stories that characterize individuals who are confronted with discrimination and prejudice. Discuss the children's similar and different experiences as a result of their social group memberships.

- Provide a forum for the parents of the children of diverse social group memberships to interact with one another. Invite parents into one of the discussions with the children about the various social group memberships and identifying their understanding and awareness of similarities and differences. In this way, children and parents can both learn to develop and model UDO from each other.

These activities will help children develop UDO by helping them absorb beliefs about themselves and others that highlight similarities common to all people as well as unique differences that set oneself and others apart, ideally in positive ways. Such activities also help lay the groundwork for identity development in adolescence based on more accurate knowledge of social groups as well as acceptance of others as part of the larger group of humanity. Direct experiences with diverse others are key to establishing friendships and developing a genuine understanding of how people are both similar and different from each other.

School is a time for learning and socialization. Children learn from watching and interacting with their teachers and peers. They acquire attitudes from the absence as well as the presence of diversity in the student body and staff, in the curriculum, and in the physical environment. The above interventions can be effective only in a school setting whose administrators and teachers also express positive social attitudes and are trained to promote multiculturalism and UDO. It is further assumed that the children in the setting have diverse social group memberships. Schools with less diverse school populations must make efforts to create diverse group contact, for example, by developing sustained interventions across schools or districts. Finally, although schools are one of the major socializing agents of children, they cannot be alone in eradicating prejudice and discrimination. The active support of policymakers, the media, and family members is needed to combat prejudice and develop UDO.

Higher Education Settings

Another ideal period during which to foster UDO is late adolescence, particularly in higher education settings. Today's college students are the most diverse of any generation in terms of race, gender, age, socioeconomic status, and so on. Despite this fact, or because of it, more tension on campus regarding diversity issues exists today than previously. Indeed, research shows that students are more willing to talk about the intimate details of their sex lives than to talk about race relations on campus (Levine & Cureton, 1998). Thus, UDO interventions may be critical to helping not only foster positive social attitudes among individual students but also promote a more positive campus climate.

The college years are an important time for the crystallization of identity. Identity development is generally associated with decisions and commitments regarding career, relationships, lifestyle, values, and sexual identity (White & Porterfield, 1993). Healthy identity involves two important elements: a persistent sense of sameness within oneself and a persistent sharing with others. Erikson (1968) theorized that identity develops best when students are given a psychosocial moratorium—a time and a place in which they can experiment with different social roles before making permanent commitments to an occupation, intimate relationships, social and political groups and ideas, and a philosophy of life (Gurin, Dey, Hurtado, & Gurin, 2002). For students of color, issues of racial/ethnic identity are particularly relevant, and it is important that all students see themselves represented in the environment around them to avoid feelings of invisibility or marginality that can undermine positive identity development and genuine UDO (Tatum, Calhoun, Brown, & Ayvazian, 2000). Thus, UDO interventions in higher education should relate to enhancing identity development and building healthy relationships among college students.

To help deal with the psychosocial development of college students, many universities have departments or divisions of student affairs (SA). SA departments are generally responsible for developing interventions through programming that enhances student development, particularly around identity issues and positive social attitudes (Howard-Hamilton, Phelps, & Torres, 1998). The American College Personnel Association and the National Association for Student Personnel Administrators developed seven core principles for student development on which interventions should be based. Interestingly, the seventh principle states that "student learning occurs best in communities that value diversity, promote social responsibility, encourage discussion and debate, recognize accomplishments, and foster a sense of belonging among their members" (Howard-Hamilton, 2000). Thus, the conceptual framework for promoting UDO in higher education settings already exists.

In recent years, many SA interventions have focused on multicultural education and diversity awareness, including reducing prejudice and increasing positive social attitudes. However, while many SA departments wish to be perceived as promoting more positive attitudes and raising awareness about multicultural issues, few actually have developed a unified and sustained vision within the department of what positive and accepting attitudes among college students truly entail. Many units within SA departments create diversity programming, but little communication or planning across these units seems to exist on many campuses. Thus, better communication across units would help create a more coherent framework for changing attitudes and ultimately lead to longer-lasting results.

As well, some existing programs are more successful than others in reducing prejudice and fostering positive social attitudes. Critical factors for success include incorporating any number of the conditions previously described, such as level of sustained contact with diverse others and the ongoing nature of the program. Programs also vary according to their intentionality. Some programs clearly articulate and plan prejudice reduction as a goal for participants, while other programs exist whose consequences might include reducing prejudice and developing UDO, but were not recognized as such by program planners. Intramural sports are one of the most salient examples on most campuses of this latter type of programming. Large and diverse numbers of students are drawn annually to this activity; a common enjoyment of sports and friendly competition provide a formal way of bringing students of all backgrounds together with the goal of exercise and perhaps to create a winning team. These activities meet many of the conditions outlined for developing UDO: particularly positive intergroup contact, the opportunity to develop friendships, the possibilities of activating both recategorization (as members of a common team) and cross-categorization (team members plus other social group members) processes, and the enhancement of social identity development.

A goal of many SA programs is to assist students in feeling a sense of connectedness through shared experiences, another characteristic of UDO. Such programs begin with freshman, minority, and transfer student orientations, and continue with residence hall floor meetings and activities. Also, specific diversity programming focusing on various social groups (for example, Hispanic Heritage month) is a component of many SA programs, emphasizing meaningful differences among university students. Both types of interventions seem to foster aspects of UDO, although this goal could be more clearly stipulated and integrated into program activities.

On-campus housing provides one of the best environments for fostering long-lasting positive social attitudes and behaviors. Close intergroup contacts based on race and gender occur every day in campus housing. Students also are afforded the opportunity to interact with members of other social groups through "theme" housing such as a Native American floor, African American floor, or "foreign language" floor. Students from any cultural or ethnic background may reside on the floor; the only requirement is that each individual be interested in learning about the highlighted opportunity. Whether these contacts in campus housing are positive, however, depends on the degree to which the conditions of positive intergroup contact exist (Bennett, 1993). Well-trained staff and student leaders should be available to aid in the necessary discourse associated with negative contacts that are a natural component of any community. Ideally, a faculty member is also assigned as an advisor to the floor.

Intentional multicultural programming nationwide ranges from single program approaches to semester-long or even lengthier programs. Examples of offering opportunities to explore similarities and differences among ethnic and cultural environments include such programs as "focus nights," in which students from various countries present an educational program on their country followed by a variety of homemade "home" foods. Still other SA programs directly challenge underlying prejudices based on race, gender, and sexual orientation and include more confrontative elements. Discussions on hate crimes and male/female differences as well as stereotype awareness activities (for example, a "Racism 101" course) are common examples of these interventions. The goals of these programs are to increase awareness of one's own stereotypes and prejudices and to provide more accurate information and understanding of different social groups. These programs influence social identity development of participants by increasing the cognitive complexity surrounding social group perceptions. These latter activities likely need to be led by a professional.

With some adjustments, many existing multicultural programs can include fostering UDO more directly as a goal. Ultimately, participants of UDO programs will be able to develop more complex social identities that allow oneself and others to be seen as part of many and simultaneous groups; participants also might come to see that some groups converge with each other regarding similar values or purposes, while others do not and may even conflict. As well, the opportunity to interact with diverse others, particularly to confront tough issues of oppression and privilege and to participate in dialogue necessary to express feelings of anxiety and discomfort in a safe setting, will bring about the ability to withstand anxiety and ambiguity and even to learn from these experiences. To devote time to facilitating knowledge of one another in conversation is to create shared values of respect, trust, and dignity (Healy & Liddell, 1998). The key to creating effective UDO interventions in higher education is creating situations that allow for the deceptively simple task of facilitating common discourse.

Finally, instructors can develop UDO in the classroom. Anderson and Miville (2002a) conducted research on the effectiveness of organizing a multicultural education course using UDO as the conceptual framework. Beginning with the first class, students were oriented to learning about multicultural issues from the framework of shared commonalities and unique and meaningful differences. Course themes and discussions facilitated by the study's first author utilized this emphasis throughout the semester. Results demonstrated that by the end of the semester, students expressed stronger UDO attitudes, greater multicultural awareness, and lower prejudice.

Organizational Settings

The workplace is another seemingly ideal setting in which to apply interventions that reduce prejudice and foster UDO. By adopting a more socially accepting approach, both within the workforce as well as in marketing products, organizations stand to reap greater profits economically as well as psychologically. Workplaces have attempted to enhance the psychological functioning of their workers for some time, particularly with social attitudes. The growth of so-called "diversity training" programs in the last three decades has been documented in numerous studies. By the mid-1990s, it was estimated that 60 percent of Fortune 500 corporations had initiated some kind of diversity training program. The general effectiveness of these interventions on workers appears to be mixed, however, with rising harassment and discrimination lawsuits and the appearance of "backlash" attitudes among many white male employees, viewed by some as pointing to failure (Combs, 2002). Reasons cited for the mixed effectiveness of current approaches range from too minimal an intervention (the classic one-shot approach), too little administrative support for genuine changes in organizational culture (Bendick, Egan, & Lofhjelm, 2001), too much glossing over or over-generalizing of significant differences among people (Zhu & Kleiner, 2000), and too little emphases on teaching concomitant behavioral/skill-based changes along with increased awareness (Arai, Wanca-Thibault, & Shockley-Zalabak, 2001). Indeed, "mishandled training . . . [can serve] to exacerbate low morale and a negative diversity climate" (Gilbert & Ivancevich, 1999, p. 31) for both majority and minority workers. A recent study found that 64 percent of black women felt that diversity programs were not effective in addressing subtle racism (Grossman, 2000).

Most experts agree that a key condition for the success of such interventions is support from top management: "Organizations can develop rationales for training that recognize [that] nurturing the potential of a diverse employee workforce can help in adapting their products and services to diverse market groups" (Lindsley, 1998, p. 304). Without the support of top management, most diversity training programs are doomed to fail, or worse, to exacerbate existing tensions in the work climate.

UDO provides an ideal framework for organizations to couch prejudice-reduction interventions and increase social attitudes of awareness and acceptance of diverse others. A focus on similarities among people is likely to be embraced by administrators and many workers because of the lower likelihood of creating negative and defensive reactions from the start. As well, the emphasis on commonalities, if conducted in a genuine and meaningful manner, can bring people together in ways that create emotional bonds and attachments.

Because workplaces typically employ adults, developmental interventions previously described as utilizing emerging cognitive processes or social identities are not likely to be as effective here. Instead it is important to presume that adults already have various social attitudes that are deeply held and social identities that are salient and central to their self-concepts. UDO interventions must therefore allow for these attitudes and identities to be meaningfully involved and expressed. Indeed, adults are ideally suited for UDO interventions, since part of the process necessarily involves grappling with ambiguities and anxieties that emerge when focusing on social attitudes and identities present in a diverse work group. Such strong emotions are likely to emerge when confronting important differences (of opinions and beliefs, of behaviors and customs, of emotional reactions to events):

> After all, learning about diversity is tough business. It tangles with issues that are deeply emotional, uniquely personal, powerfully systemic, and firmly rooted in our psyches and institutions. It asks us to engage in an uncomfortable struggle with life's paradoxes and to live contentedly with contradictions. Valuing diversity requires learning to hold tenaciously onto core beliefs while freely letting go of rigid views of self and world. It demands the ability to see differences and similarities at the same time. It requires complex developmental capacities and a worldview [often] at odds with Western thinking. Diversity is steeped in ambiguity and challenge. (Gallos, 1997, p. 153)

Thus, fostering UDO in the workplace must include adequate processing of emotional reactions in ways that encourage honesty and comfort with ambiguity and change. There need to be both "feel good" experiences (such as enjoying music and food from other groups) and "feel not so good" experiences (such as feeling angry, sad, and confused) that are processed openly and with few repercussions in the workplace. The presence of a professional in these latter activities is essential for success.

As has been suggested by Loden and Rosener (1991, in Lindsley, 1998), organizations that utilize a multilayered identity model also are more apt to effectively change workers than those that focus on single identities. This model promotes cross-categorization processes and helps create the cognitive complexity necessary for developing genuinely accepting social attitudes. A multilayered identity model also allows for diversity among the workforce not only in terms of the type of social group identifications but also of the quality of these identifications. Workers will differ in the importance and salience of their various identities.

Interventions emphasizing the development of common ingroup (or universal) identity typically involve activities that utilize cooperative techniques (Slavin & Cooper, 1999). Such interventions can be "special" programs or experiential activities whose express purpose is developing such an identity. More long-lasting results, however, will come from weaving cooperative techniques into the actual work of the organization so that rewards of employment are given based on collective efforts that cut across pre-existing social groups. These interventions create cognitive dissonance from having positive social interactions across social groups, leading to changes in attitudes toward both one's own groups and other groups (Pettigrew, 1998).

The primary challenge of developing organizational interventions that foster UDO is to simultaneously focus on critical similarities and differences among people in genuine and sustained ways, a task that often can be derailed for many reasons (such as diminishing resources that drive up competitive motivations within the organization and lead to outgroup denigration). The greater the extent to which workers perceive diversity programs are due to genuine belief in change by top administrators, rather than cynical avoidance of legal troubles, the more likely workers will buy into the approach (Bendick et al., 2001).

Counseling/Clinical Settings

Fostering UDO in counseling/clinical settings can be approached from at least two levels: attitudes of the counselor/clinician and attitudes of the clients. Sue and Sue (2003) have presented a model for understanding culturally different clients (and counselors) that incorporates three dimensions of identity: individual, group, and universal. Training programs that emphasize the development of UDO might utilize a multidimensional view to help lay the cognitive basis for developing sophisticated and genuine positive social attitudes of awareness and acceptance. A multidimensional model helps provide the cognitive framework that allows for both cross-categorization and recategorization of group memberships of oneself and others. This approach creates the language and the cognitive categories that allow counselors/clinicians to perceive how people may be both similar and different from each other.

As well, the need to interact with diverse others as part of the training program is essential to promoting UDO. Contact with people in a variety of social statuses including faculty, peers, and clients enables counselors/clinicians to develop multiple emotional bonds/attachments, create necessary dissonance and anxiety, and develop interpersonal attraction for a more profound change of not only attitudes but also of one's identity. Current efforts in many graduate training programs have emphasized the importance of meaningfully examining worldviews, cultures, and so on that are different from one's own (Sue & Sue, 2003). Emphasizing commonalities adds complexity to this understanding as well as allowing bridging to occur across people and communities (however, the limits of such bridging efforts must also be addressed). As with previous settings, the more sustained these training efforts are, the deeper the change in social attitudes.

Fostering UDO among clients at both individual and group levels also might be potentially helpful goals in therapy. Some research already exists to show that UDO is linked with well-functioning variables such as openness, self-efficacy, coping, and positive thinking (Miville, Romans, Johnson, & Lone, 1998; Thompson, Brossard, Carlozzi, & Miville, 2002). Universality has long been recognized as an important variable in establishing group process (Yalom, 1995). Fostering UDO would be in line with therapeutic foci of developing a more positive social/collective identity or in preparing clients to deal more effectively with an increasingly diverse social world.

CONCLUSION

The current chapter has described a hopeful alternative to prejudice: universal-diverse orientation that represents a social attitude characterized by awareness and acceptance of the similarities and differences that exist among people. A number of conditions have been described that are believed to be critical for prejudice reduction and the development of UDO. Suggestions for fostering UDO were made for a number of settings, including schools, higher education, organizations, and counseling/clinical settings.

Evaluation of the success of UDO interventions can be conducted in several ways. Pre- and post-assessment of UDO among individuals can be measured using the Miville-Guzman Universality-Diversity Scale (M-GUDS) (Miville et al., 1999). Given the social desirability possible in responses to using paper-and-pencil measures, more indirect or covert assessment might be conducted as well. These include behavioral measures, such as observing participant interactions pre- and post-intervention (for example, examining social interactions in less formal settings, such as the lunchroom, or assessing the number of diversity-based conflicts) as well as qualitative approaches in which participants are asked in a variety of ways (interviews, journals) about their experiences with the intervention. Qualitative approaches are ideal for describing the process of change and what stood out to participants as aiding or interfering with the development of UDO.

The background of individuals (age, race, gender, etc.) as well as type of existing conflict should guide UDO interventions. For example, if homophobia or racist jokes regarding Latinos/as have been a concern in a setting, interventions should be targeted to deal directly with these specific issues, versus a generic "we are all different" message. Such a focus does not disallow for emphasis on identifying similarities among participants but only creates a context for genuinely doing so.

The experiences of participants who are from culturally different or oppressed group experiences must be recognized in fostering UDO. People of color and other minority group members (such as lesbian, gay, bisexual, or transgendered persons, or persons with disabilities) are often numerical minorities, and are sometimes, disastrously, called upon to "speak" for their communities. It is important to use activities that prevent rather than encourage such incidences, allowing for more equalized opportunities to learn among the participants. It is also important to recognize the centrality and salience of social identities based on group memberships for minority participants. Indeed, as Miville et al. (1999) noted:

> The overall experience of oppression may . . . affect the expression of UDO in that there are times when it is realistic and adaptive to perceive social group boundaries as existent and impermeable, as in the instance of overt hostile and discriminatory behavior or in the establishment of identity and acceptance based on one's group memberships. That is, there may be times or circumstances when UDO simply is not psychologically adaptive or salient. (p. 305)

Thus, fostering UDO must be approached from a perspective that recognizes the importance of social identities (and differences), rather than minimizing them. An effective approach is to focus on enhancing social identities based on true commonalities of the participants—work setting, age, gender, etc.—thus building in opportunities to recognize a larger superordinate group of common humanity.

Indeed, fostering UDO can be highly positive for minority or oppressed group members:

> It may . . . be healing for a person in the face of hostile social group behavior to realize that whereas members of other social groups (e.g., based on race or gender), particularly those that are nonoppressed, may hold different or even contradictory values, these individuals also may strongly reject hostile, discriminatory behaviors. As well, members of oppressed social groups may appreciate bridging with others from differing social groups, particularly with individuals who genuinely attempt to understand their perspective (e.g., nonracist Whites, nonsexist men, or nonhomophobic heterosexuals). (Miville et al., 1999, p. 305)

UDO interventions need to include activities that blend well with the values, customs, and general worldview of the participants. For example, not all cultures utilize effectively a small group approach where everyone must talk. A part of processing the intervention might involve learning how activities did or did not blend well with participants' backgrounds.

Toolbox for Change

For	Images/perceptions	Strategies for change
Individuals	Understand multiple social group memberships of self and others. Perceive self and others as part of common group.	Own areas of growth. Have opportunities for positive interactions/contact with diverse others (see section on critical conditions).
Community/ society	Celebrate diverse and common group memberships of community members.	Use of multiple settings (school, work, social agencies). Provide social context, rewards to reinforce UDO.
Practitioners/ educators	Understand cognitive complexity of multiple social group memberships. Understand complexity of the process of developing UDO. Understand developmental processes of participants.	Allow for sufficient time. Allow expression of variety of emotional reactions, both positive and negative. Emphasize both individual and group approaches.

Finally, it is important to be realistic about the impact of programs that are created to foster UDO. As has been noted, the more sustained the program, the more hope for long-lasting change in attitudes. As well, institutional support is essential for creating genuine attitude change (for example, giving concrete rewards for expressing more positive attitudes). Clear goals help to maintain realism of what can be accomplished via UDO interventions. For example, one setting may wish to develop more cordial or courteous interactions of participants to replace overt hostility (even a minimal "agreement to disagree"). Other settings may wish to delve deeper emotionally and psychologically and foster understanding and acceptance. Interventions for these latter settings must include adequate processing of thoughts and feelings, and at the same time, focus on commonalities viewed as important by participants. Effects of such interventions include a broadening of one's identity (via both recategorization and cross-categorization) along with friendships across prescribed social lines. These latter interventions have better chances of effecting truly felt social attitude change among their participants.

It is simply not realistic to establish as a goal of UDO interventions eliminating all tension and conflict regarding prejudice. Instead, a more achievable goal is to create a social context that allows for a coming together of participants when there is tension and hostility, in order to have open and healthy dialogue (such as ownership of feelings and behaviors); and where relevant, to create strategies that promote continuing dialogue and acceptance of others. At the same time, settings may wish to establish policy that specifies concrete behavioral criteria of what harmful or discriminatory behaviors are unacceptable under any conditions and will be sanctioned (Grossman, 2000). As well, it is important to be realistic about what "acceptance" of others entails in UDO. Acceptance does not necessarily mean adopting the same worldview or customs, though, at a minimum, it describes understanding and accepting that another person has a worldview that, while different from one's own, is valid.

REFERENCES

Aboud, F. E., & Fenwick, V. (1999). Exploring and evaluating school-based interventions to reduce prejudice. *The Journal of Social Issues, 55*(4), 767–785.

Allport, G. W. (1948). *Psychology, in college reading and religion: A survey of college reading materials* (pp. 80–114). New Haven, CT: Yale University.

Anderson, A. L., & Miville, M. L. (August, 2002a). *UDO in the classroom: A framework for teaching multiculturalism.* Poster session presented at the annual meeting of the American Psychological Association, Chicago, IL.

Anderson, A. L., & Miville, M. L. (August, 2002b). *Developmental correlates of universal-diverse orientation using a Dabrowski framework.* Poster session presented at the annual meeting of the American Psychological Association, Chicago, IL.

Arai, M., Wanca-Thibault, M., & Shockley-Zalabak, P. (2001). Communication theory and training approaches for multiculturally diverse organizations: Have academics and practitioners missed the connection? *Public Personnel Management, 30*(4), 445–466.

Banks, J. A. (1995). Multicultural education: Its effects on students' racial and gender role attitudes. In J. A. Banks & C. A. McGee Banks (Eds.), *Handbook of research on multicultural education* (pp. 617–627). New York: Macmillan.

Bendick, M., Egan, M. L., & Lofhjelm, S. M. (2001). Workforce diversity training: From anti-discrimination compliance to organizational development. *Human Resource Planning, 24*(2), 10–26.

Bennett, C. (1993). Issues of race and culture on the college campus. In G. Bliming (Ed.), *The experienced resident assistant* (pp. 17–41). Dubuque, IA: Kendall/Hunt.

Bigler, R. S. (1999). The use of multicultural curricula and materials to counter racism in children. *The Journal of Social Issues, 55*(4), 687–705.

Brewer, M. B. (2000). Reducing prejudice through cross-categorization: Effects on multiple social identities. In S. Oskamp (Ed.), *Reducing prejudice and discrimination* (pp. 165–184). Mahwah, NJ: Lawrence Erlbaum.

Brown, R. (1995). *Prejudice: Its social psychology.* Oxford, UK: Blackwell.

Byrnes, D. A. (1988, April/May). Children and prejudice. *Social Education, 52*(4), 267–271.

Carter, C., & Rice, C. L. (1997). Acquisition and manifestation of prejudice in children. *Journal of Multicultural Counseling Development, 25,* 185–194.

Cass, V. C. (1979). Homosexual identity formation: A theoretical model. *Journal of Homosexuality, 4,* 219–235.

Combs, G. M. (2002). Meeting the leadership challenge of a diverse and pluralistic workplace: Implications of self-efficacy for diversity training. *Journal of Leadership & Organizational Studies, 8*(4), 1–16.

Cross, W. E. (1971). The Negro-to-black conversion experience: Towards a psychology of black liberation. *Black World, 20*(9), 13–27.

Cross, W. E., & Phagen-Smith, P. (1995). Nigrescence and ego identity development: Accounting for differential black identity patterns. In P. B. Pedersen, J. G. Draguns, W. J. Lonner, & J. E. Trimble (Eds.),

Counseling across cultures (4th ed., pp. 108–123). Thousand Oaks, CA: SAGE Publications, Inc.

Dovidio, J. F., & Gaertner, S. L. (1986). *Prejudice, discrimination, and racism.* New York: Academic Press.

Dovidio, J. F., & Gaertner, S. L. (1999). Reducing prejudice: Combating intergroup biases. *Current Directions in Psychological Science, 8*(4), 101–105.

Downing, N. E., & Roush, K. L. (1985). From passive acceptance to active commitment: A model of feminist identity development for women. *Counseling Psychologist, 13*(4), 695–709.

Erikson, E. (1968). *Identity: Youth and society.* New York: W. W. Norton.

Gaertner, S. L., Dovidio, J. F., Anastasio, P. A., Bachman, B. A., & Rust, M. C. (1993). The common ingroup identity model: Recategorization and the reduction of intergroup bias. *European Review of Psychology, 4,* 1–26.

Gallos, J. V. (1997). On learning about diversity: A pedagogy of paradox. *Journal of Management Education, 21*(2), 152–155.

Gilbert, J. A., & Ivancevich, J. (1999). Organizational diplomacy: The bridge for managing diversity. *Human Resource Planning, 22*(3), 29–40.

Grossman, R. J. (2000). Is diversity working? *HR Magazine, 45*(3), 46–51.

Gurin, P., Dey, E., Hurtado, S., & Gurin, G. (2002). Diversity and higher education: Theory and impact on educational outcomes. *Harvard Educational Review, 72*(3), 330–367.

Healy, M., & Liddell, D. (1998). The developmental conversation: Facilitating moral and intellectual growth in our students. *New Directions For Student Services, 82,* 39–48.

Helms, J. E. (Ed.). (1990). *Black and white racial identity: Theory, research, and practice.* New York: Greenwood Press.

Howard-Hamilton, M. (2000). Programming for multicultural competencies. *New Directions for Student Services, 90,* 67–78.

Howard-Hamilton, M., Phelps, R., & Torres, V. (1998). Meeting the needs of all students and staff members: The challenge of diversity. *New Directions for Student Services, 82,* 49–64.

Khmelkov, V. T., & Hallinan, M. T. (1999). Organizational effects on race relations in schools. *Journal of Social Issues, 55*(4), 627–645.

Levine, A., & Cureton, J. (1998). What we know about today's college students. *About Campus, 2,* 4–9.

Levy, S. R. (1999). Reducing prejudice: Lessons from social-cognitive factors underlying perceiver differences in prejudice. *Journal of Social Issues, 55*(4), 745–765.

Lindsley, S. L. (1998). Organizational interventions to prejudice. In M. L Hecht (Ed.), *Communicating prejudice* (pp. 302–310). Thousand Oaks, CA: SAGE Publications, Inc.

Lynch, J. (1987). *Prejudice reduction and the schools.* New York: Nichols Publishing.

Miville, M. L., Gelso, C. G., Liu, W., Pannu, R., Holloway, P., & Fuertes, J. (1999). Appreciating similarities and valuing differences: The Miville-Guzman Universality-Diversity Scale. *Journal of Counseling Psychology, 46*, 291–307.

Miville, M. L., Romans, J. S. C., Johnson, D., & Lone, R. (1998, August). *Exploring correlates of well-functioning using the Universality-Diversity Scale.* Poster session presented at the annual meeting of the American Psychological Association, San Francisco, CA.

Ossana, S. M., Helms, J. E., & Leonard, M. M. (1992). Do "womanist" identity attitudes influence college women's self-esteem and perceptions of environmental bias? *Journal of Counseling and Development, 70*, 402–408.

Pate, G. S. (1995). *Prejudice reduction and the findings of research.* East Lansing, MI: National Center for Research on Teacher Learning. (ERIC Document Reproduction Service No. ED383803)

Pettigrew, T. F. (1998). Intergroup contact theory. *Annual Review of Psychology, 49*, 65–85.

Schofield, J. W. (1995). Improving intergroup relations among students. In J. A. Banks & C. A. M. Banks (Eds.), *Handbook on multicultural education* (pp. 628–634). New York: Macmillan Publishing.

Slavin, R. E. (1995). Cooperative learning and intergroup relations. In J. A. Banks & C. A. M. Banks (Eds.), *Handbook on multicultural education* (pp. 628–634). New York: Macmillan Publishing.

Slavin, R. E., & Cooper, R. (1999). Improving intergroup relations: Lessons learned from cooperative learning programs. *Journal of Social Issues, 55*(4), 647–663.

Stephan, W. G. (1999). *Reducing prejudice and stereotyping in schools.* New York: Teachers College Press.

Sue, D. W., & Sue, D. (2003). *Counseling the culturally different: Theory and practice* (4th ed.). New York: Wiley.

Tajfel, H., & Turner, J. (2001). An integrative theory of intergroup conflict. In M. A. Hogg & D. Abrams (Eds.), *Intergroup relations: Essential readings* (pp. 94–109). Philadelphia, PA: Psychology Press.

Tal-Or, N., Boninger, D., & Gleicher, F. (2002). Understanding the conditions and processes necessary for intergroup contact to reduce prejudice. In G. Salomon & B. Nevo (Eds.), *Peace education: The concept, principles, and practices around the world* (pp. 89–107). Mahwah, NJ: Lawrence Erlbaum.

Tatum, B., Calhoun, W., Brown, S., & Ayvazian, A. (2000). Implementation strategies for creating an environment of achievement. *Liberal Education, 86*(2), 18–25.

Thompson, R., Brossard, D., Carlozzi, A. F., & Miville, M. L. (2002). Five-factor model (big five) and universal-diverse orientation in counselor trainees. *Journal of Psychology, 136*(5), 561–572.

Turner, J. C. (1987). *Rediscovering the social group: A self-categorization theory.* Oxford, UK: Basil Blackwell.

White, D., & Porterfield, W. (1993). Psychosocial development in college. In R. Winston & S. Anchors (Eds.), *Student housing and residential life* (pp. 65–94). San Francisco: Jossey-Bass.

Wotorson, M. (2001). *Partners against hate program activity guide: Helping children resist bias and hate.* Washington, DC: Partners against Hate. (ERIC Document Reproduction Service No. ED464966)

Yalom, I. (1995). *Theory and practice of group psychotherapy* (4th ed.). New York: Basic Books.

Zhu, J., & Kleiner, B. (2000, May/June). The failure of diversity programs. *Nonprofit World, 18*(3), 12–14.

CHAPTER 9

The Chicago Dinners: A Model for Community Engagement and Social Change

Dietra Hawkins
Terri Johnson
Josefina Alvarez

> The problems signified by prejudice and racism in the United States are not new, not simple, and certainly not gone. . . . Race is a subject of emotional, volatile, vexing, and frustrating dimensions in this society. It seems that no matter how much things change, the problem of race remains.
>
> (Jones, 1997, p. 2)

Social psychologist James Jones (1997) summarized the vast amount of research and theory written about prejudice and racism. He began by describing how the "problem of the color line" as first noted by W. E. B. Du Bois in 1903 could be applied to the period from the sixteenth century through the twenty-first century. Jones stated, "The problem of the color line endures—in stark defiance of all our efforts to contradict its reality or destroy the problem" (p. 23). As America embraces this new millennium, the issue of race has indisputably remained embedded in the threads of our culture despite the tremendous technological and economic advancements of the twentieth century.

This chapter presents some of our ideas about why this conversation is so difficult. We also talk about the Chicago Dinners program, which has succeeded in building connections and creating a setting for uncomfortable questions and experiences with racism to be expressed. We begin this chapter by focusing on the evolution of the race problem, and we describe past and current attempts at rectifying the effects of racism. The history and evolution of the Chicago Dinners project are then presented before we conclude with some practical lessons learned from this program's unique approach toward racial healing.

THE CONCEPT OF RACE

One can only address *racism* when the concept of race is first understood. The race concept, according to Jones (1997), comes from two perspectives: biological and social. Originally the concept of race provided an explanation for the human diversity that Europeans encountered, and it served to create distance between the oppressor and the oppressed. The biologic or genetic basis for race was meant to introduce a "rationale" for the hierarchical value judgments. The concept was used to justify the exploitation and dispossession of theoretically inferior peoples (Akintunde, 1999; Smedley, 1993).

The socially constructed concept of race only gained biological support during the eighteenth century. At this time, a Swiss botanist named Carolus Linnaeus wrote the first recorded instance of scientifically categorizing racial characteristics. His 1735 work *Systems of Nature* originally grouped humans with higher primates such as monkeys and sloths without subdividing humans. In the second edition, five years later, he divided Homo Sapiens into four geographic regions: the Americas (*americanus*), Europe (*europaeus*), Asia (*asiaticus*), and Africa (*afer*) (D'Souza, 1995). His description of each set a clear hierarchical arrangement where whites were at the top, blacks at the bottom, and Asians and Americans in between (Akintunde, 1999).

Johann Blumenbach, a protégé of Linnaeus and one of the most honored scientists of his time, altered the four-race classification scheme in his doctoral dissertation. Blumenbach identified five races of man: Caucasoid, Ethiopian, Mongoloid, American, and Malay, based on the study of human skulls. His classification scheme breaks down into the familiar colors white, black, yellow, red, and brown, which have likely contributed to the ongoing popularity of his terms. Blumenbach and Linnaeus both used the biblical account of a single creation and of the unity of man to reason that if God had created humans in His image, he would have chosen Europeans as the variant. His mistaken belief that Europeans were the original humans, who evolved from the region of the Caucasus Mountains in Russia, led him to name this "variety" of people Caucasians. Any observed defects in other human types were blamed on "degeneration" caused by climate and circumstances (D'Souza, 1995). Blumenbach's five groups were ranked along a gradient of superior to inferior based on their closeness to the alleged epicenter of the original human being; Caucasian was unquestionably first (Akintunde, 1999; Cameron & Wycoff, 1998; Smedley, 1993). These early attempts at racial taxonomy to support the notion that one group was superior to another led researchers to seek biological differences between the African and the Caucasian. They created these distinctions by observing the "other's" history, manners, temperament, and morals; we now use the word "culture" to make these distinctions (Jones, 1997).

In summary, the concept of race is based on the assumption of biological differences that are unique to a group, attached to observable temperament and character traits, and believed to be relatively stable or fixed. Ironically, rigorous research has shown that the concept is based on false beliefs (Jones, 1997). Why does the concept persist? Jones suggests that:

1. Race is a way of valuing one's own group over others.
2. Race is a handy way to encapsulate and rationalize social conflict.
3. Race is useful as a means of talking about group differences, values, social hierarchy, and competition.
4. Race is bound up in our worldview. It gives meaning and value to our culture and preserves a social hierarchy that accords privilege and dominance to those in power. (1997, p. 352)

Despite abundant scientific evidence to debunk the concept of race, it persists on the social and cultural levels because it is a habit and it preserves the power of those who traditionally benefited from racial categorizations. In addition, the concepts of "culture" and "ethnicity" confuse us. These concepts are new, unfamiliar, complex, and hold little social meaning. In contrast, the social construct of race more easily distinguishes "us" from "them" (Jones, 1997). Therefore, racism is derived from a flawed concept of race now instituted into the framework of our society.

DEFINITION OF RACISM

Jones distinguishes three levels of racism: individual, institutional, and cultural. He notes that to define racism as a singular concept is difficult and likely the "wrong approach" due to the many ways the concept of race has become salient in our country (Jones, 1997, p. 12). Therefore, he continues, there may be many "racisms" and not a singular definition.

Jones extrapolates the main elements of racism as the following:

1. Belief in racial superiority-inferiority, based implicitly or explicitly in biological differences

2. Strong ingroup preference, solidarity, and the rejection of people, ideas, and customs that diverge from the ingroup's customs and beliefs

3. Doctrine (or cultural or national system) that conveys privilege or advantage to those in power

4. Elements of human thought and behavior that follow from the abstract properties, social structure, and cultural mechanisms of racialism

5. Systematic attempts to prove the rationality of beliefs about racial differences and the validity of policies that are based on such beliefs. (p. 373)

Racism is a complex, multifaceted phenomenon in our society. It cannot be taken lightly. As Feagin and Sikes also note, the term *racism* in the broad sense extends beyond the prejudices and discriminatory actions of particular "white bigots" but also includes institutionalized discrimination and the recurring far-reaching ways in which white people dominate people of color in this society. The notion of power cannot be left out of the definition, for it is this ability to maintain a social structure that endorses those in power, either consciously or unconsciously. They control legal, cultural, religious, educational, economic, political, environmental, and military institutions (Feagin & Sikes, 1994; Jones, 1997).

The definitions offered by these authors help clarify the type of racism that now exists in our society. In addition, their perspective speaks to a new racism that may not be fully recognized, nor easily addressed or healed. They draw a distinction between "old-fashioned racists" who hold negative stereotypes of others and support open acts of discrimination, and "modern racists" who see their beliefs as factual and feel that they do not hold old-fashioned racist views. This new racism is generally subtler but nevertheless preserves the power status quo. Essentially, there is a "profound undercurrent of racial animosity not only in those overt bigots but among more friendly people," who nevertheless believe in the dominant ideology of opportunity and personal responsibility (Jones, 1997, p. 130).

This new racism is less about the devaluing of a racial or ethnic group and more about the ingroup's values and morals and an unconscious or conscious need to maintain power. Therefore, anything that is anti-racism, such as multiculturalism and cultural diversity, challenges the heart of what it means to be American (Jones, 1997). Historically, we have tried to address racism as if a singular law or decree could right this embedded problem. Jones notes that it will take more than tolerance, education, or sympathy to address this multifaceted phenomenon that must be attacked on multiple levels.

For many people, racism is like murder: the concept exists but someone has to commit it in order for it to happen (Akintunde, 1999). When it is simply conceived as the conscious employment of certain taboo "racist" acts, then one can ignore its true essence. Racism conceptualized from this limited perspective ignores the societal, systemic, institutional, and political institutions that protect and maintain white racism, white privilege, and the construction of "other" (Akintunde, 1999). Most people see racism as only individual acts of meanness, not "invisible systems" conferring power to certain groups. Peggy McIntosh (1988) describes white privilege as "an invisible weightless knapsack of special provisions, amps, passports, code books, visas, clothes, tools and blank checks" (p. 1). White privilege is the package of benefits granted to people in society who have white skin. The privileges allow them certain benefits that are not easily available to people of color.

INITIATIVES FOR ENDING RACIAL DISCRIMINATION

The resurgence of the affirmative action and reparations debates are strong indicators that the problem of the color line persists. Ironically, the current debate for reparations actually began in 1854 with Sojourner Truth (Allen, 1998). It emerged again in the 1890s with Callie House and the support of Frederick Douglass, who challenged Congress to pay black Americans for past wrongs. According to author Derrick Bell, it appears that the plight of blacks is no better now than it was in 1866 when Thaddeus Stevens recognized that his "bright hope of forty acres and a mule for every freedman had vanished" (as quoted in "The Debt," 2000, p. 76). Historically, some movement occurred in 1875 when the Civil Rights Act was enacted and gave blacks the right to equal treatment in public inns, theaters, and public amusement places (Jones, 1997). However, 1877 brought a compromise and 1883 brought the Jim Crow Supreme Court ruling, which supported the mass discrimination and continued oppression of blacks. Then the 1896 doctrine of "separate but equal" was set by the case *Plessy v. Ferguson*. Unfortunately, in an effort to right another wrong, the 1954 reversal of this ruling in *Brown v. Board of Education* seemed to create more racial conflict and antagonism.

Civil rights activists once again pushed for justice and, in the 1960s, things started to change. The 1964 civil rights movement addressed the overt expression of racism in society, preventing overt institutional discrimination in schools, restaurants, and other public places. Governments, educational institutions, and corporations developed affirmative action programs to address institutionalized racism and required institutions to diversify their employees. Many instituted quota systems, which have given rise to feelings that discrimination in any case is unconstitutional. Affirmative action is now a bigger public issue than it has ever been, mainly because it has been intensely under attack for the past several years, most recently in the Supreme Court cases involving the University of Michigan. On the surface it appears that we as a nation have steadily addressed the problem of the color line. Yet, when we take a broader look at the complexity and history of racism, there are ever-present disparities that indicate that race-based differences persist.

Jones suggests that our nation needs to understand how racism is maintained in the culture and that it needs to approach the inherent diversity of our country from a perspective that does not categorize and create polarization. He gives a compelling plea that we learn to decategorize by breaking down barriers, recategorize by creating a "we," and move toward unity, and he emphasizes the importance of generalizing from an interpersonal experience with an individual from a different group (Jones, 1997). These suggestions lead us to the central focus of this chapter. How do we as individuals in our society begin to interact with someone different from ourselves? How do we have a conversation about this race issue and begin to address its complexity? Is conflict resolution the answer? What about diversity training? According to the multifaceted definition of the problem, neither of these is a sufficient solution to these complex problems. However, through meaningful dialogue, we can take the first step toward racial healing by moving toward an appreciation of diversity and diminishing the notion of the "other."

NEED FOR CONVERSATIONS ON RACE

The National Conference for Community and Justice (formerly the National Conference of Christians and Jews) conducted a survey that uncovered a "central willingness on the part of a sizable majority of the American people to give racial, religious, and ethnic matters a front and center place in the priorities of the nation" (McCoy & Sherman, 1994, p. 112). The people surveyed also noted a lack of opportunity and little encouragement to pursue this interest in their everyday lives. It seems that a large majority of our society would like to have better relationships with their diverse neighbors and that there is a need for opportunities to be created. If we can approach this sensitive issue of race with the perspective that we are engaging in a dialogue and not a debate, maybe the customary resistance can be lowered and a common ground found.

Shelly Berman (2003) prepared a list of distinctions between dialogue and debate from discussions with the Dialogue Group, the Boston chapter of Educators for Social Responsibility (ESR). Some particularly relevant points about racial dialogue are highlighted in Berman's contrasting definitions. Dialogue is collaborative, where two or more sides work together toward common understanding; a debate is oppositional, where two sides oppose each other and attempt to prove each other wrong. In dialogue, the goal is to find common ground. People sit down and listen to each other in order to understand and find meaning and agreement. Additionally, dialogue encourages introspection by the participants. There are many positive and empowering aspects to dialogue that may help people find answers to the conflicts in our society. For example, despite the critical commentary about former President Bill Clinton's call for a "national dialogue," some described positive outcomes and examples of conversations that have led to change. The following author's remarkable experience highlights the important distinction between dialogue and other forms of verbal exchange while also indicating the potential for healing:

> The Conversation taught me that blacks and whites in America cannot know each other without knowing what part race plays in the life of the other. . . . The Conversation was personal. We sat together, looked at each other, read each others' eyes, body language, tones of voice. The stories and feelings were our own. It was voluntary. No one made us do it: We were there because our hearts were there. The group controlled what the group did. We had no leader and no agenda. . . . And

so, more than any book or history class, its lessons have stayed with me, because they are not lessons at all, but people who were seen, felt, known in explicitly racial ways. (Franklin, 1996)

Many other groups have been working to create dialogue and promote understanding between groups by creating opportunities for better race relations (Hawkins, 1997). Several of these groups have found successful models for creating dialogues that have led to social action, greater awareness, and mutual understanding.

MODELS FOR DIALOGUES ON DIVERSITY

Programs such as The Study Circle's "Can't We All Just Get Along?" (Niedergang & McCoy, 1992), Kramer and Weiner's (1994) Dialogue on Diversity, Capowski's (1996) Guidelines for Managing Diversity, Norman's (1994) Cultural Model for Mixed Group Dialogue, and Sanford's (1983) approach to beginning a dialogue in South Africa have noted several suggestions that should be incorporated and found to be effective. These models emphasize the need to have open communication through focus groups, study circles, or among community leaders. Common themes suggested in these programs exemplify the needed social exchange and a space for stereotypes to be explored and mutual understanding to be achieved, as suggested by Jones (1997). Successful dialogue coordinators do the following:

1. Stress the differences between a dialogue and a debate and encourage participants to speak from their own experiences, without resorting to expert opinion.

2. Help participants recognize that the process of dialoguing is not easy and that they must commit to the difficult, emotional work of engaging their own biases.

3. Stress the necessity of a safe and open environment where participants can speak honestly and candidly. Facilitators help the process by monitoring the group, not allowing any one person's biases to dominate the conversation, while stimulating deeper exploration of the topic and ensuring that everyone's views are respected.

4. Explain that the purpose of a dialogue on race is not to end racism. Nevertheless, the process of dialoguing is a beginning. Through sharing and mutual understanding, the establishment of common ground can lead to racial healing.

5. Recognize the role and importance of a neutral facilitator who can keep all members present during the conversation and not allow his/her views to dominate the conversation.

6. Engage a balanced group of participants. If the group is not well balanced with diverse people and opinions, the facilitator may use additional materials to challenge the group by presenting diverse views.

7. Incorporate an educational piece. The topic of race has different historical significance for different groups. For example, if two groups are unaware of the other's historical struggles, education could help them see how they have been alienated and oppressed and struggled and survived. Hopefully this education will instill a new appreciation for the other group as well as highlight their common struggles.

8. Use flexible materials and schedules. Different formats may be interchanged throughout a session, such as personal stories, expert presentations, or current articles and editorials.

9. Prepare the participants for the process; all the basics such as time, place, and a basic format should be addressed before beginning the conversation.

10. Allow participants to express their concerns about the process before beginning. This opportunity to express their pessimism or anxiety is often cathartic. Participants may also share why they came and what they hope to gain from the experience. The process of sharing helps normalize the experience and allows the facilitator to know where people may want to begin.

11. Establish ground rules or guidelines. The use of ground rules helps keep discussions on track and fair. For example, the facilitator can refer to a specific ground rule to refocus a domineering participant.

12. Acknowledge that feelings of anger and fear are natural because the topic of race is difficult to discuss.

Hawkins (1997) offers four principles that are appropriate for any program that addresses the emotional race problems of America.

Rule 1: There is a commitment to work hard.

Rule 2: There is a commitment to the long term, not the short term.

Rule 3: The race dialogue requires the proper historical context.

Rule 4: Talking eventually means doing.

In addition, it is helpful for dialogue coordinators to also learn from the mistakes others have made. Frost (1999) discusses ten traps to be avoided when dealing with the issue of race in a business environment. Many of these traps apply to other environments. For example:

5. Expanding the dialogue focus to include all "individual differences" when race, gender, and sexual orientation have yet to be resolved.

6. Using euphemisms such as "ethnic" or "culture" when you mean "race." Direct language indicates comfort with the topic.

7. Arguing that diversity and efforts to embrace it are the "right thing to do." Resistance is not due to a lack of education or exposure but to a reaction to dismantling old prejudices.

8. Focusing on excluded non-majority groups. Programs must engage the dominant group by aiming to change group behavior and organizational values and norms that ultimately excluded the minority groups.

9. Believing that this work can be done without making people uncomfortable.

10. Assuming that dialogues and trainings automatically change behavior, while research continues to show that raising awareness alone will not shift behavior.

THE CHICAGO DINNERS CONCEPT

In November 1995, to ameliorate local intergroup tensions in the midst of a growing national racial divide, the Human Relations Foundation of Chicago and its parent organization, The Chicago Community Trust, created The Chicago Dinners: A Night of Unity. The Chicago Dinners, as the project is now known, brings together civic, business, and community leaders from a variety of racial, ethnic, and religious backgrounds to discuss race and racism. Nearly 11,000 people have participated in the Dinners dialogue process throughout metropolitan Chicago and the nation.

The concept was co-developed by Clarence N. Wood, then the president of the Human Relations Foundation, and Bruce Newman, then the CEO of the Chicago Community Trust. They developed it to (1) support the work of the Human Relations Foundation to eradicate racism, bigotry, and prejudice by creating sustainable dialogue opportunities; (2) provide safe spaces for people to gather in an informal, normalized setting to "break bread"; and (3) challenge myths and stereotypes by creating an intentional dialogue among peers of different groups, making it harder to label people as exceptions to stereotypical rules.

The Chicago metropolitan area is profoundly segregated, with a majority-minority city surrounded by majority white suburbs; there is very little interaction across the color lines. The creators of the Chicago Dinners model understood that for the model to work, it would have to make what was abnormal, normal. To that end, they determined that a meal would be the centerpiece of the process.

Eating and fellowship with one another are cherished activities for all humanity. They also understood that since race and racism were such difficult topics, the dialogue would have to be as focused as possible. Other issues such as socioeconomic status, class, ethnicity, gender, sexual orientation, etc. are not the central theme of the dialogue process. This is made clear throughout the process. Finally, from its inception, the model has helped participants understand the complexity of the issue, making linkages between individual responsibility and systemic impact.

FORMAT OF THE CHICAGO DINNERS

Twice a year, the Night of Unity is held. On this night, dinner parties are sponsored throughout the metropolitan Chicago area. Dinner parties range in size from ten to fourteen people. Parties are as formal or informal as the hosts desire. Over the years, dinner parties have been in homes, church basements, rectories, community organizations, and restaurants and are catered using the finest china and linen napkins, or home-cooked using paper plates and paper napkins. Every dinner is unique, brimming with the potential for great insight and new relationships among people with diverse experiences and ideas for change. Hosts serve as facilitators for the dialogue and attend a briefing session to outline the goals of the dinner, share suggestions for how to manage the conversation, and share their concerns about the process. After each dinner, hosts attend another meeting to share their experiences with the process.

In addition to the two Nights of Unity, throughout the year, the Chicago Dinners model is used by the Foundation to convene issue-specific community dialogues. Some examples of these efforts include examinations of the role of the arts and cultural institutions in challenging myths and stereotypes to create a new, inclusive vision of the world; the role of women of color in the women's movement and the intersection of race, culture, and gender in the lives of all women; and the intersection of race, economics, and culture in the lives of immigrant communities (this effort was part of President Clinton's *One America* initiative in 1998).

Over the years, the Foundation has worked with other organizations and agencies that have found the model useful and adapted it for their own purposes. For example, the YWCA of metropolitan Chicago and the Cook County public defender's office have used the model in-house with staff members. Another local organization,

Public Allies Chicago, adapted the model to incorporate specific questions about leadership and young people, targeting all factions of the Public Allies family (staff, volunteer, donor, client, etc.) Other organizations and institutions throughout the Chicago metropolitan area, such as Governor's State University, Queen of Peace High School, College of DuPage, Bartlett High School, North Park University, the School of Social Service Administration of the University of Chicago, Lookingglass Theatre, Girl Scouts of Chicago, the Beverly Area Planning Association, the South Regional Leadership Center, Evanston Neighborhood Conference, Villages of Park Forest and Matteson, and the Chicago Park District have sponsored community-wide dialogues. Various churches in the area, such as St. Thomas the Apostle Catholic Church, Fourth Presbyterian Church, St. Gertrude's, Immanuel United Church of Christ, and Holy Name Cathedral, have worked within their congregations and surrounding communities to advance interracial dialogue.

In addition to agencies within the Chicago metropolitan area who have adapted the model, Foundation staff have consulted with agencies throughout the nation about ways to use the model in places such as St. Louis, Ottawa Hills, Columbus, Miami, Racine, San Francisco, Flint, Milwaukee, New Haven, South Bend, and Prince George's County. The House of Blues Foundation sponsored dinners in New Orleans, Los Angeles, and Boston. During the most recent Society for Community Research and Action conference, a group of participants experienced the Chicago Dinners process on one night and later in the week participated in a session designed to debrief their experiences and discuss the format of the Dinners.

Over the years, participants have been surveyed for their feedback about their experiences. This information has been used to modify the process. Assessments of the Dinners indicate that despite the challenges and tensions in the dialogue, participants enjoy the exchange. Many dinner participants return as guests or hosts every time the Dinners are scheduled.

One reason for the success of the Dinners is that they incorporate the twelve key elements previously outlined in this chapter while avoiding the pitfalls outlined by Frost (1999). The four "rules of engagement" outlined by Hawkins (1997) to facilitate a conversation on race are also incorporated into the program. These rules also provide some insight into some of the challenges faced in the process of implementation.

Hawkins's first two rules of commitment—to working hard and in the long term, not just the short term—are difficult in a society that embraces the "quick fix" approach to problem-solving. Where instant gratification is valued, the complexity of working on racial issues can be overwhelming. Many Dinners participants have expressed feelings of "not knowing what to do next" and being confronted by the complexity of an issue that they thought was solved already.

There is also a tendency for participants to limit the dialogue to issues of personal responsibility, ignoring the institutional and systemic impact of racism. To address this challenge, the Dinners have recently been restructured to address questions related to the institutional and structural nature of racism. Continuous efforts are made with the hosts/facilitators and guests to remind them of the complexity of the issue on both the individual and systemic levels.

Hawkins's (1997) rule for a historical context to the dialogue is challenging in a country that does not tell the truth about race and racism. Despite recent efforts to tell the stories of oppression of people of color in the "land of the free and the home of the brave," the stories of the oppressed remain marginalized. The learning curve for many people is very high. One way that this challenge has been addressed in the Chicago Dinner model is to share essays and articles that have not just a historical context but a contemporary one as well. This helps participants to understand that the realities of racism, bigotry, and prejudice remain.

Hawkins's (1997) fourth rule, of talking leading to action, is the premise from which the Chicago Dinners began. The dialogue to find common ground is a process that supports real, sustainable efforts to solve our social problems. It is a way to develop genuine relationships that can weather the difficulties for the long haul.

Many people suggest that either one *talk* or one *do*. Many people of color see talking by the majority community as an excuse not to do anything; they see it as something that makes them feel better. Often the willingness to talk does not translate into doing or into a willingness to do. As the team responsible for implementing the Chicago Dinners, we recognize that participants fall along different places in this continuum and must be valued wherever they find themselves. Open and honest dialogue is critical to the Dinners, but so is action. For that reason, we supply Dinners participants with suggestions of things they can do that will tear down racial barriers. For example, when the topic for the Dinners was the educational system, participants were given a list of agencies working to advocate for educational reform in metropolitan Chicago as well as volunteer opportunities for agencies working directly with students.

Like the "either we are talking or we are doing" dichotomy, there are other dichotomy paradigms that challenge effective dialogues on race. Previously we have outlined the idea that dialogues about race must encompass both the system and the individual. There is also the tension between one's identity as an individual and one's group identity. Tension also exists in whether to focus on diversity or racial justice (Blackwell, Kwoh, & Pastor, 2002). Perhaps the most difficult of these paradigms to address is the tension between the black/white paradigm and one that embraces different cultures and communities.

Racism has, for this nation, been embedded in the oppression of the descendents of African slaves over the centuries. The continued racial disparities between blacks and whites are reminders that racism is alive and well. The unfinished agenda of the civil rights movement, continued societal anti-black sentiment, and the continued violence against black people remain critical issues. However, oppression of communities of color has never been limited to that mistreatment and misuse of blacks. Native Americans, Latinos, and Asian Americans have legitimate stories to tell about their abuse by the dominant culture. Immigration has increased the numbers of people of color who live at the bottom rungs of our society and may be trapped there. Their needs are both similar to and different from those of blacks who remain marginalized. These needs must also be addressed in a racial and social justice agenda.

Therefore, when a table is appropriately set to include all of these races, colors, and ethnicities, the dialogue becomes more challenging. The impacts of color, culture, and language as experienced by Asians and Latinos place them in a parallel paradigm where there are many similarities but as many differences. The unique experience of Native Americans raises other issues. Latino and Asian participants and hosts tell us that they sometimes disconnect from the dialogue because they have difficulty finding their place in the black-white paradigm. In the "Oppression Olympics," where people compare their pain to assess whose is most worthy, they often "lose" when there are blacks in the room. This behavior should be expected and should be addressed, as it is one of the tensions that arise when addressing the deep-seated reality of racism.

Another dichotomy that has been raised recently in the Chicago Dinners dialogues is whether the issue is race or class. While acknowledging that some of the rationale for raising this question may be the denial of the insidious nature of race, we have chosen to add this dynamic to the dialogue not because we see it as a dichotomy, but because we see it as an intersection. In twenty-first-century America, class must also be considered as we shape a new racial dialogue. America is home to the best-educated, wealthiest group of black people in the world. The group identity of blacks erodes as growing numbers of them have adopted the principles of individualism and pursued the trappings of the American dream. The gap between haves and have-nots that grows within our nation grows among blacks as well. The impact of race can be ameliorated by class.

Differences can also be seen when there is an intergenerational representation in the dinner dialogue. The elders in the room tell stories about oppression that younger people do not understand. When those who fought in the civil rights movement join together with those who benefited from the fight and know nothing else, the nature of racism is then questioned. Do the young white, Asian, and Latino who go to school with a diverse group of young people and listen to hip-hop see a racial divide? What is the role of the person who brings a multi-racial or bi-racial identity to the room? The challenge is to ensure the flexibility of the dialogue to gather the range of voices.

One key issue that needs to be raised in effective racial dialogue is power and privilege. Most people, regardless of race, do not admit to having either power or privilege. The American myth tells us that we are equal, even in the face of our inequality. After all, any of us can make it if we try hard enough. Acknowledgment of a different reality, where life is not fair and where all that communities of privilege possess was not necessarily earned, requires a shift in self-image that can be very painful. How does one admit in front of members of other groups that he or she lives a better quality of life at the expense of those other groups? How does a woman who carries white skin privilege in the context of her gender oppression see herself as part of the problem? How easy is it for a black American to admit that he or she carries the same stereotypes about other communities of color and is in the position to make hiring decisions, give grades, and make other choices that negatively impact them? These are just a few natural questions that arise; it is not for us or the facilitator to always give answers to these questions but to facilitate a process in which answers can be sought.

Perhaps the greatest challenge of effective racial dialogue is the pervasiveness of denial, not just of the magnitude of racism, but the role we may play in its survival. In each round of the Dinners, someone asks, "Aren't we preaching to the choir?" There are several implications in this statement that reflect this denial. First, the person asking the question believes that his willingness to participate in the dialogue makes him a member of the choir—a good guy. Therefore, he believes he has little to learn. This often translates into a discomfort with information that might challenge his sense of good. Second, it diminishes the process by suggesting that the "real work" needs to be done with another group. This assumes that racists are those who live on the extremes—people who commit hate crimes and wear white hoods. It absolves the vast majority of people who do not participate in these activities but benefit from a system of white privilege and work to maintain those systems either actively or passively. The more important question to raise may be, What is the function of the choir? The Chicago Dinners process is, in fact, choir rehearsal. People with similar values choose to gather together to practice. In that process, they learn that even though they may have similar values, there are instances when they do not. They learn that even though they may all know the song, they sing it differently. They learn that getting it right takes a lot of time and commitment. They begin to recognize that they are not alone and have support systems in other groups. With practice, they begin to work better together.

CONCLUSION

The Chicago Dinners experience confirms the theories of the social scientists outlined in this chapter. What these social scientists have learned about racial prejudice and discrimination, along with our work with the Chicago Dinners, has led us to the following conclusions:

- Racism is a complex social problem created and sustained by individuals and organizations. There are no quick fixes. Efforts to end bigotry, prejudice, and racism are ongoing processes that require long-term investments.
- Open and honest dialogue among diverse groups of people is critical.
- Value and nurturing come from sharing a meal that tears down some of the barriers and discomfort inherent in this difficult discussion.
- Discomfort, tension, and denial should be expected and acknowledged as a critical part of the process. It should not be avoided. Facilitators and participants can be prepared to handle this energy.
- For some people, there will be great changes as a result of the dinner experience. For others, changes will take longer. For most of us, one dinner will not be enough, and the dialogue and self-reflection that the dinner process entail will be an ongoing endeavor.

While racism is a complex and persistent problem, we believe that as individuals and as a society we have the tools to do away with the racial divisions that now more than ever threaten our society. The toolbox that follows summarizes some of the lessons learned from our experiences with the Chicago Dinners and presents the highlights of the vision that guides this innovative program. Individuals engaging in dialogues such as the Chicago Dinners will need to remember that participating in such a program requires honesty, ongoing self-awareness, and a commitment to moving away from race-based privilege. At the societal level, racial justice will require a vision for confronting a complex problem with no easy "quick fix" solutions,

Toolbox for Change

For	Images/perceptions	Strategies for change
Individuals	Raise awareness of issues related to prejudice and discrimination. Participate in dialogues, workshops, and forums related to the above. Seek more education and connections with people different from yourself. Acknowledge privilege based on skin color and learn to be an ally.	Introduce awareness into work, home, and community environments. Work within institutions (work, children's school, religious institutions, etc.) to promote racial justice. Monitor media outlets. Contact your local papers when you see examples of racist or unfair reporting. Create "safe spaces" for dialogue.
Community/ society	Challenge "us/them" thinking. Provide educational opportunities raising the issue of the community impacts of racism, bigotry, and prejudice. Create "safe spaces" for people of difference to gather.	Sponsor dialogues and other antiracism interventions. Provide support for social action activities aimed at racial justice.
Practitioners/ educators	Update (and develop where missing) antiracist curricula that emphasize privilege.	Support and evaluate antiracism programs.

and leadership for implementing a variety of efforts to eradicate racism. Creating settings where people can come together, eat, talk, and work with one another to move beyond "us" and "them" and to challenge privilege based on skin color provides a way to begin the process of change.

REFERENCES

Akintunde, O. (1999). White racism, white supremacy, white privilege, and the social construction of race: moving from modernist to post-modernist multiculturalism. *Multicultural Education, 7,* 2–8.

Allen, R. L. (1998). Past due: The African American quest for reparations. *Black Scholar, 28,* 2–17.

Berman, S. (2003). *Dialogue and debate: A comparison.* Retrieved October 31, 2003, from http://64.89.140.177/ecw/dialogue_is_collaborative.htm

Blackwell, A. G., Kwoh, S., & Pastor, M. (2002). *Searching for the uncommon common ground: New dimensions on race in America.* New York: W. W. Norton.

Cameron, S. C., & Wycoff, S. M. (1998). The destructive nature of the term race: Growing beyond a false paradigm. *Journal of Counseling and Development, 76,* 277–285.

Capowski, G. (1996). Managing diversity. *Management Review, 85,* 12–19.

The debt: What America owes to blacks. (2000). *Essence, 30*(10), 76, 80, 159–160.

D'Souza, D. (1995). *The end of racism.* New York: The Free Press.

Feagin, J. R., & Sikes, M. P. (1994). *Living with racism: The black middle-class experience.* Boston: Beacon Press.

Franklin, R. (1996, February 23). Conversation in black and white. *Commonwealth, 123,* 9–10.

Frost, D. D. (1999). Review worst diversity practices to learn from others' mistakes. *HR Focus, 76,* 11–12.

Hawkins, J. A. (1997, October 22). Dialogue on race: The rules of engagement. *Education Week, 28.*

Jones, J. (1997). *Prejudice and racism* (2nd ed.). New York: McGraw-Hill.

Kramer, M., & Weiner, S. S. (1994). *Dialogues for diversity: Community and ethnicity on campus.* Phoenix, AZ: ORYX Press.

McCoy, M. L., & Sherman, R. F. (1994, Spring–Summer). Bridging the divides of race and ethnicity. *National Civic Review,* 111–119.

McIntosh, P. (1988). White privilege: Unpacking the invisible knapsack. In *White privilege and male privilege: A personal account of coming to see correspondences through work in women's studies* (Working Paper 189). Wellesley, MA: Wellesley College Center for Research on Women.

Niedergang, M., & McCoy, M. L. (1992). *Can't we all just get along? A manual for discussion programs on racism and race relations.* Pomet, CT: Study Circle Resource Center, Topsfield Foundation.

Norman, A. J. (1994). Black-Korean relations: From desperation to dialogue, or from shouting and shooting to sitting and talking. *Journal of Multicultural Social Work, 3,* 87–99.

Sanford, R. (1983). The beginning of a dialogue in South Africa. *The Counseling Psychologist, 12,* 3–14.

Smedley, A. (1993). *Race in North America: Origin and evolution of a worldview.* Boulder, CO: Westview Press.

CHAPTER 10

When Diversity Becomes the Norm

Donald Daughtry
Denise Twohey
David H. Whitcomb
Cindy Juntunen
Michael Loewy

Multiculturalism can have the most positive social impact when it is used to promote change in organizations and institutions (D'Andrea & Daniels, 1995; Sue, 1995; Sue et al., 1998), in addition to increasing awareness and multicultural competency among individuals. The goal of this chapter is to illustrate the efforts of one academic department to change from an ethnocentric to a multicultural organization. We will be describing an evolution of organizational diversity and individual experiences in a department of counseling, which is home to a master of arts in counseling and a PhD in counseling psychology, and is staffed by six full-time faculty and two part-time faculty.

In our department's effort to evolve to an environment where diversity is the norm, we have chosen to explore how multicultural competency impacts our work as a group, as well as our work as individuals. The changes we have made over the last decade reflect the developmental stages of organizational multicultural development described by Sue (1995): monocultural, nondiscriminatory, and multicultural.

A MONOCULTURAL ORGANIZATION: EARLY HISTORY

Monocultural organizations are defined as primarily ethnocentric and Eurocentric. Minorities, women, and other oppressed groups are excluded, the dominant group is privileged, culture is not considered in decisions, and assimilation is expected (Sue, 1995). Up until the early 1990s, the composition of our department faculty (and to a lesser degree, students) reflected very limited attention to diversity or cultural differences of any type. The six-member faculty, for much of its history, had consisted of five men and one woman, all white and heterosexual. One woman hired in the mid-1980s was a lesbian, and one male faculty member in the early 1990s was Native American, but both stayed for only brief periods of time. Cultural diversity was inconsistently sought in the student admissions process, and no system was in place to support students of color in an overwhelmingly dominant-culture institution. Further, criteria favoring dominant culture applicants were generally upheld. Importantly, efforts to increase diversity were not integrated into department functioning, and isolated attempts that did occur were easily frustrated.

These attitudes toward diversity reflected a lack of awareness, rather than intentional avoidance of multicultural representation or training. Nonetheless, the overall effect was the neglect of multiculturalism, limited advocacy for multicultural training, and minimal attention to multicultural competencies. Further, the department existed within a university setting that at times seemed to exhibit active neglect (D'Andrea & Daniels, 1995) of multiculturalism, demonstrating a lack of sensitivity or awareness to the needs of multicultural issues. Essentially, our department exhibited ethnocentric monoculturalism (Sue et al., 1998), relying on dominant-culture attitudes, strategies, and methods in our training and evaluation. However, due to increased attention to multiculturalism in the psychology and counseling professions and the need to meet student training demands, changes began to develop by the beginning of the 1990s, allowing the opportunity for significant evolution over the following decade.

Transitions: Moving to Nondiscriminatory Practices

In 1994, a critical change occurred in the department. Three men retired from the department, and three women were hired, resulting in a six-member faculty that consisted of four women, one of whom was Native American, and two men. Further, the newly hired faculty members had substantial training in multiculturalism and diversity issues and were focused on changing departmental policies and procedures to reflect their commitment. This resulted in the department's transition to a nondiscriminatory organization (Sue, 1995). Several behaviors changed on an organizational level during this stage. Diversity considerations became the first level of discussion in admissions meetings, hiring decisions, and curriculum planning. Although we continued to offer separate courses in multicultural counseling and gender issues, diversity was also systematically integrated into each course in the curriculum.

This period of departmental history represented several clear improvements from the previous stage, as we were actively struggling with ethnocentric attitudes and a monocultural training environment. However, we also exhibited those characteristics of a nondiscriminatory organization that maintained some barriers to true multiculturalism. As described by Sue (1995), nondiscriminatory organizations have inconsistent policies on multicultural issues and lack systematic policies to address issues of bias. Furthermore, changes to improve the organizational climate can be superficial, and affirmative action policies may be implemented without enthusiasm.

In our case, several key indicators were present. Although we developed statements about our commitment to diversity, specific strategies to implement our goals were not systematically developed. We relied on a legalistic approach to multiculturalism, driven more by affirmative action than an inherent appreciation of diversity. Further, the process of becoming a multicultural group was not explicitly addressed. Importantly, values, background, and individual differences between faculty members were rarely acknowledged or discussed. Even though individual faculty members were authentically committed to multicultural values, we did not make a strong organizational commitment.

Toward a More Multicultural Organization

Fortunately, a second major shift in departmental functioning occurred over several semesters from the late 1990s to the early 2000s. During this time, several new hires occurred, and open positions were filled by two people with disabilities (one white man and one black woman) and two gay men, one of whom was fat and Jewish. In addition, one long-time faculty member developed a significant physical disability. This resulted in our present-day faculty, which consists of four women and four men, seven white persons and one black person, two gay faculty (one fat and Jewish), and three persons with disabilities. More important than demographics, however, each faculty member is a willing advocate for diversity, and our own individual experiences help the group to look at diversity broadly and consider how we function as a unit that is actively addressing multiple sources of diversity.

This change in our faculty membership resulted in diverse group representation as the norm, but more was required in order to actually represent a multicultural organization. According to Sue (1995), multicultural organizations are developing a vision that reflects multiculturalism, views diversity as an asset, engages in planning and problem-solving that will lead to equal accesses to opportunity, does not confuse equal access with equal treatment, and works to consistently diversify the environment. In order to continue our organizational development, we needed to engage in several important processes. Specifically, we had to address our own inconsistencies and biases about sources of diversity that might not be salient to each of us individually, yet were of immediate importance to our functioning as a group. This became apparent the first time a faculty member with a disability was hired, necessitating several adaptive technology accommodations. Initially, this was an issue addressed almost exclusively by the faculty member, chair, and to a lesser extent the university's affirmative action officer. However, over time, the entire faculty became involved in the discussion. Now, disability accommodation is an issue that is more routinely attended to by all faculty members when planning departmental activities or allocation of resources. With increased exposure and experience, accommodation has become salient for each of us, regardless of our individual ability status. This experience exemplifies how group recognition of the importance of diversity has resulted in both behavior and attitude changes.

This recognition has been formalized in our department's mission statement and strategic planning process. Recently, we have begun to discuss the ways in which various sources of diversity converge and diverge, and the impact that has on our curriculum development, research activities, and resource allocation decisions. In all hiring and admissions decisions, perspectives on the diversity of candidates are thoroughly discussed and treated with respect, moving away from the legalistic "quota based" discussion of the past. These behaviors, which build on the attitudes that we have developed through this transition, demonstrate our multicultural values to students and to colleagues throughout our college and university.

Next Steps

We continue to seek ways to increase our awareness of barriers that we are unknowingly supporting. Some conversations around multiculturalism can still be very difficult, and tender feelings emerge, so we struggle at times to find the right balance of support and confrontation with colleagues within our organization. Sometimes, competing values and perceived needs cause tension within our organization. For example, recently two of our top candidates for a job search were of sexual orientation and racial minority status, respectively. Although there seemed to be consensus that having a second faculty member of racial minority status would be an asset, there was an indirectly stated concern that hiring a third openly lesbian or gay faculty member would actually reduce the diversity within our department. The prospect of a minority group becoming a dominant group seemed to create discomfort among some members of our department. Our faculty had to re-establish what diversity meant to us and the academic climate we created for our students, a process that is still continuing as we seek to reinforce our advancement from a nondiscriminatory organization to a multicultural organization (Sue, 1995).

Also, despite our overall diversity, ethnic and racial diversity is not readily apparent in our faculty or students, and the fact that we live in a very racially homogeneous region of the country makes this an on-going challenge for us. Finally, it is critical to note that our organizational multicultural development is also occurring within a larger organization, which is attempting to maintain nondiscriminatory practices, but still has several monocultural characteristics in place. This highlights for us the need for continued advocacy and change at even larger institutional levels (D'Andrea & Daniels, 1995; Sue et al., 1998), and provides context for the evolution within our own group's history.

The transition toward a multicultural organization is a profound experience in the life of our department. It is made possible, in large part, by the critical experiences of each individual member of the faculty, who together are motivated to foster and continue that transition. In the following sections of this chapter, individual stories will illustrate the personal and professional nature of these transitions. Several faculty members involved in this ongoing evolution share personal perspectives of their experience within the context of organizational change. Together, this overview and those individual stories are designed to illustrate how diversity can become the norm, to great benefit for individuals and organizations alike. We also discuss the ways in which conversations across various group identities can play out within an organization where diversity is normative. We conclude by providing our toolbox for change focusing on helpful strategies for developing a multicultural organization.

JOURNEY OF A BLIND PROFESSOR

Disability: A Silent Voice

I entered academia seven years ago and, since then, have held two faculty appointments in counseling psychology programs. I was surprised that, within these diversity-friendly climates, the voice of disability was silent. I gained this awareness through a variety of interactions with colleagues and students. I began noticing that a consideration of disability was absent in faculty conversations dealing with student recruitment and training issues. Although other diversity variables such as gender and ethnic origin came up frequently, any mention of disability issues was conspicuously absent. At the same time, it became apparent that faculty did not regard me as having minority status. This was best illustrated through a conversation with a female Asian American student who had noted to our program director that none of our training clinic material was in alternative format. The director responded that an alternative format was not appropriate, since that would be treating me differently. Obviously, the director was not familiar with the concept of "reasonable accommodation." As we processed the interaction in terms of the need for greater awareness and inclusion, the student commented, "You should be an ethnic minority, then you would be treated much better" (Daughtry, in press).

Disability issues are also frequently neglected in training. This was brought home during a doctoral practicum class I was supervising. A student was seeing a couple in which the female member was afflicted with a degenerative disease. As the disease progressed, she was losing stamina and the ability to perform daily activities. Yet, as we were conceptualizing the case after the second session, I had to introduce the disease as an issue meriting consideration. I was amazed that five doctoral students with previous clinical experience did not recognize the impact of the disease on this couple. I was more amazed that I had to point out the salience of the disease more than once, since most did not seem to get it the first time.

These types of training issues lend substance to the claims made by various disability scholars (Vace & Clifford, 1995; Reeve, 2000). Reeve has argued that disability issues receive insufficient attention in training programs. She asserts that current diversity training focuses primarily around areas such as ethnicity and gender. Inattention to disability issues is counter-intuitive, since individuals with disabilities are one of America's largest minorities, comprising about 14.3 percent of the total population (Hahn & Beaulaurier, 2001; Olkin, 2000). Yet, inattention to disability issues by training programs is well documented by other authors (Bluestone, Stokes, & Kuba, 1996). Olkin compared program application material for all APA-accredited graduate training programs for clinical and counseling psychology for the years 1989 and 1999. She found that the modal number of required courses on disability was zero. Only 11 percent of programs offered at least one course on disability. Even with the greater emphasis being given to diversity considerations, the voice of disability is relatively silent (Daughtry, in press). It is in this context of silence that my experiences with students and faculty are played out.

Relationships with Students

The silencing of disability contributes to students being ill prepared regarding interactions with disabled professionals. Subsequently, my interactions with students are often confusing and contradictory. Some interactions suggest appropriate and positive student perceptions, and my work with students as a teacher, advisor, and research supervisor is generally positive and productive. These types of mentoring opportunities are important in that they expose students to a professional disabled role model.

However, a notable proportion of interactions indicate negative or mixed student perceptions, demonstrated primarily by avoidance and oversight of my professional role. For example, students have approached the department chair about questions regarding fieldwork placements, even though they know that I am the fieldwork coordinator. As the chair outlined the areas of student confusion, I could not help but wonder why the questions had not been directed to me. My chair also had the impression that students had not been attempting to contact me, despite being told to do so. A similar dynamic has occurred when I teach courses with graduate teaching assistants, who have reported being the recipients of questions that would typically be directed to faculty. On several occasions, assistants have told me that students were asking them questions about grading policy, assignment formats, or scheduling. The teaching assistants have generally replied that students need to talk with me. Sometimes, however, several weeks pass before students are finally willing to discuss it with me, despite my repeated efforts to address the questions in class (Daughtry, in press). Although these types of incidents can be attributed to causes other than disability-related avoidance, the pattern is noteworthy. The pattern also is consistent with what various authors have called the "invisibility of disability" (Olkin, 2000).

Of course, I do not automatically assume that patterns of avoidance are always related to my disability. Separating student reactions that may be related to disability from those that may be related to personal attributes can be confusing. On more than one occasion, I have attempted to clarify this confusion by processing student reactions to my disability. However, such efforts are often frustrating. They are typically met with responses like "It does not bother me," or "I forget you have a disability." As noted by Olkin (2000), such comments serve to discount an individual's disabled experience, redefining it as something that does not merit discussion. By redefining blindness, students can excuse themselves from any self-examination of their own discomfort or bias around disability. It sometimes angers and sometimes amuses me that this pattern of avoidance is so common in a profession where being immediate and genuine are supposedly core values. However, I do not mean to imply any hostility or resentment toward students. While specific interactions may be confusing, one advantage of my presence in the department is that it guarantees opportunities for disputing stereotypic images of disability.

Relationships with University Faculty

If relationships with students are confusing, those with university faculty are much more consistently marked by a message of "invisibility." As noted in the chapter overview, the university is best described as an ethnocentric monocultural organization (Sue, 1995). Therefore, it is not surprising that interactions reflect that context, and multicultural differences are regularly overlooked. For example, during committee meetings, my presence is often ignored, and colleagues rarely initiate conversation on personal or professional matters. Never at a loss for words, I will often begin a conversation, which then flows along what would be considered socially appropriate lines. Yet, oddly, in subsequent meetings the same people rarely initiate dialogue. It is as if I am invisible and people do not notice my presence until I speak.

During the course of a meeting, if I offer input it is acknowledged, but often brushed quickly aside. Of course, in some cases my ideas probably should be brushed aside. Even so, it is hard to believe that they are consistently bad. In cases where I feel my thoughts are particularly relevant, I am more persistent in asserting them. Frequently, colleagues seem surprised that I am disagreeing with them or perhaps are even surprised to hear an idea from a person with a disability. They seem more surprised that I am willing to assertively defend a position and not simply let it be dismissed. This can be best described as an example of "self-advocacy." Individual self-advocacy is one key to advancing our department's diversity message within the broader university.

Self-Advocacy and Multicultural Development

The capacity to act as a self-advocate is of particular importance for disabled individuals (Daughtry, in press). Self-advocacy is a necessary mechanism for giving increased voice to disability. There has been a reciprocal interaction between our department's multicultural development and my capacity for self-advocacy. In other words, each has aided and facilitated the other.

When first arriving at the University of North Dakota (UND), I would have described our department as a "friendly monocultural" organization relative to disability issues. It was evident that no thought had been given to accommodation concerns, and departmental faculty thought existing university mechanisms would naturally attend to them. I had considerable doubt, but took a wait-and-see attitude. When my doubts were confirmed, I became more persistent in presenting my needs. Early conversations with my chair centered largely on needs for adaptive equipment and reading assistance. While she was naive on such matters, she wanted to be supportive. These early conversations focused on educating her about the nature and importance of adaptive technology. This is an easy form of self-advocacy: interactions are typically not emotionally charged.

However, raising accommodation matters set the stage for increasing departmental awareness of disability. It aided in reinforcing the reality that experiences of disabled people differ significantly from those of the mainstream. These differences were again made evident by taking advantage of opportunities to make comparisons between experiences related to disability and ethnic or women's issues. Seizing opportunities to point out similarities such as differential economic or political power helped make the case for greater inclusion of disability in the department.

Although slow at first, change began to occur. For example, the multicultural class began giving increased emphasis to disability. Conversations related to student admissions and faculty hires increasingly included disability issues. Conversations around disability issues became more common in the department, culminating in their prominent inclusion in our symposium submission to the 2003 Multicultural Summit. All of these types of interactions were playing out within the context of an organization evolving into a multicultural developmental phase. Upon reflection, I cannot say the increased awareness of disability was fraught with tense emotional conflict. While there were at times struggles that were more difficult, the road was relatively clear. The main implication of these interactions for self-advocacy was a sense of being accepted. The accepting environment provided by faculty acted as a support at times when interactions required more self-assertion.

This self-assertion was particularly important at times when I needed to exercise authority in dealing with students. It has been key in preventing external faculty from dismissing my ideas, as if I did not exist. Self-advocacy is one mechanism that potentially allows disabled individuals to be perceived in non-stereotypic ways. Authors such as Olkin (2000) have commented on the socialization of individuals with disabilities. Olkin noted that emotions such as anger are not considered acceptable for the disabled. People's expectations are that individuals with disabilities will not get angry or engage in assertive behavior. Instead we will be "cheerful overcomers," happy in spite of disability and certainly not willing to rock any boats. We will be passive and willing to gladly accept any crumbs society hands us. Self-advocating forces one to confront these types of internalized, self-defeating messages.

A supportive climate has been key in helping make the cognitive and emotional shifts needed to offset these types of "disabling attitudes." To be certain, eliminating self-defeating messages is my responsibility. However, the opportunity to self-advocate within the context of a department that is becoming increasingly disability-friendly makes the process easier. The organization facilitates the reprogramming of messages such as "be reasonable" and "you can't expect to be treated differently from anyone else." It does this by re-inforcing internal dialogue such as "you have a right to be heard" and "you don't have to submit."

The capacity for self-advocacy is necessary for achieving what some authors have termed an "integrated disability identity" (Daughtry, in press; Gill, 1997). The cognitive and emotional re-programming needed to confront internalized prejudice parallel those needed to incorporate disability into a healthy self-concept. Gill (1997) has commented that advanced stages of disability identity development are characterized by a perception of disability as strength—a source of creativity and insight. Such attitudes have resulted in my increasingly incorporating the advocate role into my professional identity, through mentoring students with disabilities as well as increased self-advocacy.

Not Always Accessible: Disability and Gender

In 1982, the year I entered graduate school, there was no way to predict that in 1998 I would be diagnosed with oligoastrocytoma, a type of brain tumor. Although my work experience prior to graduate school included a stint as a rehabilitation counselor, I could have never anticipated the impact a physical disability and life-threatening illness would have on my career, and particularly my relationship with students.

The Quotes

I will begin with a discussion of student reactions to an article I wrote about having a life-threatening illness (Twohey, 2001). The article summarized my feelings about five important areas: relationships, boundaries, denial, sexuality, and existential issues. Below are the students' actual reactions as written, followed by my responses to these reactions. I wrote my responses two years after the article was published.

Reaction 1

I suspect that this piece may serve as a catalyst that will bring about closer examination of issues surrounding life-threatening illnesses. It seems odd that we are so ill prepared to deal with this when it is one thing that has been around since the beginning of time.

My Response

The irony of our "ill preparedness" in dealing with the angst that we feel when confronting our own mortality becomes the topic of this reader's response. I heartily agree, and note that it parallels my colleague's earlier comment about students' lack of preparation to discuss issues of his disability. Mortality and disability have both been neglected in our training models, as well as professional literature. Student responses to my first-hand accounts reflect the lack of certainty they have for addressing these concerns with clients.

Reaction 2

I agree with the idea that part of our discomfort lies in fear of death and mortality, but I think there might be more to it. . . . Our society puts so much value in youth; beauty and health that it seems each day we grow older we all lose some worth (as measured by society). Having a terminal illness seems to speed this factor up so that your worth is diminishing at a more rapid rate because so many feel you have nothing more to offer. . . . I am also wondering how you (Denise) fight for the social change when you have to continually fight a disease in your own body and also adjust the physical and cognitive changes post-illness?

It reminds me of my 82-year-old grandmother who had broken almost every bone in her body at least once and was almost blind when she died. Most people thought she was just a housewife who had never written out a check before my grandpa died or obtained a drivers license, but underneath the quaint exterior was someone with more wisdom, courage, and faith than anyone else I have ever known. I did enjoy the article but thinking about these types of issues makes me sad. I feel helpless and am not sure how to help bring about change! Maybe that is another reason why people avoided you?

My Response

This reader offers a fresh perspective on my situation, which at first I did not quite appreciate; but after multiple readings, and the passage of time, I have come to respect and even appreciate the reader's sentiments. At first I resented being compared to the reader's 82-year-old grandmother. But the weekend after returning from a professional conference, in early February 2003, I suffered a seizure that put me in the hospital, once again. I have not, to date, fully regained the use of my entire right side, despite the devoted efforts of both physical and occupational therapists. It took me a little while to "digest," but I have come to believe that I might never regain this use. I perceive this turn of events as just one more loss. So, when I first read this reaction, I was quite defensive. After six months or so, I realized that I really could "go on fighting for social change" as this reader points out, in spite of having to fight with my body. However, I don't like the metaphor of fighting. I would rather say, "go on working with my body, mind and soul."

Reaction 3

I wanted to comment that I thought that it was brave to discuss these personal things with the class. I think that although it may be uncomfortable as a class to hear about this, it is invaluable information. Sex is an important aspect of an adult's life, and as counselors I think that we must be comfortable talking about it. People are socialized that sex should be a private thing and should not be talked about. This is not beneficial for some clients because some of their distress could be from sexual difficulties or concerns.

My Response

This reader focused only on the sexual part of the article and ignored the other four strands. Once when I had shared this article with a previous class, two students threatened to report me to the APA for violation of the ethical code, although they did not say exactly how I had done so. However, it seems that they may have been responding with discomfort to my self-disclosure. Self-disclosure as a teacher may be understood as modeling how therapists would self-disclose with their clients. However, these students may have been responding to the content of my self-disclosure—talking frankly about sex and, specifically, my personal feelings about my own sexuality as a woman with a disability.

Frustrated by student response, I decided to consult the literature. In numerous articles I found that, contrary to what we teach, self-disclosure often enhances the therapy relationship (Barrett & Berman, 2001; Hill & Knox, 2002). One article, written specifically for physically ill or dying therapists, examines the ethical issues embedded within the decision about whether or not to self-disclose (Bram,

1995). The dilemmas the therapists face could be summarized as (1) precautions about abandoning clients, (2) self-disclosure to clients about the illness, and (3) decisions about returning to practice. Thankfully, I never had to face any of those issues, because I terminated my practice after discovering the cancer. However, the reactions of students suggest that similar considerations are relevant to teachers. Of course, I found articles arguing the other side. One such article, written from a psychoanalytic perspective, warned novice therapists not to attempt this higher-level task (self-disclosure) without "judicious execution" (Bishop & Lane, 2001). The issue of self-disclosure is widely debated, but it is worth noting that, at one level, I have no choice but to self-disclose any time I am in a teaching situation. My physical disability is visibly apparent, and so students are always in a position of responding to something about my personal life whenever they interact with me.

Maybe all of the readers are a bit uncomfortable with my self-disclosures. After all, we train them not to disclose any secrets to their clients. But if we can believe the literature, there are both pros and cons to self-disclosure (Peterson, 2002). In a world of diversity, the pros of self-disclosure may be more important than the cons.

GAY MAN ON CAMPUS: WHAT ALL THE FUSS IS ABOUT

Out on the Prairie

The perspective I bring to this chapter is that of a middle-aged man who enjoys the privileges of being without a disability and who is of a white, Anglo-Saxon, Protestant background, but who struggles with issues of being openly gay in a conservative, rural region. For the first four years at my current position as a tenure-track assistant professor, I was the only openly gay male faculty member on campus. Being from the East Coast, I faced a different culture after moving to the northern plains region, and it took a few years to adjust to living in a small city lacking a strong gay-lesbian-bisexual-transgendered (GLBT) community. With a predominant "don't ask, don't tell" mentality, it is harder for GBLT persons to develop a strong sense of identity in rural communities than in major urban areas (Beard & Hissam, 2002), so my openness about my sexual orientation is often not welcomed by either heterosexual or GLBT persons. Fellows (1996), writing about life for gay men in rural and small-town midwestern settings, noted that being gay is often thought to be exclusively an urban experience. Since moving here, I have discovered that a reticent tolerance of GLBT people is the norm in this rural, conservative region, in contrast to the overt hostility that friends and family back home continually feared I would face.

A recent national survey demonstrated that a favorable opinion of gay and lesbian persons is much less common in the Midwest than in the East or West (Pew Research Center for People and the Press, 2003). Tolerance seems to be the limit of my social integration among most men in the area, including the male faculty at my university. Among most women faculty on campus I have always felt accepted, but overall I still sense that I am an outsider here. Although my career is productive and rewarding, I am still somewhat socially isolated and professionally marginalized. This is a university where the non-discrimination statement includes sexual orientation, but where most gay male staff and faculty leave within several years of hire, often feeling cast aside, subtly or directly, due to their sexual orientation. This irony appears to be a consequence of the university's surface level of commitment to diversity, whereas our department aspires to a deeper commitment (Banning, 2003). Consistent with this aim, I strive to increase awareness and acceptance of GLBT persons and causes on campus and in the community. I am fortunate, in this regard, to have the support of a diverse collegial faculty in our department.

Out in the University

There are certain professional advantages to being an openly gay man at the university. For example, ever since my first semester I have frequently been asked to present on GLBT issues on campus, at nearby campuses, and in the community. These presentations have increased local awareness, knowledge, and, I hope, acceptance of GLBT persons and have helped me develop my skills as a public speaker. The downside of these service activities is that they do not contribute nearly as much as research or teaching do to one's tenure portfolio. Although I have not been able to find any data for GLBT faculty on this issue, a recent national survey reported that male faculty and white faculty spend a higher proportion of their time on research and less time on service than female, black, Latino, and Asian/Pacific Islander faculty (National Center for Education Statistics, 2002). Similarly, becoming a spokesperson for GLBT issues also appears to interfere with the time commitment needed to complete the research one must do in order to advance in an academic career.

A more unambiguously positive aspect to my minority status is that people look to me as a spokesperson on GLBT issues even when I would not claim myself as an expert. As a prime example, I have been awarded several state-funded HIV prevention grants and a university "seed money" grant on GLBT health issues, even though HIV/AIDS and other areas of health psychology were only secondary interests of mine before moving to this relatively remote location. My expertise in these areas has developed and has led to two national presentations and one publication so far (Whitcomb & Pahl, 2002), but may not have if I were in an area where more experts were already working.

Even within these advantages, however, there are disadvantages, such as never being able to be invisible. Although I recognize the importance of being a gay role model while in front of a classroom (in part to counter the presumption of heterosexuality) (Pobo, 1999), sometimes I am aware that I am being seen as a role model even when attending a social function. Even with a very small private practice and as a teacher of small graduate classes, clients and students sometimes attend the same social events that I do. While working within a newer ethical understanding of professional boundaries, I have learned that dual relationships are inevitable as a minority member in a small community.

Out in My Department

I turn now to reflecting upon my status as a gay man within my department, first considering relationships with colleagues. In applying to my current position, I came out as gay and felt comfortable presenting a colloquium on a LGB research area. The faculty were relatively diverse when I started the job and have become increasingly so since then, with the subsequent hire of faculty who are diverse by race, gender, disability, and sexual orientation. I did not feel like a junior faculty for long, as I became the director of our master's program in my second year, the same time that I filled a position on the college's tenure and promotion committee. Although I believe that being gay had nothing to do with assignment to these positions, even the fact that these assignments were offered to me demonstrates acceptance of my sexual orientation. That is, a homophobic department would not appoint an openly gay man as a program director in charge of student recruitment, and a homophobic college would not permit an openly gay man to vote on promotion decisions for fellow faculty.

Regarding my research agenda, I have always felt that it has been supported within our department, but I have needed to be creative to initiate collaborative diversity-related projects with my colleagues. I know that this is not different from the experience of faculty everywhere whose specialization is not shared by colleagues, but sometimes most of them had a greater understanding of the opportunities and barriers involved in conducting GLBT-focused research. Writing this chapter and developing the presentation that preceded it, however, has created wonderful opportunities to discuss with colleagues the commonalities and differences across sexual orientation, gender, religion, disability status, and size that occurred only sporadically before. Having taken the risks to engage in these sometimes-difficult dialogues clarifies our mission as a department and what we strive to offer our students and the university.

Out in the Classroom

Often I recognize the impact of my sexual orientation on relationships with students. I come out to each of my regular classes, but whereas in my first couple of years I came out almost immediately, reacting in a compulsive manner to reduce my own discomfort with anticipated prejudice, I feel more relaxed now about mentioning it when it seems appropriate, and it always does at some point early in the semester. I sometimes wonder about the level of students' comfort with my sexual orientation. Students have never publicly raised this issue, but they seem to test the issue in ways such as asking more questions about client sexual orientation issues than other important clinical issues. Recently published resources, such as the American Psychological Association's *Guidelines for Psychotherapy with Lesbian, Gay, and Bisexual Clients* (Division 44/Committee, 2000) have facilitated my teaching, but speaking from personal experience as a gay clinician working with GLBT issues helps the issues come alive for my students.

In addition to discussing my clinical work, experience has taught me how best to self-disclose anecdotes related to my sexual orientation and how to discuss in class my own perceptions of how students perceive sexual orientation issues. Occasional discussions with other GLBT faculty provide guidance, as does reading about how others use self-disclosure to create teachable moments regarding sexual orientation.

Although many students appear interested in sexual orientation issues while others appear disinterested, our department chair has sometimes wondered whether homonegativity was a factor during semesters when one or two students appeared as outliers in their negative evaluations of my classes. Although I would not attempt to try to prove that student bias has affected my evaluations, a recent study supported such a notion (Russ, Simonds, & Hunt, 2002). In that experimental study of undergraduate students, participants who thought that their instructor was gay perceived him to be significantly less credible, both in terms of competence and character, than an instructor they thought was heterosexual. The students also felt that they learned less from the gay than from the heterosexual teacher. Given these results, it is plausible that a portion of the negative evaluations could be an indirect, perhaps even unconscious, way to express disapproval for a stigmatized way of being in the world.

Researching GLBT Issues

I will conclude this section with examples of collaborative projects in which my sexual orientation has played a role. Co-teaching a course entitled The Psychology of Women, Gender, and Development with a heterosexual woman with a disability (Twohey, 2001) was a rewarding experience. Students observed and benefited, we believe, from the interaction and complementary styles of a heterosexual woman with a disability and a gay man without a disability. This learning process has continued by my co-authoring, with a male student, a book chapter on male privilege and heterosexual privilege (Whitcomb & Cummings, in press).

I have worked closely with three outstanding lesbian students, resulting in publications and presentations. Two of the students indicated, directly or indirectly, that my presence on the faculty as an openly gay person influenced their decision to attend our program. Seeking a supportive faculty relationship may be particularly important for GLBT students. One national survey of psychology graduate students (Pilkington & Cantor, 1996) and a campus climate study of undergraduate and graduate students at a large midwestern research university (Waldo, 1998) reported many instances of LGB students facing a less nurturing and sometimes hostile learning environment, pointing to the importance of LGB students having faculty they could trust concerning their sexual orientation and faculty who encouraged LGB students to work with them. In light of these data, I am encouraged to remain open about my sexual orientation as a faculty member and to promote GLBT-affirmative research and clinical practice in my work with students.

Of course, students of any sexual orientation can benefit from involvement with GLBT academic projects. Gay, lesbian, bisexual, heterosexual, and unidentified students have contributed greatly to my HIV-prevention grants, including leadership in daylong workshops with intense levels of sexual self-disclosure among mostly gay men. Students who become involved in projects like these have made a shift from non-engagement to engagement with multiculturalism—they are prepared to challenge the status quo and work on issues of social justice (Chávez & O'Donnell, 1998).

THE CASE OF THE FAT, GAY JEW

Judaism in Academia

As a fat, gay, Jewish, white man in his early 50s, currently able-bodied (though less so than in the past), and recently relocated from a lifetime in urban, southwestern, U.S. cities to the rural Midwest, I have witnessed changes in prejudices and their manifestation. As a child, living in Jewish neighborhoods and attending Jewish parochial schools protected me from overt anti-Semitism, for the most part. My first conscious encounters with this prejudice (other than the internalized anti-Semitism in my family) were as an adult in the workforce. Even at its worst, however, it always occurred in isolated incidents, and I never had to look far for an ally to support me in confronting this type of bigotry.

Certainly, Jews have been overrepresented in U.S. academia in my lifetime (not so in previous generations when quotas were in place), and though there are many negative stereotypes about Jews still prevalent, having so much contact with members of such a small minority group tends to mitigate the negative stereotyping (Loewy, 1995). The biggest problem I have faced in the academy in this regard is that of being cast in the role of "model minority"—mostly by Christians (in statements such as "I love your people," "You people are so smart, learned, etc.," "You are God's chosen people"). It is difficult to integrate this rhetoric into my reality while simultaneously being shown no regard for scheduling important academic events on our holiest of days or just living with the daily assumption that everyone is Christian. Christmas is a national holiday, and still Christian privilege is invisible and unacknowledged in this country.

I have had a graduate student ask me whether it is true that Jews are cheap. I have been asked whether my Judaism makes me anti-Christian. I have felt obligated to participate in Christian ritual (often disguised as "holiday" ritual) or risk being cast as a "Scrooge" or "Shylock." I am faced every year with decisions about whether to ask for release from classes during the Jewish holy times.

Coming Out at the University

However, these experiences of prejudice and discrimination pale in comparison to the experiences of growing up gay in the United States. Though I probably had it better than most gay boys, growing up in the 1950s and 1960s in a neighborhood that has since incorporated into a city that elected the first gay majority city council in the United States, the homophobia of the time did not escape me. Heterosexism and homophobia generally start in the family (Hunter & Mallon, 2000), and mine was no exception. Coming out was a long and difficult process for me.

Upon entering academia, however, I found a forum for talking about the politics and psychology of homosexuality. I encountered many educated people who could see past their stereotypes and fears to the real issues that faced lesbian, gay, and bisexual people. I entered the field of psychology just as multiculturalism was becoming a force and was fortunate to find a graduate program that was leading the way in multicultural education in counseling psychology.

For the first time, I felt valued as a gay man. My experience of openly dealing with my sexual orientation and coming to see homosexuality as a political issue made me a valuable resource to my colleagues and professors. I was respected for having the courage to be "out" in an academic environment that was just beginning to accept openly gay people and embrace diversity as a positive force in the academy.

On the other hand, though my very private life has been a resource for the university, my relationships were not seen as valid then and still are not. My same-sex spouse cannot receive the same benefits as my heterosexual colleagues' spouses. We could not live together in family student housing, and we still cannot live together in faculty housing.

I have had students call me a sinner. Often I am accused of "pushing my own agenda" by bringing issues of sexual orientation into my courses. Unlike Jews (who are only 1–2 percent of the U.S. population), lesbian, gay, and bisexual people make up a sizable minority in the United States. We are in all segments of society. It is safe to say that almost all psychologists will work with someone who is a sexual minority. Most students appreciate having a professor who is willing to share her or his own experiences as they relate to the material to be learned. Yet every year I have some students who complain that I talk too much about gay issues. I wonder how much is too much when it is a topic that has never been discussed in any class they have ever taken before.

I face the decision every year about whether and when to come out to my students. I spent the first several years of my teaching experimenting with different ways and different times during the semester to come out to my classes. If I come out too soon, many students just see me as a stereotype and discount what I say because I'm the "gay professor." If I wait too long, then students can feel betrayed, and I feel stifled by missing "teachable moments" because it is "too soon" to come out to the class yet and still maintain credibility. Ironically, many times it is out of my control anyway, since students will gossip with each other.

Overcoming Fat Phobia

As a gay Jew, I have had many barriers to overcome. However, none of the prejudice I have faced as a Jew, as a gay man, or as a gay Jew, has come close to affecting me as much as the oppression I have faced as a fat person. Unlike anti-Semitism and heterosexism, anti-fat bias is not abating in this culture, but getting worse. However, much like homophobia, sizism is rooted in fear and misinformation.

This bias is one that I have found even my colleagues to be unaware of in themselves. Poor body image is so pervasive in our culture that most of us project our bad feelings about our own bodies onto fat people. Even colleagues who have been working in the area of multiculturalism have trivialized my work in this area. Much as racism, sexism, and heterosexism were not seen as legitimate areas of study until recently, sizism is still seen as not worthy of study by many, and for many of the same reasons.

The cultural messages regarding fat bodies are so strong and overt that even after spending considerable time explaining both the health risks of obesity and the complete failure of any and all weight loss programs in the long term—short of surgery, which is often riskier than being fat—students still regularly want to challenge the credibility of my size-positive message by stating that being fat is unhealthy. They somehow cannot accept the idea that diet and exercise might make one healthier but will usually not result in permanent weight loss. Raising people's awareness that one can be fat and fit does not seem to help them accept larger bodies.

Shedding light on the fear and loathing that most of us feel about being fat and about fat people makes us feel uncomfortable in the same ways that pointing out personal and institutionalized racism, sexism, and heterosexism makes us uncomfortable when we have to look at ourselves. Many students (and professors) squirm in their chairs at the thought that it may be okay to be fat: that one can be fat and happy, healthy, and fulfilled.

Multiple Group Identity Development

Academic institutions, as agents of socialization, reinforce the status quo (Hall, Lopez, & Bansal, 2001). Western psychology has supported and promoted a rather narrow, Eurocentric view of mental and social health (D'Andrea & Daniels, 1991). As such, developing and maintaining a positive identity as a fat, gay Jew has presented many challenges. In fact, people are so uncomfortable with these identities that I am almost always met with nervous laughter when I identify myself this way. Finding a department that was more advanced in its understanding and appreciation of diversity was important to my development as a multicultural counselor as well as my personal group identity development. Rather than being seen in a problem-saturated way, my colleagues and I have been able to learn much from each other as we grapple with the issues that advocating for diversity brings to a small department in a very traditional academic environment.

Identity development models do not take into account the complex multiple identities that we all have (Constantine, 2002). Though we are all certainly still evolving in our multicultural competence and group identity development, being in a work and learning environment where everyone is exploring the nuances and implications of our identity development establishes an environment wherein one is eager to do so. For example, recently I have begun to think about the connections and continua that fat people have with people who have certain physical disabilities or limitations. Many fat people require accommodations like elevators instead of stairs, or armless chairs. Yet even as we learn to embrace our fat identities, most fat people still reject the "disabled" label.

The most current direction of identity development for the profession of multicultural counseling psychology is that of counselor/ psychologist as advocate. The need for this new role is a reflection of an increasing awareness of the complexity of the contextual variables that affect our mental health and growth (Toporek & Liu, 2001). The normative nature of multicultural values in the Department of Counseling at UND has fostered a commitment to social action that is inherent in the role of advocate.

CONVERSATIONS ACROSS IDENTITIES

In this section we will describe the ways in which our diverse identities and values form the foundation for collegial dialogue. Like any academic program, we are routinely faced with competing demands regarding resource and workload allocation. In addition, there exists the potential to encounter diversity-related conflicts. In the case of resource and workload allocation, as with our research foci, conversations dealing with how our energies are directed could easily become ultimatums on whose identity is most important. Instead, all five authors believe our experiences and values are reflective of Sue's (1995) multicultural phase of organizational development—able to accommodate and support multiple diversities.

Common Experiences

Several commonalties exist among our diversity experiences. First, students and faculty have consistently identified us all in terms of our diversity identity, for example, blind professor or gay professor. Second, most of us have felt uncomfortable in being the central focus or "cause" of a lot of trouble, or even change for others. We don't want to feel like others have to make adjustments "just for us." These feelings tend to arise when requesting disability accommodations or considering the appropriateness of celebrating mainstream religious holidays and not others. My Jewish colleague and I (Daughtry) have drawn parallels between objecting to exclusive holiday traditions and advocating for accommodation measures. We feel strongly about the right to reasonable accommodation and religious parity in the workplace, but realize that others' budget needs and long-held traditions are also impacted. Third, students have often judged many of us as "grinding a personal axe" when presenting class material. Two gay colleagues commented on challenges encountered when students perceived them as advocating personal views while presenting class material. Last, we each belong to a marginalized group that is valued less than the dominant group and often discriminated against. This marginalization extends to our research agendas. University hierarchies have traditionally regarded research areas such as disability, sexual orientation, body size discrimination, or women's issues as less worthy of scientific study than research areas with a narrower view of human diversity. Historically, individual differences have been studied in terms of deviation from the (white, male, heterosexual, able-bodied) norm, rather than from a perspective that celebrates diversity and could advocate for a minority group (Sue & Sue, 1999). People choosing to conduct research with a social justice focus risk being considered less worthy of tenure or promotion.

Common experiences form the core connections of our shared multicultural identity. We all are acquainted with experiences such as marginalization and discrimination. Shared understanding helps us realize that each others' experiences of discrimination are real and must be taken seriously. Shared understandings also serve to promote a mutual respect and empathic buffering that aids in negotiating potential conflicts.

Unique Experiences

Our multicultural identity is also characterized by recognition of uniqueness. Our experiences of discrimination are not identical. For example, able-bodied, average-sized colleagues do not encounter physical barriers or other accommodation considerations. In a similar fashion, male colleagues do not have to cope with objectification, safety issues, or harassment to the extent that female colleagues might. Unique experiences help create an "awareness of not knowing." At times, we each have had to assume the role of educator to help the rest understand our unique group experience. Hence a departmental norm has evolved that it is "okay" not to know, at least when "not knowing" is combined with a willingness to learn. Often discussions of our unique diversity experience lead to broader dialogues related to our uniqueness as human beings. This is valuable for

Toolbox for Change

The following are strategies we believe can be used to reinforce the value of diversity as the norm, as well as to challenge group and individual preconceptions and biases. The first four strategies (real listening, believing in the experience, identification of similarity, and continual introspection) are processes that build on each other to develop a diversity-friendly environment. The last three strategies (discussion and modeling, publicizing, and increasing numbers) are more practical organizational tools that can be implemented once a safe and accepting environment exists. These latter three strategies represent institutional actions necessary to create more diverse work settings.

1. Real listening

Listening in a sincere and authentic fashion to facilitate dialogue and develop an atmosphere in which diversity is acknowledged and appreciated. Do not mentally tune out when colleagues present views you disagree with.

2. Believing in the experience

Believe the perspectives of others by assuming that their experiences are valid. Do not discount experiences just because they differ from ours and are therefore unfamiliar.

3. Continual introspection

Actively introspect about your own biases and prejudices to increase openness to individual differences. Increase self-awareness by having the courage to challenge personal biases and prejudices, thus defusing their power within the group.

4. Identification of similarity

Actively focus attention on similarities between differing diversity identities while continuing to appreciate the differences.

5. Discussion and modeling

Actively discuss issues of diversity and identify how they are affecting the group's cohesion and productivity. Openly process diversity issues related to student admissions and faculty hiring.

continued

Toolbox for Change (continued)

6. Documenting and publicizing	Record diversity expectations in departmental documents and university or other outlets that perpetuate diversity awareness and codify multiculturalism. This practice increases the degree of departmental accountability while challenging the status quo. Accountability creates a platform for advocating for diversity needs and helps ensure that none are overlooked.
7. Increased representation	Increase the number of diverse members in the group. Critical mass facilitates change.

reminding us that no one can be defined solely by membership in a demographic category. It is the recognition of individual uniqueness, within a group context, that facilitates movement beyond simple nondiscrimination.

Practical Implications

So how does this blend of diversity experiences and values become manifest in daily departmental interactions? Put another way, what are the practical implications of becoming a multicultural organization? This can be seen from our interactions around disability. We have recognized that disability has been given significantly less attention than other diversity considerations, such as race or gender. One area in which this was noted was student admissions. An abled colleague has candidly shared that reviewing applicant files does not bring the same "gut" reaction when reviewing an application from a student with a disability relative to other aspects of diversity. Another abled colleague has shared reactions related to practical issues. How does one accommodate in the classroom? How do I act with an interpreter in the classroom?

Our commitment to diversity has helped us process such reactions in a respectful fashion. Beyond respectful, our conversations have been productive. Our norms and values helped create a climate where potentially problematic perceptions can be shared and worked through. Our "empathic glue" is grounded in the shared knowledge that we all have our learning curves.

REFERENCES

Banning, J. H. (2003). The institution's commitment to diversity: An aid or hindrance to teachers of diversity. In W. Timpson, S. Canetto, E. Borrayo, & R. Yang (Eds.), *Teaching diversity: Challenges and complexities, identities and integrity* (pp. 207–216). Madison, WI: Atwood Publishing.

Barrett, M. S., & Berman, J. S. (2001). Is psychotherapy more effective when therapists disclose information about themselves? *Journal of Consulting and Clinical Psychology, 69*, 597–603.

Beard, K. W., & Hissam, A. (2002). The use of Erikson's developmental theory with gay men from rural communities. *Journal of Rural Community Psychology, E5*(2). Retrieved February 1, 2004, from www.marshall.edu/jrcp/JRCP%20Intro%20GLBT/JRCP%20Erikson.htm

Bishop, J., & Lane, R. C. (2001). Self-disclosure and the therapeutic frame: Concerns for novice practitioners. *Journal of Contemporary Psychotherapy, 31*, 245–256.

Bluestone, H. H., Stokes, A., & Kuba, S. (1996). Toward an integrated program design: Evaluating the status of diversity training in a graduate school curriculum. *Professional Psychology: Research and Practice, 27*, 394–400.

Bram, A. D. (1995). The physically ill or dying psychotherapist: A review of ethical and clinical considerations. *Psychotherapy: Theory, Research, Practice, Training, 32*, 568–580.

Chávez, R. C., & O'Donnell, J. (Eds.). (1998). *Speaking the unpleasant: The politics of (non) engagement in the multicultural education terrain.* Albany, NY: State University of New York Press.

Constantine, M. G. (2002). The intersection of race, ethnicity, gender and social class in counseling: Examining selves in cultural contexts. *Journal of Multicultural Counseling and Development, 30*, 210–215.

D'Andrea, M., & Daniels, J. (1991). Exploring the different levels of multicultural counseling training in counselor education. *Journal of Counseling and Development, 70*, 78–85.

D'Andrea, M., & Daniels, J. (1995). Promoting multiculturalism and organizational change in the counseling profession: A case study. In J. G. Ponterotto, J. M. Casas, L. A. Suzuki, & C. M. Alexander (Eds.), *Handbook of multicultural counseling* (pp. 17–33). Thousand Oaks, CA: SAGE Publications, Inc.

Daughtry, D. (In press). Should I just tell them I can't find the door? In D. Cleveland (Ed.), *When minorities are especially encouraged to apply: Addressing diversity and affirmative action in PWI's.* New York: Peter Lang.

Division 44/Committee on Lesbian, Gay, and Bisexual Concerns Joint Task Force on Guidelines for Psychotherapy With Lesbian, Gay, and Bisexual Clients. (2000). Guidelines for psychotherapy with lesbian, gay, and bisexual clients. *American Psychologist, 55*, 1440–1451.

Fellows, W. (Ed.). (1996). *Farm boys: Lives of gay men from the rural Midwest*. Madison, WI: University of Wisconsin Press.

Gill, C. J. (1997). Four types of integration in disability identity development. *Journal of Vocational Rehabilitation, 9*, 39–46.

Hahn, H., & Beaulaurier, R. L. (2001). Attitudes toward disabilities: A research note on activists with disabilities. *Journal of Disability Policy Journal, 12*(1), 40–46.

Hall, G. C. N., Lopez, I. R., & Bansal, A. (2001). Academic acculturation: Race, gender, and class issues. In D. B. Pope-Davis & H. L. K. Coleman (Eds.), *The intersection of race, class, and gender in multicultural counseling* (pp. 171–188). Thousand Oaks, CA: SAGE Publications, Inc.

Hill, C. E., & Knox, S. (2002). Self-disclosure. In J. Norcross (Ed.), *Psychotherapy relationships that work: Therapist contributions and responsiveness to patients* (pp. 255–265). London: Oxford University Press.

Hunter, J., & Mallon, G. P. (2000). Lesbian, gay, and bisexual adolescent development. In B. Greene & G. L. Croom (Eds.), *Education, research, and practice in lesbian, gay, bisexual, and transgender psychology* (pp. 226–243). Thousand Oaks, CA: SAGE Publications, Inc.

Loewy, M. I. (1995). Size bias by mental health professionals: Use of the illusory correlation paradigm. (Doctoral dissertation, University of California–Santa Barbara, 1994). *Dissertation Abstracts International, 56*(3), 1704.

National Center for Education Statistics. (2002, September 10). *Gender and racial/ethnic differences in salary and other characteristics of postsecondary faculty: Fall 1998*. (U.S. Department of Education Office of Education Research and Improvement, NCES, 2002-170). Retrieved February 1, 2004, from http://nces.ed.gov/pubs2002/2002170.pdf

Olkin, R. (2000, August). *What do we talk about when we talk about disability?* Presentation at the U.S. Department of Education, National Institute of Disability and Rehabilitation Research, Washington, DC.

Peterson, Z. D. (2002). More than a mirror: The ethics of therapist self-disclosure. *Psychotherapy: Theory, Research, Practice, Training, 39*, 21–31.

Pew Research Center for People and the Press, Pew Forum on Religion and Public Life. (2003, November 18). *Republicans unified, Democrats split on gay marriage: Religious beliefs underpin opposition to homosexuality*. Washington, DC: Author. Retrieved February 1, 2004, from http://pewforum.org/publications/surveys/religion-homosexuality.pdf

Pilkington, N. W., & Cantor, J. M. (1996). Perceptions of heterosexual bias in professional psychology programs: A survey of graduate students. *Professional Psychology: Research and Practice, 27*, 604–612.

Pobo, K. (1999). The gay/lesbian teacher as role model. *Humanist, 59*(2), 26.

Reeve, D. (2000). Oppression within the counseling room. *Disability & Society, 15,* 669–682.

Russ, T. L., Simonds, C. J., & Hunt, S. K. (2002). Coming out in the classroom . . . An occupational hazard: The influence of sexual orientation on teacher credibility and perceived student learning. *Communication Education, 51,* 311–324.

Sue, D. W. (1995). Multicultural organizational development: Implications for the counseling profession. In J. G. Ponterotto, J. M. Casas, L. A. Suzuki, & C. M. Alexander (Eds.), *Handbook of multicultural counseling* (pp. 474–492). Thousand Oaks, CA: SAGE Publications, Inc.

Sue, D. W., Carter, R. T., Casas, J. M., Fouad, N. A., Ivey, A. E., Jensen, M., et al. (1998). *Multicultural aspects of counseling* (Vol. 11). Thousand Oaks, CA: SAGE Publications, Inc.

Sue, D. W., & Sue, D. (1999). The politics of counseling and psychotherapy. In *Counseling the culturally different* (3rd ed., pp. 3–26). New York: Wiley.

Toporek, R. L., & Liu, W. M. (2001). Advocacy in counseling: Addressing race, class, and gender oppression. In D. B. Pope-Davis & H. L. K. Coleman (Eds.), *The intersection of race, class, and gender in multicultural counseling* (pp. 385–413). Thousand Oaks, CA: SAGE Publications, Inc.

Twohey, D. (2001). Feminist therapy in cases of life-threatening illness. *Women & Therapy, 23,* 11–120.

Vace, N. A., & Clifford, K. (1995). *Individuals with a physical disability.* In N. A. Vance, S. B. De Vaney, & J. Wittmer (Eds.), *Experiencing and counseling multicultural and diverse populations* (3rd ed., pp. 251–271). Bristol, PA: Accelerated Development.

Waldo, C. R. (1998). Out on campus: Sexual orientation and academic climate in a university context. *American Journal of Community Psychology, 26,* 745–774.

Whitcomb, D. H., & Cummings, J. (In press). Exploring male privilege: Journey of two white middle-class men. In S. K. Anderson & V. A. Middleton (Eds.), *Explorations in oppression, diversity and privilege.* Pacific Grove, CA: Books/Cole.

Whitcomb, D. H., & Pahl, P. (2002). Safe connections: Planning, organizing, and running an HIV prevention workshop for MSM in a rural region. *Journal of Rural Community Psychology, E5*(2). Retrieved February 1, 2004, from www.marshall.edu/jrcp/JRCP%20Intro%20GLBT/JRCP%20Safe%20Connections/safe_connections.htm

Index

Accountability, 174–177, 197
Affirmative action, 237
African Americans, 96–97, 175
Akaka Bill, 144
"Alien self disorder" syndrome:
    case study of, 171–172;
    description of, 166
Allport, Gordon, 33
Americans with Disabilities Act: in
    education, 60; history of, 57, 59;
    Individuals with Disabilities
    Education Act vs., 63–64;
    provisions of, 61–62; purpose of,
    59–60
Asthma, 67
"Aversive racism reaction"
    syndrome: case studies of, 173–174,
    176–177; description of, 166
Avoidance, 260
Awareness, 150–151

Bias: intergroup, 80–81, 83–84; in
    language, 150–151
Blacks: intimidation against, 175;
    life expectancy of, 177–178;
    physical health of, 177–178;

racial profiling against, 174–175.
    See African Americans
Body mass index, 112–113
Body weight: facts about, 113–115;
    lifestyle influences, 114; myths
    about, 113–115; negative
    stereotypes based on, 112;
    terminology associated with,
    112–113; in western society,
    112
Body weight–related discrimination:
    case study of, 271–275;
    examples of, 111–112; research
    regarding, 115–132
Buddhism, 41
Buddhist psychology, 39

Categories of disabilities, 53
Central traits, 75–76
Cerebral palsy, 65
Change: in attitudes, 79–80; by
    community, 154–155; by
    individuals, 153–154
Chicago Dinners: background of,
    242–243; conclusions made after,
    248–250; format of, 243–248;

power-related discussions, 247;
rules of engagement for,
244–245; success of, 244
Children: development of,
215–216; learning by,
217–218; school influences
on, 215–217; shared value and
responsibility for, 181–183,
193–194, 200; vulnerability of, 181
Children with disabilities: barriers
to services for, 67–68; mental
disabilities, 67; physical
disabilities, 64–65; prejudice
against, 64–65
Clinical settings, universal-diverse
orientation in, 224–225
Cognitive dissonance, 77
Collective identity, 211
College, 218–221
Community change, 154–155
Community inclusion, 169–170,
196
Compassion, 42, 44
Contact theory, 80–81
Counseling settings, universal-
diverse orientation in, 224–225
Crisis of meaning, 29, 33, 36
Cross-categorization, 209
Cultural diversity, 20
Cultural groups, 14–15
Cultural identity: description of, 2;
dress as form of (see Dress);
evolution of, 2–3
Cultural myths, 54–55
Cultural relational paradox, 163
Culture: definition of, 2; dress
based on, 3, 16; subjective, 31
Culture swapping, 166
Cystic fibrosis, 66

"Dangerous minds" syndrome: case
studies of, 169–170, 173–174,
176–177; description of, 165

Decategorization, 210–211, 238;
description of, 162
Dieting, 113
Direct intergroup conflict, 71
Disability: definition of, 52, 74;
health and, 99; International
Classification of Functioning
definition of, 64; as a loss, 76–77;
low-income jobs as cause of,
104; medical model of, 58, 60,
62–68; minority model of, 58,
68; models of, 58; moral model
of, 58; people with (see Persons
with disability); self-advocacy,
261–263; social construction of,
73–74, 79; training about,
258–259
Discrimination: ability status-based,
97; body weight–related,
111–112, 115–132; case studies
of, 87–90; definition of, 52;
examples of, 52–54; factors
associated with, 54; history of,
54–56; images and perceptions
that facilitate, 145–149; leaders'
influence on, 144–145;
low-income background and,
96–97; racial, 237–238; social
class-based, 101;
universal-diverse orientation
for (see Universal-diverse
orientation); varied experiences
of, 276
Diversity: commonality of
experiences, 74, 275–276;
dialogues on, 240–242; respect
for, 170–172, 196; training
programs regarding, 222
Domestic violence, 162–163
Dominance, 169–170
Douglass, Frederick, 237
Dress: changes in, 18; cultural
differences reflected by, 8–9;
cultural identity derived from, 3,

14–18; cultural influences on, 3, 16; definition of, 3; description of, 1; ethnic, 16; ethnocultural context of, 9–11; European standards of, 4, 17, 24; heterogeneity in, 21; homogeneity of, 24; mute assimilation effects on, 17; personal narrative of, 5–8; professional identity and, 5–8; psychological resources and meaning derived from, 3–4; self-image and, 16; social visibility of, 21–24; in United States, 4

Economic abuse, 172–174, 192–193
Economic empowerment, 172–174
Economic globalization, 138–141
Education: access to, 56, 102–105; Americans with Disabilities Act in, 60; Individuals with Disabilities Education Act, 57
Educators, 155–157
Emotional abuse, 170–171, 188–189
Emotional affirmation, 170–172, 196
Empathy, 168
Employment, Americans with Disabilities Act provisions for, 61
Equal opportunity, 186–187, 199
Erikson, Erik, 32–33
Ethnic dress, 16
Ethnic identity, 2
Ethnocentric narcissism, 146–147
Ethnocentrism: description of, 141–142; methods to counteract, 147
Existential psychology, 37–38
Extrinsic spirituality, 33

"Fly in the buttermilk" syndrome: case studies of, 169–170,

173–174, 176–177; description of, 164–165
Fromm, Erich, 33

Gallaudet University, 78–79, 84
Gay-lesbian-bisexual-transgender persons, 266–271
Genocidal fascism, 148
Globalization: backlash against, 138–141; description of, 135–136; economic, 138–141; educators' role in, 155; hegemonic, 139; interdependencies created by, 140; nationalism and, 139; responses to, 140; spirituality affected by, 27–30
Government, 61
Groups: power differentials among, 16; surface markers used to differentiate, 15, 22

Hate crimes, 161
Head and face anomalies, 66
Hegemonic globalization, 139
Heterogeneity, 21
Higher education: on-campus housing, 220; student affairs, 219; in United States, 156; universal-diverse orientation in settings of, 218–221
Honesty, 174–177, 197

Identity development, 218
Immigrants: description of, 103–104; post-colonization stress disorder, 166
Impairment, 74
Incarceration, 97
Individual change, 153–154
Individuals with Disabilities Education Act: Americans with Disabilities Act vs., 63–64; description of, 57, 59

Institutions, 55
Intergroup bias, 80–81, 83–84
Intergroup differences, 14–15
International Classification of
    Functioning, 64
Internationalism, 136
Intimidation, 174–175, 189–190
Intrinsic spirituality, 33
"Invisibility" syndrome: case studies
    of, 169–170, 173–174,
    176–177, 182–183, 184–186;
    description of, 165
Isolation, 169, 188

James, William, 32
Jones, James, 233
Jung, Carl, 32
Jungian psychology, 40–41

Knowledge, 151–152

Low-income background, 96–97,
    104

Male privilege, 186, 194–195, 200
"Man enough" syndrome: case
    studies of, 182–183, 184–186;
    description of, 165
Maslow, Abraham, 33, 38–39
Meaning: crisis of, 29, 33, 36; in
    patients' lives, 36; search for, 42
Medical model of disability, 58, 60,
    62–68
Meditative state, 39
Meningomyelocele, 65
Mental health, 178; religion and,
    33–34; spirituality and, 29–30
Mental impairment, 53
"Might is right" belief, 147–148
Minority model of disability, 58, 68
Monocultural organizations:
    definition of, 253–254;
    multicultural shift in, 255–258;
    transitions in, 254–255

Moral model of disability, 58
Multiculturalism: description of, 8,
    20; literature about, 136; social
    impact of, 253; in United States,
    136
Multicultural organization:
    case studies of, 258–278;
    gay-lesbian-bisexual-transgender
    case study, 266–271;
    monocultural organization
    transition to, 253–258
Multilayered identity model, 223
Multiunilateral agreements, 140
Mute assimilation, 17
Mutuality, 168

Narrative(s): cultural diversity and,
    20; of ethnic dress, 5–8; purpose
    of, 20
Narrative identity model, 3
National Association for Retarded
    Children, 56
Nationalism, 139, 142
Negative stereotyping, 171
Neural tube defects, 65
Noble-savage myths, 142–143
Non-threatening behavior,
    183–186, 198
Normalcy, 62

Obese people: coping by, 120,
    122–124, 128; descriptive
    terminology associated with,
    113; dieting by, 113; negative
    attitudes toward, 115–116;
    in non-Western countries,
    116–117; research about,
    115–132; stereotypes about,
    115–116; stigmatization
    associated with, 115–132
Obesity: definition of, 112;
    demographics of, 114; dieting to
    reduce, 113; discrimination for,
    112; income levels and, 114;

lifestyle influences, 114; myths about, 113–115. *See also* Body weight–related discrimination; Obese people

On-campus housing, 220

Oppression: definition of, 163–164; origins of, 163; personal trauma and, 163; of persons with disability, 74; racism and, 246

Oppression reactive syndromes: "alien self disorder," 166, 171–172; "aversive racism reaction" syndrome, 166, 173–174, 176–177; "dangerous minds" syndrome, 165, 169–170, 173–174, 176–177; description of, 162; "fly in the buttermilk" syndrome, 164–165, 169–170, 173–174, 176–177; "invisibility" syndrome, 165, 169–170, 173–174, 176–177, 182–183, 184–186; "man enough" syndrome, 165, 182–183, 184–186; "post-colonization stress disorder," 166, 173–174, 184–186; "stereotyped threat" syndrome, 165–166, 169–170, 171–172, 176–177; symptoms of, 164; "woman enough" syndrome, 165

Organizations: monocultural (*see* Monocultural organizations); multicultural (*see* Multicultural organizations); universal-diverse orientation in, 221–224

Outgroup homogeneity, 72–73

Overweight, definition of, 112

Pathology, 62

Persons with disability: access to education for, 56; affective norms for, 76; Americans with Disabilities Act (*see* Americans

with Disabilities Act); asthma, 67; barriers for, 97; behavioral norms for, 76; case studies of, 87–90, 258–266; celebrating our differences, 83; central traits of, 75–76; cerebral palsy, 65; children, 64–65; commonality of experience among, 74, 275–276; community formation by, 77–78; community response to, 81–82; contact theory for, 80–81; cystic fibrosis, 66; definition of, 52; devaluation of, 74; disability as defined by, 74; Gallaudet University for, 78–79, 84; grateful feelings by, 76; head and face anomalies, 66; Individuals with Disabilities Education Act, 57, 59; loss associated with, 76–77; mass media portrayal of, 82; medical advances for, 51–52; medical issues for, 60, 62–68; medical professionals' relationship with, 62–64, 82; meningomyelocele, 65; models of, 58; myths about, 75; nationality effects on attitudes toward, 84; neighbors' response to, 81–82; neural tube defects, 65; notions commonly held about, 75–76; oppression of, 74; physical defects, 64–65; political involvement by, 82–83; problems experienced by, 74–75; public education effects on, 82; self-identity of, 77; skin disease, 66; strengths and skills of, 81

Physical abuse, 178, 190

Physical health, 177–181, 197

Physical impairment, 53

Politics, persons with disability in, 82–83

"Post-colonization stress disorder": case studies of, 173–174, 184–186; description of, 166

Power abuse, sociocultural model of: description of, 162–163; domestic violence similarities with, 162–163; oppression reactive syndromes caused by (*see* Oppression reactive syndromes); overview of, 161–162; survivors of, 166–167

Practitioners, 155–157

Prejudice: attitude changes and, 79–80; awareness and, 150–151; beliefs affected by, 71, 73; case studies of, 87–90; clusters of, 141–143; community change for reducing, 154–155; definition of, 52; educators role in reducing, 155–157; ethnocentrism and, 141–142; examples of, 51; expectations affected by, 71, 73; factors associated with, 54; of "haves" vs. "have-nots," 143–144; history of, 54–56; images and perceptions that facilitate, 145–149; individual change for reducing, 153–154; institutionalized, 136; intergroup bias and, 80–81; knowledge for reducing, 151–152; leaders' influence on, 144–145; literature about, 136; "might is right" belief and, 147–148; nationalism and, 139, 142; persistence of, 72–73; practitioners role in reducing, 155–157; public education to reduce, 82; reduction of, 79; skills for reducing, 152–153; social theories regarding, 69–77; strategies for combating, 150–157; universal-diverse orientation for (*see* Universal-diverse orientation); "we are the ideal" belief and, 146–147; "world is just too complicated" belief and, 149; "world is quite simple" belief and, 148–149; xenophobia and, 142

Prejudiced person, 52

Privilege, 186–187, 194–195, 200

Psychological violence, 183

Psychologists: religion as viewed by, 32–33; religious competency of, 34–37; spiritual competency of, 34–37, 41–44

Psychology: Buddhist, 39; existential, 37–38; Jungian, 40–41; religion and, 30–32; transpersonal, 38–39

Psychotherapy: Buddhist approach to, 39; existential psychology approach to, 37–38; Jungian approach to, 40–41; meditative state in, 39; spiritual approach to, 33, 37–41; spiritual attitude to, 41–44; transpersonal psychology approach to, 38–39

Public accommodations, Americans with Disabilities Act provisions for, 61

Race: assumptions of, 235; concept of, 234–235; conversations about, 239–240; dialogues on, 240–242; social construction of, 234

Racial animosity, 236

Racial discrimination, 237–238

Racial profiling, 174–175

Racism: definition of, 235–236; denial of, 247–248; elements of, 236; levels of, 235; oppression and, 246

Relational cultural model, 168

Religion: definition of, 31; demographics of, 28; importance of, 28–30; influences of, 28; mental health and, 33–34;

psychologists' view of, 32–33; psychology and, 30–32; societal perspective of, 30; spirituality vs., 31
Religious competency, 34–37
"Religious or spiritual problems," 35
Religious practices, 32

Safety, 183–186, 198
School settings, universal-diverse orientation in, 215–218
Self-advocacy, 261–263
Self-concept, 72, 211
Self-fulfilling prophecy, 73
Self-identity, 42
Self-image: acceptance of, 129; ethnic dress and, 16
Sexual abuse, 178–179, 190
Sexual harassment, 179–180
Sexuality, 177–181, 197
Shared power: accountability, 174–177, 197; community inclusion, 169–170, 196; components of, 168–169; description of, 167; economic empowerment, 172–174; emotional affirmation, 170–172, 196; equal opportunity, 186–187, 199–200; honesty, 174–177, 197; non-threatening behavior, 183–186, 198; physical health, 177–181, 197; principles of, 167–168; respect for diversity, 170–172, 196; safety, 183–186, 198; sexuality, 177–181, 197; shared value and responsibility for all children, 181–183, 200
Skill, 152–153
Social categorization, 70, 209
Social class: access to education and, 102–105; access to work and, 102–105; discrimination

based on, 101; economic stability and, 102–105
Social class identity, 101
Social context, 211–212
Social dominance theory, 167
Social identity, 211
Social identity theory, 71
Social isolation, 169
Social learning, 70
Sociocultural model of power abuse: description of, 162–163; domestic violence similarities with, 162–163; oppression reactive syndromes caused by (see Oppression reactive syndromes); overview of, 161–162; survivors of, 166–167
Sociocultural model of shared power and control: accountability, 174–177, 197; community inclusion, 169–170, 196; components of, 168–169; description of, 167; economic empowerment, 172–174; emotional affirmation, 170–172, 196; equal opportunity, 186–187, 199–200; honesty, 174–177, 197; non-threatening behavior, 183–186, 198; physical health, 177–181, 197; principles of, 167–168; respect for diversity, 170–172, 196; safety, 183–186, 198; sexuality, 177–181, 197; shared value and responsibility for all children, 181–183, 200
Spiritual competency: in clinical training of psychologists, 41–44; description of, 34–37
Spiritual diversity: description of, 27; impact of, 29
Spiritual history, 30
Spirituality: crises of, 27; definition of, 31–32; extrinsic, 33;

globalization effects on, 27–30;
  intrinsic, 33; lack of, 29; mental
  health and, 29–30; practices
  associated with, 32;
  psychotherapy and, 33, 37–41;
  religion vs., 31
"Stereotyped threat" syndrome:
  case studies of, 169–170,
  171–172, 176–177; description
  of, 165–166
Stigmatization of obese people:
  coping with, 120, 122–124,
  128; mental health effects, 127;
  research regarding, 115–132
Student affairs, 219
Subjective culture, 31
Substantially limits, 53
Surface markers: cultural identity
  based on, 15, 22; group
  differentiation using, 15, 22;
  types of, 15

Telecommunications, 62
Threats, 183–184, 191–192
Transpersonal psychology, 38–39
Transportation, 61

United Cerebral Palsy
  Organization, 56
United States: dress in, 4;
  ethnocentrism by, 141–142;
  higher education in, 156;
  intergroup differences in, 14–15;
  "might is right" belief in, 147–
  148; multiculturalism in, 136;
  mute assimilation in, 17;
  nationalism by, 139, 142;
  persons with disability in, 84;
  privilege in, 187, 194–195, 200;
  social influences in, 14; "we are
  the ideal" belief in, 146–147;

"world is quite simple" belief in,
  148–149
Universal-diverse orientation:
  characteristics necessary for,
  212–214; in clinical settings,
  224–225; conditions for, 212–214;
  in counseling settings, 224–225;
  decategorization for, 210–211;
  definition of, 207–208;
  evaluation of, 225–226;
  fostering of, 208–225; in higher
  education settings, 218–221;
  impact of, 228; ingredients for,
  208–212; interventions for,
  213–225; in organizational
  settings, 221–224; in school
  settings, 215–218; settings for,
  213–225; summary of, 225–228;
  in workplace, 221–224

Vocational rehabilitation programs,
  98–99

"We are the ideal" belief, 146–147
White privilege, 186–187, 237
"Woman enough" syndrome, 165
Women: discrimination against, 95;
  sexual abuse against, 178–179;
  social class identity of, 101
Workplace: diversity training
  programs in, 222; economic
  abuse in, 172–173; stereotypes
  in, 172–173; universal-diverse
  orientation in, 221–224
"World is just too complicated"
  belief, 149
"World is quite simple" belief,
  148–149

Xenophobia, 142, 148

About the Series and the Series Editors

It is expected that nearly half of the entire U.S. population will be of nonwhite ethnic and racial minorities by the year 2050. With this growing diversity, clinicians, researchers, and, indeed, all Americans need to understand that the Eurocentric psychological views particular to Caucasians may or may not be relevant or adequate to address mental health issues in racial and ethnic minorities. This series addresses those issues, aiming to better understand how these factors affect mental health, and what needs to be done, or done differently, to heal disorders that may arise.

JEAN LAU CHIN is a licensed psychologist and systemwide dean of the California School of Professional Psychology at Alliant International University. She is also president of CEO Services, which offers clinical, educational, and organizational development services emphasizing cultural competence and integrated systems of care. She holds a doctorate from Teacher's College of Columbia University. Dr. Chin's past positions include associate professor of psychiatry at the Center for Minority Training Program, Boston University School of Medicine; regional director of the Massachusetts Behavioral Health Partnership; executive director of the South Cove Community Health Center; and codirector of the Thom Child Guidance Clinic. She has authored, coauthored, or edited books including *Relationships among Asian American Women* (2000), *Community Health Psychology*

(1998), and *Diversity in Psychotherapy: The Politics of Race, Ethnicity and Gender* (1993).

VICTOR DE LA CANCELA is associate clinical professor of medical psychology at the College of Physicians and Surgeons, Columbia University. He is also deputy executive director of Tremont-Crotona Child Development Center, and a clinical psychologist serving with the United States Army Reserve.

JOHN D. ROBINSON is a professor in the Departments of Psychiatry and Surgery at the College of Medicine and Hospital at Howard University. He is a fellow of Divisions 1, 12, 38, 44, 45, 49, 51, and 52 of the American Psychological Association. In 1998, he received a letter of commendation from the president of the United States for teaching excellence. Robinson is a distinguished visiting professor at the Walter Reed Army Medical Center and at the Tripler Army Medical Center. He earned his EdD in counseling psychology at the University of Massachusetts–Amherst, completed a clinical psychology residency at the University of Texas Health Sciences Center at San Antonio, and earned an MPH at Harvard School of Public Health. Robinson worked earlier as chief of interdepartmental programs in the Departments of Psychiatry and Surgery at Howard University, and has also served as dean of the Division of Graduate Studies and Research at the University of the District of Columbia, clinical professor in the Department of Psychiatry at Georgetown University School of Medicine, and clinical attending faculty in the Department of Psychiatry at Harvard University School of Medicine at the Cambridge Hospital.

About the Advisers

JESSICA HENDERSON DANIEL is an assistant professor of psychology in the Department of Psychiatry at Harvard Medical School, and both director of training in psychology and associate director of the LEAH (Leadership Education in Adolescent Health) Training Program in Adolescent Medicine at Children's Hospital of Boston. She is also an adjunct associate professor of psychology in the clinical psychology program at Boston University. Daniel is the past president of the Society for the Psychology of Women, Division 35, APA; and is coeditor of *The Complete Guide to Mental Health for Women* (2003). Her awards include the 1998 A. Clifford Barger Excellence in Mentoring Award from Harvard Medical School; the 2001 Education Distinguished Alumni Award from the University of Illinois; the 2002 Distinguished Contributions to Education and Training Award from APA; and the 2003 Professional Award from the Boston & Vicinity Club, Inc., National Association of Negro Business and Professional Women's Clubs, Inc.

JEFFERY SCOTT MIO is a professor in the Department of Behavioral Sciences at California State Polytechnic University–Pomona, where he also serves as the director of the master of science in psychology program. He received his PhD from the University of Illinois–Chicago in 1984. He taught at California State University–Fullerton in the counseling department from 1984–1986, then taught at Washington State University in the Department of Psychology from 1986 to 1994 before accepting his current position at CSPU–Pomona. His interests are in the teaching of multicultural issues, the development of allies, and how metaphors are used in political persuasion.

NATALIE PORTER is vice provost for academic affairs systemwide at Alliant International University. She is also an associate professor of psychology. She received her PhD from the University of Delaware. Porter's research interests include feminist and anti-racist models of clinical training and supervision, cognitive and emotional developmental changes in individuals abused or traumatized as children, and feminist therapy supervision and ethics.

JOHN D. ROBINSON is a coeditor of *Race and Ethnicity in Psychology*, a Praeger series.

JOSEPH EVERETT TRIMBLE is a professor of psychology at the Center for Cross-Cultural Research at Western Washington University. Trimble was a fellow in the Radcliffe Institute for Advanced Study at Harvard University in 2000 and 2001. He is a research associate for the University of Colorado Health Sciences Center, in the Department of Psychiatry, National Center for American Indian and Alaska Native Mental Health Research. He is also a scholar and adjunct professor of psychology for the Colorado State University Tri-Ethnic Center for Prevention Research. In 1994, he received the Lifetime Achievement Award from the Society for the Psychological Study of Ethnic Minority Issues, Division 45, American Psychological Association. In 2002, he was honored with the Distinguished Psychologist Award from the Washington State Psychological Association. He has authored eighty-two journal articles, chapters, and monographs, as well as authored or edited thirteen books, including the *Handbook of Racial and Ethnic Minority Psychology* (2002).

MELBA J. T. VASQUEZ is in full-time independent practice in Austin, Texas. A past president of APA Divisions 35 (Society for the Psychology of Women) and 17 (Society of Counseling Psychology), she has served in various other leadership positions. She is a fellow of the APA and a diplomate of the ABPP. She publishes in the areas of professional ethics, psychology of women, ethnic minority psychology, and training and supervision. She is coauthor, with Ken Pope, of *Ethics in Counseling and Psychotherapy: A Practical Guide* (1998, 2nd ed.). She is the recipient of several awards including Psychologist of the Year, Texas Psychological Association, 2003; Senior Career Award for Distinguished Contributions to Psychology in the Public Interest, APA, 2002; Janet E. Helms Award for Mentoring and Scholarship,

Columbia University, 2002; John Black Award for Outstanding Achievement in the Practice of Counseling Psychology, Division 17, APA, 2000; and the Distinguished Leader for Women in Psychology Award, Committee of Women Psychology, APA, 2000.

HERBERT Z. WONG has provided management consulting, diversity training, and organizational assessments to over 300 government agencies, businesses, and other organizations. He was the cofounder and president of the National Diversity Conference, Inc., which presented contemporary issues and future directions of workforce diversity. He was a consultant to the President's Commission on Mental Health (1977), the White House Conference for a Drug Free America (1989), and the President's Initiative on Race–White House Office of Science and Technology (2000). In the past twenty-five years, Wong has written extensively on multicultural leadership, cross-cultural communication, and diversity issues. Wong received his PhD in clinical and organizational psychology from the University of Michigan.

About the Contributors

JOSEFINA ALVAREZ is a research associate at DePaul University's Center for Community Research. She has been a visiting assistant professor at DePaul University and director of the Center for Intercultural Clinical Psychology at the Chicago School of Professional Psychology. Her professional training includes a predoctoral fellowship at Yale University School of Medicine. Alvarez has, in practice and research, focused often on Latino mental health issues. She earned her PhD in clinical psychology at DePaul University.

LEENA BANERJEE is an associate professor of multicultural community clinical psychology in the doctor of psychology program at Alliant International University. She is also in private practice as a consultant to the mental health program at Bienvenidos Children's Center. She has authored or coauthored many journal articles or chapters, and is an editorial board member for the *Journal of Research and Applications in Clinical Psychology*. She earned her PhD in marriage and family therapy from Virginia Polytechnic Institute and State University.

MARTHA E. BANKS is an associate professor of black studies at the College of Wooster and a research neuropsychologist in the research and development division of ABackans DCP, Inc., in Akron, Ohio. She has been instrumental in developing the Ackerman-Banks Neuropsychological Rehabilitation Battery and the Post-Assault Traumatic Brain Injury Interview and Checklist. Banks has also served as a clinical psychologist with the Brecksville Department of Veterans Affairs Medical Center and as associate professor of psychology at the College of Wooster. She has published widely in books and professional journals, including *Women & Therapy, Topics in Geriatric Rehabilitation*, and *Social Science Computer Review*. Banks is a member of numerous professional organizations, including the American Psychological Association, serving on its Committee on Ethnic Minority Affairs (CEMA), Committee on Women in Psychology (CWP), and the Council of Representatives. She has also been president of the Society for the Psychology of Women's Section on Psychology of Black Women. In 2003, she received the American Psychological Association's Sue Rosenberg Zalk Award for Distinguished Service from the Society for the Psychology of Women. Banks is the Ethics Member of the Rosalynn Carter Institute for Human Development's Expert Panel on Caregiving for People with Disabilities. She has a forthcoming book chapter, "Ethical Issues in Caregiving for People with Disabilities," in Ms. Carter's book series on caregiving. Banks' recent publications include the book *Women with Visible and Invisible Disabilities: Multiple Intersections, Multiple Issues, Multiple Therapies* and "The Role of Neuropsychological Testing and Evaluation: When to Refer" in *State of the Art Reviews: Adolescent Medicine*. She is an associate editor for *Women & Therapy*.

DONALD DAUGHTRY is an assistant professor in the Department of Counseling at the University of North Dakota. He is a higher education representative to the North Dakota Board of Counselor Examiners and assistant director for the Global Rural Autism Information Network. He earned his PhD in counseling psychology from Texas Tech University.

BRAVADA GARRETT-AKINSANYA is president of Brakins Consulting and Psychological Services in Plymouth, Minnesota. Garrett-Akinsanya has served as board member for the Minnesota Psychological Association, board president for the Minnesota Association of Black Psychologists, and board president for the Multicultural Specialty Providers Mental Health Network. Garrett-Akinsanya's BA in psychology, MA in counseling psychology, and PhD in clinical psychology are all from Texas Tech University.

DONALD E. GREYDANUS is pediatrics program residency director at the Kalamazoo Center for Medical Studies at Michigan State University. He is also a professor of pediatrics and human development at Michigan State University's College of Human Medicine. He is co–editor in chief of *State of the Art Reviews: Adolescent Medicine.* He has authored or coauthored 103 journal articles, fifty-seven book chapters, and eight books. Greydanus is a diplomate for the American Board of Pediatrics and the National Board of Medical Examiners, as well as a fellow for the American Board of Pediatrics.

DIETRA HAWKINS is a postdoctoral fellow at Yale University School of Medicine. She works on policy development for Connecticut's Department of Mental Health and Addiction Services. She also consults with several community-based agencies in their development of programs to reduce the health disparities among ethnic and racial low-income populations. Her primary interests include health care disparities related to race, ethnicity, and income. She continues to address racism as a facilitator for the Middlesex County Institute for Healing Racism, and through her community presentation Black Hair and Slavery. She is a graduate of the Chicago School of Professional Psychology, where she received a PsyD in clinical psychology. She completed her predoctoral clinical internship at Yale University School of Medicine, with a placement at West Haven Mental Health Clinic and the Consultation Center, where she worked with children, families, and local community centers. Her dissertation, *The Chicago Dinners: A Noble Affair*, explored experiences with race dialogues from the perspectives of the facilitators.

TERRI JOHNSON is the executive director of the Human Relations Foundation/Jane Addams Policy Initiative. A program of Jane Addams Hull House Association, this initiative works to eradicate racism and poverty in metropolitan Chicago using research, public education, community dialogue, organizational consultation, and social policy reform advocacy. She managed the initial development team for the Chicago Dinners model and has consulted with organizations throughout the metropolitan area and the nation on methods to adapt the model. She has consulted various organizations and agencies on inclusion and cultural competence. Johnson is an accomplished speaker and moderator on issues of race, inequality, and systemic change. She is a graduate of Northwestern University with a BA in political science.

CINDY JUNTUNEN is chair of the Department of Counseling at the University of North Dakota. A licensed psychologist, her MA in pre-counseling psychology is from Ball State University, and her PhD in counseling psychology was earned at the University of California–Santa

Barbara. She coedited *Counseling Across the Lifespan* (2002) and has authored numerous journal articles.

ANGELA B. KIM is a doctoral student in the counseling psychology program at Teachers College, Columbia University. She holds an MA and an EdM.

MICHAEL LOEWY is professor of counseling and counseling psychology at the University of North Dakota. He earned his master's and PhD degrees in counseling psychology at the University of California–Santa Barbara. He has been a professor at San Diego State University and the University of Missouri–Columbia. Loewy's primary interest and emphasis is multicultural competence. His recent research aims at understanding the components of competent multicultural clinical supervision, the campus social climate for underrepresented groups, factors making up unearned social privilege, motivation for individuals to participate in social/political action on behalf of their own groups, mental health and adjustment issues for immigrants and refugees, and the cultural influences on Native American resiliency.

CATHERINE A. MARSHALL is a research professor in the Department of Educational Psychology at Northern Arizona University (NAU), and has a joint appointment as professor with the Mel and Enid Zuckerman College of Public Health. She holds an adjunct professor position at Griffith University near Brisbane, Australia. Marshall was the director of research and a professor at the American Indian Rehabilitation Research and Training Center at Northern Arizona University in Flagstaff, Arizona, where she has worked since 1989. She cofounded the Work Group on American Indian Research and Program Evaluation Methodology and has been involved in rehabilitation research for twenty years, working as either a counselor or educator in rehabilitation for twenty-five years. Marshall's research interests include the needs of persons with severe and persistent psychiatric disabilities, family and disability issues, the rehabilitation needs of indigenous people in Latin America, and women and disability. Marshall was selected for a Fulbright Scholar Research and Teaching Award in 1997. She has published more than twenty juried articles or chapters. She edited *Rehabilitation and American Indians with Disabilities: A Handbook for Administrators, Practitioners, and Researchers* (2001). She obtained her PhD at the University of Arizona–Tucson. Marshall is also a graduate of Berry College (1972) in Mt. Berry, Georgia, and of Boston University

(1977). She is founder and president of a nonprofit organization, the Women's International Leadership Institute (http://www.wili.org).

ASIAH MASON is associate professor of psychology at Gallaudet University. His past positions include clinical psychologist at the University of Pittsburgh Medical Center, chief psychologist for the Commonwealth of Massachusetts Department of Mental Retardation, and program director at Western Pennsylvania School for the Deaf. Mason's PhD, MA, and BA were all earned at Western Michigan University at Kalamazoo.

MARIE L. MIVILLE is an associate professor of psychology and education at Teachers College, Columbia University. She is also the program coordinator and director of training of counseling psychology programs at Teachers College. Miville received her doctorate in counseling psychology from the University of Maryland–College Park. Her doctoral research involved exploring the interrelations of collective identity (gender, cultural) and personal identity among Latinos and Latinas. She also developed the Miville-Guzman Universality-Diversity Scale (M-GUDS), which measures social attitudes of awareness and acceptance of how people are both similar and different from each other. Miville is currently on the editorial boards of *Journal of Counseling Psychology* and *Assessment*. She is the co-coordinator of professional development of the National Latina/o Psychology Association.

TERU L. MORTON is academic affairs associate for international education at Alliant International University. Morton is also a professor of psychology for the PhD program in clinical psychology, and also a feedback coach and facilitator at the Center for Creative Leadership in San Diego. Morton is in independent practice in organizational consulting and executive coaching. Earlier positions held include founding faculty member and associate director for the International Center for Psychosocial Trauma at the University of Missouri School of Medicine, clinical associate professor in the Department of Psychiatry and Neurology at the University of Missouri School of Medicine, research fellow at the Vanderbilt Institute for Public Policy Studies, visiting associate professor of psychology at Vanderbilt University, and administrative officer of state relations and consultant to the Office of Professional Development for the American Psychological Association. Morton has also been an associate professor of psychology at the University of Hawaii, as well as a consultant to the psychiatry residency program at Hawaii State Hospital. Morton has also contributed to a number of volumes, including *Practicing Multiculturalism* (2002), *The Clinical Psychology Handbook* (1991), and *Childhood Aggression and Violence* (1987).

ANNA M. MYERS is a licensed clinical psychologist practicing in northern Vermont. Currently, she provides intensive treatment and psychological assessment services in an acute mental health care setting. Her research and writing have focused on issues of women's mental health as well as the psychology of prejudice and discrimination.

DILIP R. PATEL is director of adolescent and sports medicine, professor of pediatrics and human development, and assistant program director at the Pediatric Residency Program at Michigan State University–Kalamazoo Center for Medical Studies. He is board certified in pediatrics, adolescent medicine, and sports medicine. Patel attended medical school in India. He was a fellow at Newark Beth Israel Medical Center, Iowa Methodist Medical Center; Iowa Methodist Sports Medicine Center; Michigan State University–Kalamazoo Center for Medical Studies; and Southwestern Michigan Sports Medicine Clinic. Patel has also been an attending staff in pediatrics or adolescent psychiatry at Bronson Methodist Hospital, Borgess Medical Center, Newark Beth Israel Medical Center, and Elizabeth General Medical Center. Patel provides physician coverage for the Kalamazoo Central High School football program, and is an editorial board member of *Adolescent Medicine: State of the Art Reviews*, and a reviewer for *Pediatrics*, the *Archives of Pediatrics and Adolescent Medicine*, and *Medicine and Science in Sports and Exercise*. Patel is a fellow of the American Academy of Pediatrics, and he has coedited one book, *Course Manual for Adolescent Health* (2002).

HELEN D. PRATT is director of the Behavioral Developmental Pediatrics Program and professor of pediatrics and human development at Michigan State University–Kalamazoo Center for Medical Studies. She is a diplomate in clinical psychology for the American Board of Psychological Specialties, a licensed psychologist and certified domestic violence counselor, a cognitive behavioral therapist, and a behavioral therapist. She is on the editorial advisory board for the *Journal of Adolescent Health*, and is also consultant and owner of Pratt & Associates. She earned her PhD in clinical psychology at Western Michigan University.

JILL M. ROHRBACKER is coordinator of the Family Resource Center at Oklahoma State University. She is responsible for administration and program development for a clientele that is 70 percent ethnic minority and international. She has worked in a variety of positions with residential life and student affairs for over twenty years.

ESTHER D. ROTHBLUM is a licensed psychologist and professor of psychology at the University of Vermont, where she has also served as director of clinical training and chair of the Women's Studies Committee. During sabbatical in 2003–2004, she was a visiting professor at the Lesbian Health Research Center at the University of California–San Francisco; is the Beatrice M. Bain Affiliated Scholar at the University of California–Berkeley, and is a visiting scholar at the Women's Leadership Institute, Mills College, Oakland, California. She has also been visiting scholar at the Institute for Research on Women and Gender at Stanford University, visiting scholar at the Institute for Women's Studies at the University of Minnesota–Duluth, and visiting fellow at Clare Hall, Cambridge University. She completed her PhD in clinical psychology at Rutgers University and held honorary and postdoctoral fellowships at Yale University. She is a founding mother of the women's studies program at the University of Vermont. She is editor of the *Journal of Lesbian Studies* and an editorial board member of *Body Image*, the *Journal of Homosexuality*, the *Journal of GLBT Family Studies*, *Women and Therapy*, and *Contemporary Perspectives on Lesbian, Gay and Bisexual Psychology*.

ILENE SERLIN is a licensed clinical psychologist, a visiting professor at the Colorado School of Professional Psychology, and an adjunct faculty member at the Institute of Imaginal Studies in California. She has also taught at Lesley College in Boston, the University of California–Los Angeles, and Antioch University in San Francisco. A dance therapist, she started the movement therapy program at the University of California–San Francisco. She is a member of the Executive Board for Humanistic Psychology, Division 32 of the American Psychological Association. She is also an editorial board member for the *American Journal of Dance Therapy*, the *Journal of Humanistic Psychology*, and the *Moscow Psychotherapy Journal*. She has written ten book chapters and numerous journal articles. Serlin has also served on managed care panels for Blue Cross/Blue Shield, HealthNet, Behavioral Health Systems, and other organizations. Her PhD is from the University of Texas–Dallas.

DENISE TWOHEY holds an EdD in counseling psychology and is pursuing an academic career at the University of North Dakota. She is completing an internship at the University of Illinois at Urbana-Champaign, where her focus was a qualitative study on women and depression. After her first year of teaching, the university sent her to Harvard for a week to study with Carol Gilligan. In 1990, she taught her first class, Psychological Development of Women. Also in 1990, Denise attended a meeting in Boston that was to become the future home of Division 51 of the American Psychological Association (The Society for the Study of Men and Masculinity), heralding a new twist in gender issues. The new twist was the beginning of the men's movement. However, in 1998, Denise underwent treatment for a brain tumor, permanently altering her life course. Her research interests changed from gender to disability. She has authored sixteen refereed publications, ranging from book reviews to a book chapter.

DAVID H. WHITCOMB is an assistant professor of counseling at the University of North Dakota, where he is also training director for the master of arts program. He is chair of the American Psychological Association Division 17 Section for Lesbian, Gay and Bisexual Awareness.

KAREEM Z. YAHYA is in postgraduate training at the Internal Medicine and Pediatrics Combined Residency at Michigan State University–Kalamazoo Center for Medical Studies.